The Gardens of Flora Baum

V

The Gardens of Flora Baum

Book One: By the Tree of Life
   Part 1   Sum
   Part 2   The Path Approaching
   Part 3   Epiphany
   Part 4   The Waves Receding
   Part 5   Difference

Book Two: Towards a Greek Garden
   Part 1   The Program
   Part 2   Iliad
   Part 3   The History
   Part 4   Odyssey
   Part 5   The Diagram

Book Three: Rome
   Part 1   Urbiculture
   Part 2   Floralia
   Part 3   Umbrageous Vision

Book Four: Towards Farthest Thule
   Part 1   Lay of the Last Monk
   Part 2   Sibyl
   Part 3   Lyre, Harp, Violin

Book Five: By the Tree of Knowledge
   Part 1   By the Tree
   Part 2   The Tree of Knowledge
   Part 3   Knowledge
   Part 4   Of Knowledge by the Tree
   Part 5   Tree
   Part 6   Knowledge of the Tree
   Part 7   Of the Tree

BOOKS	PARTS	PARTS
Book One	5	
		10
Book Two	5	
Book Three	3	3
Book Four	3	
		10
Book Five	7	

The Gardens of Flora Baum

✦ ✦ ✦ ✦ ✦

Book Five

By the Tree of Knowledge

Julia Budenz

Carpathia Press
Chelmsford, Mass., U.S.A.

Carpathia Press
7 Colonial Terrace
Chelmsford, Massachusetts 01824
U.S.A.

© 2011 by the Estate of Julia Budenz
All rights reserved.

Published by Carpathia Press. Except for brief passages quoted in a review, no part of this book may be reproduced by any mechanical, photographic, or electronic process without the written permission of the Estate of Julia Budenz. Address such requests to Carpathia Press, 7 Colonial Terrace, Chelmsford, MA 01824. Printed in the United States of America.

Library of Congress Cataloging-in-Publication Data has been applied for.

ISBN: 978-0-9849089-5-0 (softcover, bk. 5)

Foreword

THIS IS A posthumous publication, but Julia Budenz had meticulously prepared her five-book poem and had overseen the process of digitization and proofing, and so it has the stamp of authorial approval. It rests on the author's typed version. Only the few pieces written within a week of her death on December 11, 2010, are from manuscript, and these are inserted at the points she indicated. They are "September" and "And January" (Book Three, pages 718–720, 722) and "How shall I say this?" (Book Five, page 570).

Her long poem addresses a wide range of readers, and she would have wished this first contact to be an unmediated one. So no attempt is made here to categorize, other than to indicate, as the poet did herself, that there is a different focus in each of the five books. In a short essay called "Query Re One's Work," which appeared online in the *Poetry Porch* in 1997, she said:

> The gardens are five, comprising the five books. The first garden is the garden of the holy; its book explores transcendence, is located partially in Eden, and draws upon imagery from the Bible and the liturgy. Its title, "By the Tree of Life," indicates that despite its strong center this book may be considered a Paradise Lost, as is suggested also by the names of its five parts: "Sum," "The Path Approaching," "Epiphany," "The Waves Receding," and "Difference."
>
> The second garden is the garden of the beautiful; its book contemplates the aesthetic, is situated partially in Greece, and makes use of Greek literature, mythology, and geography. This second book, which is called "Towards a Greek Garden," has a midpoint as well as a final destination and also consists of five parts, whose names intimate both the patterned centering and the linear progression: "The Program," "Iliad," "The History," "Odyssey," "The Diagram." Since Flora Baum reaches the Greek garden, the second book may be designated a Paradise Regained.
>
> The third garden is that of the true, specifically of academic

knowledge, of scholarship, of learning. Its book, entitled "Rome," uses material from Roman literature, history, and topography. This is the pivotal book in the design and development of the poem; its three parts — "Urbiculture," "Floralia," and "Umbrageous Vision" — mark not only a center which is both city and garden but also a difficult struggle to pass through pedantry to erudition and insight.

The fourth garden is that of the good and blooms with human relations. Its book, "Towards Farthest Thule," is set partly in Britain, finally in Shetland. As might be expected, it utilizes English and Scottish literature, folklore, and geography. The book begins with a long ballad, "The Lay of the Last Monk," continues with an epyllion called "Sibyl," and concludes with a sequence of lyrics, "Lyre, Harp, Violin."

The fifth and final garden is the garden of the whole. Its book, "By the Tree of Knowledge," is the philosophical book, the one most fully placed in Flora's native America but also situated in her native world, in her homeland the earth, in her home the universe. It is the book of the elm, rooted and reaching. It grounds itself not only in a meditation upon philosophy but also in social science and physical science, in culture and nature, in the microcosm and the mesocosm and the macrocosm, in the final paracosm, the final paradigm and paradise. It is the book which I will write if I can live long enough and become wise enough to do it. "O mihi tum longae maneat pars ultima vitae," I find myself crying out with Virgil, hoping to touch this great beginning or end or center or edge.

Although no critical assessment is offered here, it can be anticipated that, in due course, *The Gardens of Flora Baum* will find a place in the history of American literature once readers have had a chance to absorb its author's new and distinctive voice and to respond fully to it.

Julia's life and writing were intertwined and the following biographical sketch may prove helpful. She was the eldest daughter of Louis Budenz and Margaret Rodgers Budenz and had three sisters. She was born on May 23, 1934, in New York City. The first break in her life came in 1945 when her father renounced the Communist party and rejoined the Roman Catholic church. The family moved briefly to South Bend, Indiana, before returning to New York. The year 1956 marked Julia's graduation with an A.B. summa cum laude from the College of New Rochelle and also the beginning of the period she spent as an Ursuline nun. In 1962, she was awarded a Master of Arts degree at Catholic University and became an instructor in classics at the College of New Rochelle.

In 1966, after leaving the convent, she studied briefly at New York University in the spring and began graduate studies in comparative literature (Greek, Latin and English) at Harvard University in the fall. She graduated A.M. in 1972 and continued working towards a Ph.D. for a time, but the pull of scholarship in isolation became less compelling than the desire to create in the light of her scholarship and her vision. She began writing *The Gardens of Flora Baum* in about 1969 and received a fellowship at the Radcliffe Institute in 1974–75 for the purpose of developing it.

For the rest of her working life, she undertook paid employment with an eye always to the opportunities offered for the combination of scholarly facilities and leisure essential for her writing. Widener Library at Harvard University had the central place in her life that she speaks of in her poem. In 1972, she had begun working in Harvard's History of Science Department with I. Bernard Cohen and Anne Whitman on their new English translation of Isaac Newton's *Principia*, and, although she left Cambridge twice to teach classics — at Colby College in 1980–81 and at Berea College in 1987–88 — she was mainly engaged on History of Science Department projects until her retirement freed her to concentrate on her poetry. She suffered from ill health in her closing years and died of cancer at the age of seventy-six.

Parts of *The Gardens of Flora Baum* have been published previously in books and periodicals. *From the Gardens of Flora Baum*, Wesleyan University Press, Middletown, Connecticut, 1984, contained "The Fire Escape" and "The Sheen" (Book Two, pages 173–250), and *Carmina Carmentis*, Pivot Press, Brooklyn, New York, 2005, contained a sequence from "January" (Book Three, pages 635–673). Shorter pieces from *The Gardens of Flora Baum* were included in these edited books: *Anthology of Magazine Verse and Yearbook of American Poetry*, ed. Alan F. Pater, Monitor Book Company, Beverly Hills, California, 1980; *A Formal Feeling Comes: Poems in Form by Contemporary Women*, ed. Annie Finch, Story Line

Press, Brownsville, Oregon, 1994; *Catullus in English*, ed. Julia Haig Gaisser, Penguin Books, London, 2001; *Emily Lyle: The Persistent Scholar*, ed. Frances J. Fischer and Sigrid Rieuwerts, WVT Wissenschaftlicher Verlag Trier, Trier, 2007; *Petrarch & Dante*, ed. Zygmunt G. Baranski and Theodore J. Cachey, Jr., University of Notre Dame Press, Notre Dame, Indiana, 2009.

Other excerpts from the work appeared between 1971 and 2010 in the following periodicals: *Akros, American Arts Quarterly, The American Voice, Amphora, Arion, Bits, Bitterroot, Boston Review, Bunting Institute Newsletter, Chapman, Cloelia, Cosmos, Crazyhorse, The Cream City Review, Cross Currents, Epos, Four Quarters, La Fusta, Harvard Advocate, Harvard Review, Italian Americana, The Kenyon Review, Lines Review, The Lyric, Mati, NEeuropa, New England Classical Journal, North Stone Review, Notre Dame Review, Other Poetry, Persephone, Poet Lore, The Poetry Porch, Radcliffe Quarterly, Rhino, Scottish Literary Journal, Society of Fellows News* (American Academy in Rome), *The Society of Institute Fellows Newsletter* (The Bunting Institute of Radcliffe College), *Southwest Review, Sparrow, Studia Mystica, The Tennessee Quarterly, The Tennessee Review, Vergilius, The Wallace Stevens Journal, William and Mary Review*, and *YIP: Yale Italian Poetry*.

Very warm acknowledgement should be made in conclusion to those bodies that, through residencies, fellowships, visiting scholar appointments, and funding, gave support to this long-term poetic project. I shall instance with gratitude the American Academy in Rome, the Authors League, the Bellagio Study and Conference Center of the Rockefeller Foundation, the Djerassi Foundation, Harvard University's Departments of Comparative Literature and English, the National Endowment for the Arts, the Radcliffe Institute, and Yaddo.

EMILY LYLE
University of Edinburgh

Publisher's Note

WHEN JULIA BUDENZ began writing *The Gardens of Flora Baum* in about 1969, she prepared master sheets on a manual typewriter. By 2005 she had switched to a laptop computer, which provided digital files. The arduous task of scanning the older material (roughly 1,700 pages), processing it with optical-character-recognition software, and proofreading it was overseen by Emily Lyle. For questions that arise, readers should consult the original typescript included among Julia's papers, which have been placed on deposit in the Houghton Library, Harvard University.

Over the years Julia told friends the schedule she'd mapped out for herself, intending to finish *The Gardens of Flora Baum* in 2015, when she would have been 81. But in January 2008 she asked me to explore the idea of an "introductory edition" of the material written to that point, much of which had not yet appeared in print. She continued work on unfinished sections, mainly in Book Four and Book Five. By late 2010, with her health in sharp decline, she identified those places in the poem where she'd intended to insert further material.

In the last few months of her life she did make sure that the start and finish of every book were completed. She also discussed her preferences as to the layout and presentation of the books.

Layout and style. In preparing this set of five books for publication, my aim has been to follow the original typescript to the greatest extent possible. In most cases short titled pieces begin on a new page, or are run on with preceding pieces. The decision whether to center a title or place it flush left also follows the original. But a typewriter does not offer the stylistic variation possible in a typeset book, and we have varied heading styles to suggest the importance of each piece in the hierarchy implied by the table of contents of each book. The scheme varies somewhat from book to book.

The author's practice of having complete stanzas on a page, whenever possible, explains why some pages end short even though the piece continues on the next page. In the case of very long stanzas and other layout problems, we occasionally did break stanzas. This is indicated by the quaint device of a "catchword," set flush right at the bottom of the page. The catchword repeats the first word or two on the next page and tells the reader that the stanza has not ended yet. (To prevent anyone from mistaking a catchword for the second part of a broken line in the poem's meter, the catchword is printed in smaller type.) No catchwords were needed in Book One, but they do occur often in later books. On pages without a catchword, the page does end in a stanza break.

Occasionally the poem contains insertions that may appear to have been added by someone other than the author. One example is the use of "[sic]" in two places on page 79 of Book Two. Another is the inclusion of several footnotes in Book Five about a missing word or illegible date in a personal letter. There are a few other cases of partially bracketed dates at the tops of personal letters. All these insertions were made by Julia Budenz herself; she clearly intended them to be considered part of her poem.

Three asterisks (* * *) centered on a line denote a *lacuna,* or gap, where Julia had intended to write more material. On several occasions she commented that the asterisks could represent one stanza, one piece, or a long section of many pieces — there's no telling.

But the poem in five books appears to be at least 90 percent finished to her satisfaction. For the record, it contains about 303,700 words in 2,254 printed pages. The original typescript has 2,282 pages (owing to some differences in the locations of page breaks).

For advice and suggestions on specific issues during the preparation of these volumes, I am grateful to Virginia Furtwangler, Rebecca and Douglas Karo, Hope Mayo, Arthur Mortensen, Cynthia Thompson, and Frederick Turner. Without the monumental effort of Emily Lyle over many years, including repeated proofreading at various stages of production, this edition would not have been possible.

ROGER W. SINNOTT
Carpathia Press

Contents

Foreword   v
Publisher's Note   ix

Book Five: By the Tree of Knowledge

Part One: By the Tree   3

  One   4
    Diary of Flora Baum: October 26   5
    Diary of Flora Baum: November 5   6
    Diary of Flora Baum: November 6   8
    Diary of Flora Baum: Thanksgiving   9
    Diary of Flora Baum: First Sunday of Advent   11
    Diary of Flora Baum: December 1   12
    Diary of Flora Baum: December 8   13
    Diary of Flora Baum: Sunday, 7 p.m., December   14
    Diary of Flora Baum: Wednesday, December   15
    Diary of Flora Baum: December 20   16

  Two   18
    Birthday Card: December 11
      Elaine Gillis Storella   19
    Birthday Card: December 23
      Alice Jane Karo   23
    Birthday Card: May 5
      Ombretta Frau   24
    Birthday Card: October 25
      David Perkins   25

  Three   26
    Invocation   27

CONTENTS

Birthday Card: May 23	
Julia Mairin Toledo Budenz	28
Diary of Flora Baum: May 24	29
Diary of Flora Baum: May 25	30
Diary of Flora Baum: June 13	31
Diary of Flora Baum: July 5	32
Diary of Flora Baum: July 6	33
Diary of Flora Baum: July 7	34
Diary of Flora Baum: Still July 7	35
Birthday Card: July 13	
Gaius Julius Caesar	36
Vocation	37
Four	38
Diary of Flora Baum: October 20	39
Diary of Flora Baum: October 21	40
Diary of Flora Baum: October 23	49
Diary of Flora Baum: Tuesday, November 7	50
Diary of Flora Baum: Wednesday, November 8	51
Diary of Flora Baum: Thursday, November 9	52
Diary of Flora Baum: Friday, November 10	53
Diary of Flora Baum: September 11	54
Diary of Flora Baum: October 11	55
Diary of Flora Baum: October 25	56
Diary of Flora Baum: October 26	57
Diary of Flora Baum: October 29	58
Diary of Flora Baum: Halloween	59
Diary of Flora Baum: November 1, All Saints	60
Diary of Flora Baum: November 8, Mundus patet	61
Diary of Flora Baum: November 11	62
Birthday Card: November 24	
Joanna Maria Budenz Gallegos	63
Five	65
Diary of Flora Baum: May 15	66
Diary of Flora Baum: May 23	67
Diary of Flora Baum: May 25	68
Diary of Flora Baum: June 13	69
Diary of Flora Baum: June 15	70

CONTENTS   xiii

> Part Two: The Tree of Knowledge   71
>
>> It might be March.   72
>> All that I loved is lost or will be lost.   73
>> Zeus. Wicked. Agamemnon names.   74
>> Deus disintegrated. Saints dissolved.   75
>> Deus meus, quare me dereliquisti?   76
>> I did not die while I stared heavenward,   78
>> The hours of mere survival   79
>> Someone Homeric might say to some other,   80
>> Was it dualistic?   81
>> Thank you, I said. To whom?   82
>> White dogwood bright by darkest purple beech   83
>> They were both standing, and the sword had shattered. 84
>> Go to him, he is shining with beauty, she said.   85
>> Robins. Lilacs. Trees   86
>> Three oaks standing. Shall I advance   87
>> The biding bloom is small.   88
>> Must the grammar of beauty   89
>> What are these marks that mark the fading page,   90
>> If little lovely multitudes of blossoms   91
>> If multitudes of blossoms   92
>> The tree of knowledge grows in Paradise.   93
>> The disintegration is also,   94
>> It is hard to imagine.   95
>> At times the measures measure out the times   96
>> Why have I failed?   97
>> Something still glows. Is it a Troy in flames?   98
>> Is sky the end? Now here on earth   99
>> The metaphor becomes the simile.   100
>> Who were the fighters? They were lusty youths   101
>> Whether the roses were the weather or   102
>> To visit the virgilias one goes   103
>> What is a failure? Such a simple thing.   104
>> Here is some sun and some blue after days of grays
>>   and rain.   105
>> Olden-time, old-fashioned,   106
>> Then must the future be forgotten and forgone   107
>> Is the smile of the roses   108

CONTENTS

Well, dear old self,	109
Yet remember.	110
Facing the absolute	111
The trouble was	112
Not yet the night.	113
What else is there? Traverse five gardens.	114
Is it not unfeeling,	115
As it becomes more difficult to live	116
The noisy sea	117
Can I face this day?	118
Why does she remember with horror	119
The picture fills.	121
These torrents merely flow from the bathroom ceiling.	122
We know well that there are	123
Homer, too, is it	124
As the water came down through the ceiling	125
The oaks are standing free, not subject to these indignities.	126
The lace-cap hydrangeas	127
The day is heavy.	128
She entered twenty-two and blonde,	129
Shall I recount the miles and hours of distance	130
The lilies are not trees. They are too small.	131
The tree fell like a wounded warrior.	132
Which tree was this? There were so many trees.	133
Even in Homer levees do not hold.	134
Is this the lore:	135
Is beauty hoar,	137
In my soul there is a lack.	138
Please come down from the chariot and pull	139
Poring over the poem of obituaries	140
Blue the skies.	141
The root is what I know.	142
If the autumn anemones were nameless	143
In September	147
An azure	148
Is this all? Is this gracious gleam the end	150
This posthumous existence	155

He brought her back.							156
But what is how							157
Homer, Virgil,							158
Did I recognize							159
Oh . . .							162
Is this enough? Can that have been enough?							163
The minute mysteries of winter buds							164

Part Three: Knowledge — 165

Section One: The Margaret-Ghost — 166

No. 1	167	No. 29	203	No. 57	254
No. 2	168	No. 30	205	No. 58	255
No. 3	169	No. 31	206	No. 59	257
No. 4	170	No. 32	209	No. 60	258
No. 5	171	No. 33	211	No. 61	259
No. 6	172	No. 34	216	No. 62	261
No. 7	173	No. 35	219	No. 63	264
No. 8	174	No. 36	221	No. 64	265
No. 9	175	No. 37	222	No. 65	266
No. 10	176	No. 38	223	No. 66	267
No. 11	177	No. 39	224	No. 67	268
No. 12	178	No. 40	225	No. 68	269
No. 13	179	No. 41	226	No. 69	270
No. 14	180	No. 42	229	No. 70	271
No. 15	181	No. 43	230	No. 71	272
No. 16	182	No. 44	231	No. 72	273
No. 17	183	No. 45	232	No. 73	274
No. 18	184	No. 46	233	No. 74	275
No. 19	186	No. 47	235	No. 75	276
No. 20	187	No. 48	237	No. 76	277
No. 21	188	No. 49	241	No. 77	278
No. 22	189	No. 50	243	No. 78	279
No. 23	190	No. 51	244	No. 79	281
No. 24	191	No. 52	246	No. 80	283
No. 25	192	No. 53	248	No. 81	285
No. 26	193	No. 54	249	No. 82	287
No. 27	196	No. 55	250	No. 83	288
No. 28	201	No. 56	253	No. 84	289

No. 85	291	No. 123	332	No. 161	371
No. 86	292	No. 124	333	No. 162	372
No. 87	294	No. 125	335	No. 163	373
No. 88	295	No. 126	336	No. 164	375
No. 89	296	No. 127	337	No. 165	376
No. 90	297	No. 128	338	No. 166	378
No. 91	298	No. 129	339	No. 167	379
No. 92	299	No. 130	340	No. 168	380
No. 93	302	No. 131	341	No. 169	381
No. 94	303	No. 132	342	No. 170	382
No. 95	304	No. 133	343	No. 171	383
No. 96	305	No. 134	344	No. 172	384
No. 97	306	No. 135	345	No. 173	385
No. 98	307	No. 136	346	No. 174	386
No. 99	308	No. 137	347	No. 175	387
No. 100	309	No. 138	348	No. 176	388
No. 101	310	No. 139	349	No. 177	389
No. 102	311	No. 140	350	No. 178	390
No. 103	312	No. 141	351	No. 179	391
No. 104	313	No. 142	352	No. 180	393
No. 105	314	No. 143	353	No. 181	394
No. 106	315	No. 144	354	No. 182	395
No. 107	316	No. 145	355	No. 183	396
No. 108	317	No. 146	356	No. 184	397
No. 109	318	No. 147	357	No. 185	398
No. 110	319	No. 148	358	No. 186	399
No. 111	320	No. 149	359	No. 187	400
No. 112	321	No. 150	360	No. 188	401
No. 113	322	No. 151	361	No. 189	402
No. 114	323	No. 152	362	No. 190	403
No. 115	324	No. 153	363	No. 191	404
No. 116	325	No. 154	364	No. 192	405
No. 117	326	No. 155	365	No. 193	406
No. 118	327	No. 156	366	No. 194	407
No. 119	328	No. 157	367	No. 195	408
No. 120	329	No. 158	368	No. 196	410
No. 121	330	No. 159	369	No. 197	411
No. 122	331	No. 160	370	No. 198	412

No. 199	413	No. 237	457	No. 275	502
No. 200	414	No. 238	458	No. 276	503
No. 201	415	No. 239	459	No. 277	504
No. 202	417	No. 240	460	No. 278	505
No. 203	418	No. 241	461	No. 279	507
No. 204	419	No. 242	462	No. 280	508
No. 205	420	No. 243	464	No. 281	510
No. 206	421	No. 244	466	No. 282	512
No. 207	422	No. 245	467	No. 283	513
No. 208	423	No. 246	468	No. 284	515
No. 209	424	No. 247	469	No. 285	516
No. 210	425	No. 248	470	No. 286	517
No. 211	426	No. 249	471	No. 287	518
No. 212	427	No. 250	472	No. 288	529
No. 213	428	No. 251	473	No. 289	530
No. 214	429	No. 252	474	No. 290	531
No. 215	430	No. 253	475	No. 291	532
No. 216	431	No. 254	476	No. 292	533
No. 217	433	No. 255	477	No. 293	534
No. 218	434	No. 256	478	No. 294	535
No. 219	435	No. 257	479	No. 295	536
No. 220	436	No. 258	480	No. 296	537
No. 221	437	No. 259	481	No. 297	538
No. 222	438	No. 260	482	No. 298	539
No. 223	439	No. 261	483	No. 299	540
No. 224	440	No. 262	484	No. 300	541
No. 225	441	No. 263	485	No. 301	543
No. 226	442	No. 264	486	No. 302	544
No. 227	443	No. 265	488	No. 303	545
No. 228	444	No. 266	491	No. 304	548
No. 229	446	No. 267	492	No. 305	549
No. 230	447	No. 268	495	No. 306	551
No. 231	448	No. 269	496	No. 307	552
No. 232	450	No. 270	497	No. 308	553
No. 233	451	No. 271	498	No. 309	554
No. 234	452	No. 272	499	No. 310	555
No. 235	454	No. 273	500		
No. 236	456	No. 274	501		

Section Two: Woman in the Nineteenth Century	557
Section Three: The Wings of the Dove	559

Part Four: Of Knowledge by the Tree — 561

Standing I clasp the trunk....	564
Question?	565

Part Five: Tree — 567

Is it the strand, the shore? It is the tree.	569
How shall I say this?	570

Part Six: Knowledge of the Tree — 573

When I had known infinity,	576

Part Seven: Of the Tree — 577

No. 1	579	No. 4	582	No. 7	585
No. 2	580	No. 5	583	No. 8	586
No. 3	581	No. 6	584		

Index of Titles — 587

Book Five

By the Tree of Knowledge

Part One

By the Tree

One

Diary of Flora Baum

October 26

What is the meaning of the golden rose?
Holding our summer sun, our summer shade,
All of our summer secrets as they fade
Around about us, for the gold that glows

From ash, elm, honeylocust, maple grows
Sparse, grows scarce, grows ragged, grows more frayed,
As if fall's flash of splendor should have stayed
The crash, its folds unfold. If autumn froze

The moment of the fall before the fall,
Would we now know? Will we now never know?
What is the sense of scents? Who will disclose

How touch of sun and taste of shade can call
Through blue, through ruby, through the tupelo?
What is the golden meaning of the rose?

Diary of Flora Baum

November 5

I bowed my head.
I wept November's gray tears
That descended, that descended, upon the gray hearth of my heart.

It was not that it was raining.
The ruddy luster of the leaves
Caught the spark that shot, that dropped,
From the gray hearth arch
Of sky, reflection
From something somewhere.

Or was it the leaves?
Was it the light of the leaves?

It does not matter.
The patter
Is not gray rain.
The pattern
Will be the branches.
The leaves leave the branches
To reformulate
Design.

The syntax is too simple.
The lexicon is too low.
Can we be satisfied with parataxis?
Would we be shallow or profound
If, when we used the neuter copulative verb,
We should feel a verve?
A verse unmetered shall we feel too free?
If I were we
Who would we be?
To rhyme is too easy.
To question is too facile.

Is to cry to weep or to shout?

Is it yet, is it now, the hour
When you look less up at the leaves
And look more down,
When you read what you walk on?

I perused gray pages of cloud.
I turned a page. I shouted.

Is to shout to scream?

I was reading a gleam
Now more brown, now more yellow, now more red,
Now less, now gone.

Was it sun or leaf?
Was it fruit?
By the fruits you shall know.
Are the acorns gone?
Are all the acorns buried by the little gray paws?

That gave me pause.

I turned a leaf.
I was reading the great gray hearth arch of the sky
And the embers of the oak in a sunset of November.

Diary of Flora Baum

November 6

The sky is bare of cloud.
There is a brown glitter in the leaves.
There is a gray gleam on the boughs.
The oak can bear the caress of the sun.
The tree can take the illumination of the breeze.
The morning's gentle blue,
Still still, still moves.
The blue crests and rests like love.

Diary of Flora Baum

Thanksgiving

The amber and the umber of November
As the month advanced were chiefly the demesne
Of the regal beech, yet the yellow willow,
Yet the gilded willow, of the golden plumage,
Of the golden fleece,
And yet the gilded fingers of the larch,
The yellow feather-fingers of the larch,
Shared in the impression
Of a verdancy that was going gold
And then going, though the willows,
To tell the truth, had not become
The umber of the beeches and the larches
Or even amber as each larch and beech became
In sun or shade but golden in the sun,
Lithesome and lightly lightsome in the sun,
Subtly illumined and illumining,
Luminously golden in the sun,
And radiantly golden in the rain.

Why do I write in the past?
Today I saw, some scattered, some amassed,
The golden things that like the month still last.

And I shall thank
The cosmic Midas.
I thank, not thinking
Of gold's old problematics.
I thank, not thinking
Of the dismal distance of the solstitial sun.
Among the streetlamps above the vast traffic of Massachusetts Avenue
Does not shadblow glow golden?
I thank, not thinking
That evening slips towards night.

I know that evening slides to night.
I know that my green has disappeared,
I know that my gold has gone,
I know that my amber vanished
After dawn and my umber after dusk.
Can I ask if there must be umber
Under the amber of the moon?
No, the moon is silver.
Yes, I can still lift my arms.
I am grateful for the oak's great bare black boughs beneath the moon.

Diary of Flora Baum

First Sunday of Advent

A Communist childhood
Prepares one for the Parousia.
That straining towards the future to be made
Is this stretching towards the eternal day to come.

Then which ensanguined flags,
Which saffron satin standards stand
At the highway's end
At the garden's gates?

And what happened
To the first bright paradise?
And what happens
In the muddy middle of the road?

Diary of Flora Baum

December 1

The American elm is the tree of December
Before the snow. It gives to winter,
Before the winter, a brilliant crispness,
Lucid exuberance, gives to winter
A vision of vigor, of elegance, of height
Fine, grand, rich, spare. It is a pulpit
From which, on which, I am tempted to preach.
I will not preach. I will drink the wine
Of the wineglass pulpit, of the wineglass, of the chalice
Of delight.

       I am inebriated.
There are fireworks here. I am dizzy with wine
And fire. I float, not falling, higher.

Diary of Flora Baum

December 8

The purity and power of the elm,
The gentle strength and splendor of the stem,
The aspiring and condescending of the branches,
Reach, preach, a spotlessness that could suggest
A thought, a concept, a conception
Wintry, pristine, once primitive,
Now presiding towards the end.

The elm is not the end, nor is December.
The elm alleges . . .

                Yes, I heard the words.
And can my version fail to name
As Adam named in paradise?

Diary of Flora Baum

Sunday, 7 p.m., December[1]

An assonance of abstraction,
A folly of embodiment,
Dance, prance, walk, stalk, whirl, twirl
Around me as,
Drunk at the trunk that mediates between hard ground and impenetrable sky,
While the little week alliterates unwinding wispily,
I await the eighth day.

---

[1] Day of the month missing.

Diary of Flora Baum

Wednesday, December[1]

Had I forgotten, or had I remembered?
I checked the elm. Could I forget
The strings attached? They dangle.
Are they entangled almost, or entangling?

Can we, shall we, say what we see?
Won't we, will we, tell how we feel?
The sun behind those strings,
Back of those hanging strands,
Dazzled enough to draw gloved hands
Up to cover and reveal.
The sun was hanging back behind the tree.
I recall all these things.

The sky I saw was a heavenly blue.
The elm's lengthening lines I felt celestial.
The angelic form mattered more, much more,
Than the matter.

---

[1] Day of the month illegible.

Diary of Flora Baum

December 20

Although two miles away another elm
Rose only in the mutilated beauty
Of the still lovely bole left lingering
By ruthless plague and cruel guillotine,
This elm is not acephalous, yet I,
Sinking, just some puppet of the sun,
Huddle, hungry. Buds that bead each string
Glint as I squint. My head goes up and droops.
My hands move up and drop. Are jewels fruits?

Is this then gravity? or levity?
Or rest? or motion? In one solar year,
Within one revolution, Galileo,
Pallid as winter, pale as winter's gleam,
Wilted, chilled, in the south, set in the east,
On January eighth, and in the north
Bloomed Isaac Newton, rising in the west,
On Christmas Day, December twenty-fifth.
The year was sixteen hundred forty-two.
But the Italian, by the English date,
Died on December twenty-ninth, a year
Before, in sixteen hundred forty-one,
And, by Italian time, the Englishman
First saw the light on January fourth,
In sixteen forty-three, a later year.
Within one solar round one went, one came:
Between the twenty-ninth and twenty-fifth
Of two Decembers or between the eighth
And fourth of two successive Januaries.
We count the days three hundred sixty-one.

How do we count our years? My years have foundered.
How do we name our days? My days are numbered.

The sun is on the elm, is in the elm.
Such subtle russet bubbles gleam, such small
Baubles along, among, strings glistening.
And I am called, am pulled, am chilled, am cold.

I have not lost my head, but I am numb,
Sinking, sunk, a puppet of the sun.

Two

Brithday Card

December 11
Elaine Gillis Storella

The eleventh day of December,
A sun's day once in Rome
(How I do love thee, sun, thou scion of the south!),
Is in New England
A day for the American elm
(How many live, still live!).

Dear friend, forgive
Parentheses, apostrophes,
Explanations, exclamations.

The sun may descend.
The golden foils may have descended.
The elm in December
Surrenders no totality of charm.
What it has lost of leafiness
It gains in subtler shapeliness,
While rising towards the sky in clarity
Of rising line,
Returning towards the earth in utterly
Relaxed returning.

Were its leaves more concrete, more material, more real?
Its foliage fallen away,
It gains in abstraction.

I know, I feel,
I see the stem and see the extended branches,
The pleasure of direction and of indirection

(How I have loved thee, sun!).

Some sun remains,
Some ray at the level of my eye
Below the elm.

The elm attains
Some space up above me in the sky,
The solar realm.

I mean I meet
The star beneath
The dome of the tree.

They are
Our special tree and star
If we are we.

We greet
Them almost with belief
As our dissimilar tremendous friends

(Friend sun, friend elm, your friendship never ends!).
Each incarnates. Each transcends.

And no disturbance of words, as of, let us say,
Ulmus, sol, olmo, sole, orme, soleil,

Rends
Such potent blends,

Can tear
Simplicities so bare.

I am not breathing Roman air.

Which is our river?
The Tiber?
The Seine? This day the Charles
Curls
Swift and swifter
Into the ice of our winter.

Tomorrow may we not be elsewhere? Where?
(Today I watch before thee, elm, abider!)

Could I neglect one curlicue, one bend?
Could I reject one gift of such a giver?

I seek to offer and am blest receiver.

Dear friend,
You comprehend.
You generously share
Your own anniversaire
With celebrations of prosopopoeia.
We (who are we?) extend
Our holy love and spiritual care
Throughout infinities
Of Uranus and Gaea
And all their progenies
Nor with this prodigality impair
What we prodigiously expend.

(Elm unpersonified and there
And standing fast and firm and free
And actual and existential,
How truly I do love thee, tree!)

Can I refuse to choose
Between the that and the what?

The elm in December
I am compelled to declare
Essential elemental elegance
Of element, of essence, of idea,
Of the ideal.

I dare
To speak as I feel.

The elm in December
Is both presence and memory.

Then shall I speak of a friend as resembling an elm?

There are friends like elms.
There are elms like friends.
There are American elms
That have survived in New England.

Dear friend, live happy ever after!
Does only Janus know the future?

Though I ignore my ignorance and bear
The agony of contradiction
I am not altogether unaware
Of limitation and affliction.

I am unable to ignore these elms.

How many live! How many I can love!
How many lived! How many I have loved!
Ideals do not die.

Birthday Card

December 23
Alice Jane Karo

The notes that flowed from body, bow, and strings
Seemed a weeping,
But now the sound,
The cry of the violin rising into the sky,
Shouted out to the sky,
Is likened to the lifting limbs of the elm,
Simple in solidity,
Variously sifting
Air, with grace
From grace to grace shifting,
Drifting into the extra seconds of the sun,
Seconding the sun.

Birthday Card

May 5
Ombretta Frau

The oaks that were so golden in November
Are golden once again. But this is May.
The man who was so golden, on this day
Was, for he was no more. Do we remember

When Bonaparte departed? Shall we tremble
As Europe trembled when his shadow lay
Across, beyond, its bounds? Can the sun stay?
Does the descending autumn shade resemble

The fragrant shade of Maytide? Shall we call
The bright, declining end a different thing
From the brief, bright beginning? Shall we claim

That oaks at start and finish are the same,
So gloriously golden in the fall,
So delicately golden in the spring?

Birthday Card

October 25
David Perkins

When the violet was sweet and low
And the oak just hinting gold
The bloom was beauty and the tree was truth.
The time was April.

There is a Persian purple in the sky.
The Mycenaean gleam, if old,
Is new as young flame fiery with new breath
Under blue heaven.

Three

Invocation

Muse, grant me madness equal to my theme,
Madness to match the madness of the dream
That is so real. Then, Muse, infuse the sound
That whirs within the atom and around
The universe. O Muse, bestow the tune,
The beauty of the music of the moon,
The music of the beauty of the dune
On which I stand, on which I hold my ground
Between the tree, the sun, the sea, the scream.
Does trumpet shriek? Will fiddle screech? I seem
To hear the runcible and rhythmic spoon
With which I run away to beat the bound.

Birthday Card

May 23
Julia Mairin Toledo Budenz

Will there be lilacs? Will we be alive
To wander through the garden of Book Five
Among the irises? Will we survive
Under laburnum?

Must purple yield to gold? Does it behoove
Dawn's car and day's to cut the selfsame groove
Down the high road to night? Do forests move,
Coming from Birnam?

Diary of Flora Baum

May 24

Having addressed my god and then my author,
I now address my work. The world is green.
The oak is verdurous, the elm is verdant,
The end, across the garden, past the meadow,
Beyond the wood, is emerald. I guess
To know is labor and to know is leisure.

The leaves in light breathe us a life of air.
Long have we lived in breeze, in trees, in seas.
Sweet is the salt wind blowing from the ocean.
Large is the sweet wisp wafted from the locust.
Among the great green blades that guard the border
Globules of rain glint silver on the iris.

Some quintessential memory or hope
Glows from gigantic fivefold leaflets spread
On our own buckeyes, some with effort planted,
Some sown with ease, and from their tall yet modest
Torches of gold transmuting blooms to fruits,
Some eaten, some reputed poisonous.

Some living beings sow, some plant, some study,
Some fight, some fence, and some philosophize.
While some are filling pages with their deeds,
Others are filling pages with their dreams.
And who are we who fill pages with words?

Diary of Flora Baum

May 25

At the grand banquet of the tulip tree
Droplets of sunset in each cup
Held up,
Held high,
Blent as we toasted publicly
The privacy descending from the sky.

Diary of Flora Baum

June 13

As in the modulations of the robin,
As in the involutions of the rose,

So in June I have felt a prelude,
So in June I have entered a depth,

Or will if I listen,
Or shall if I last.

Diary of Flora Baum

July 5

Did I then deny
The soft leaves of July
In silver wind beneath celeste of sky,

Sweeping, swaying, from the elm,
Bending gentle from the elm,
Leaning low from the elm,

In greenest lullaby,
In flickering hymn,
In fluttering psalm,

Over the lily and the rose?
Infant, enter now the realm
Where crimson speech unfolds and glows,

Where incandescent candid page
Flames towards the flourish of its age,
Where azure scripture grows,

For as you there grow silvery and dim
You will not there grow gray and grim,
Will not turn dumb.

A hum,
A balm,
Will brim,

Will whelm
The scum
With fresh, sweet glim,

Will, swinging, singing, ring and rim,
Will wing and skim,
Like scintillating leaves or seraphim.

Diary of Flora Baum

July 6

I loved the leafless, and I love the leafy.

By the elm I dwell.
Is this asphodel?

I live among the lilies and the lindens.

I have lived long, long,
In the land of song,

In which the principle of contradiction

Alone is wrong.
I must be strong.

The blooms in dulcitude are ever ringing,

Ding-dong,
Ding-dong.

The sweet is sweet, and sweet will be the bitter.

I have shown. Now I tell.
I toll the bell.

The true is true, and true will be the fictive.

Diary of Flora Baum

July 7

How the white clouds flower
On the deep blue of the sky,

How on the green catalpa
Clouds and clouds of flowers flower,

Shall I shout,
Or will I wish to whisper?

It is noon. The blue is deep. The green is wide.
The wide white deepens.

Diary of Flora Baum

Still July 7

I sup on apple, cheese, and bread,
And now the green is in the skies.
The violet, indigo, blue,
The yellow, orange, and red,
Do not surprise,
But that that green should stretch and rise
And fly high, arch far, overhead
Seems as miraculous as it is true.

Birthday Card

July 13
Gaius Julius Caesar

We celebrate you on the day before
Because Apollo claims this very day
If we are Romans. Here, so far away,
Beyond an ocean, on our alien shore
Of alien name, at Massachusetts Bay,
Our eve near midnight is already your
Gold dawning and Apollo's gold aurore.

Vocation

All night there is a pain about my heart.

My neighbor's television runs all night.
I make noise silent song, make darkness sight.

I will make the bitter sweet.
I will make the fictive true.

O, of July the light, the sweetest part,
Apollo, come, Apollo, healing, art.

If the true comes I will greet
Truth; if the sweet, greet sweetness, too.

I will walk among the softly talking trees.
Lingering lindens will greet me along the breeze.

Is this death's deadly or love's lovely dart?

Four

Diary of Flora Baum

October 20

During that rainy summer
I had forgotten that there were stars.
Or perhaps there were no nights
Or was no night.
Now on this October evening
After the clarity of the day of azure
A scattering of whites,
Of bright
Flakes up there in the clarity of blackness
In a kind of apophasis given the total eclipse of cloud
Predicated or predicted
The snows of the next month or the next,
And one celestial spot was etched in azure
As though that speck of day persisted,
And suns hung on the elm.
Had I forgotten that suns existed?

Diary of Flora Baum

October 21

She hesitates on the brink
Of meaning. If she goes too far
In that beckoning direction
Will the opposite be lost forever,
Will the sweet be sweet and the bitter bitter,
Will the land be land and the ocean ocean?

Shall she glide like a gull out over the glittering wave?
Shall she walk on the water?
Between the walls of the aqueous shall she wade?

If she advances into that sunlit region
In which the luxuriating foliated maple
Blazes aureate with reason,
Will Princess Ursula and her eleven thousand
Ladies-in-waiting wait,
Or will Saint Ursula and her eleven thousand
Valiant virgins vanish,
Banished from this day of crimson, this day of gold,
Rather than ascending towards the azure singing strains
Beyond constraints of earth and sea and air
Out to and into those horizons where
Meaning does not limit meaning,
Where the road not taken is taken too,
Where to be or not to be
Is this and that,
Is the bitter and the sweet,
And the bittersweet bits, those tidbits of delight,
Those brown-wrapped bars,
Those inch-long silver-guarded treasures,
Dark morsels of surprise and delectation
                                                    Dispensed

Dispensed for pennies in the subway station
To be savored pleasures
Amidst the screechings of the subway cars,
The odors, damps, cramps, crowds, crush, rush, rough jars,
Before the worldwide blight,
Before the war,
After that trampled flame
In some later game
Emerge once more
As minuscule miracles of taste, of name,
And even when consumed endure,
Where flamma, fiamma, llama, flamme is pure,
Where the flower, bloom, or blossom is allure,
Where the rose is ille flos, il fiore, la fleur, la flor?

Where it is causa, cause, or chose,
Will the rose be a rose,
Will the poem be prose?

Fragrance is always better on the breeze.
Incense is ever sweeter in the air.

In the air shall she sail?

Why in the sky do the droning, groaning aircraft circle
Like magnified flies, like monstrous mosquitoes, like satanic bees,
Torturing her ears and eyes and mind,
Advertising that which they desire
That she desiderate? Shall she yearn, burn, to find
The not much advertised bright sky of fire,
To find the very brightness of that sky,
Deiwos, deus, dios, dio, dieu,
Or to divinity brilliant as the shining light
Of an infinity filled with sky of sky,
Finally cry or sigh,
Adieu, addio, adiós?

This is not floss or gloss.
Maybe distant, maybe close,
There is a reply.
She will make it by and by.

Higher and higher the shadow climbs
Up the oak of greens, reds, bronzes, golds,
Up to alps of paradise,
Up above everests of heaven.

In the ethereal she feels at home.

She is out of her element among the machines.
Is she un-American? She does not drive.
If only she drove, how she could go
Somewhere. How she could go.

Would she encounter, would she express,
Ecstasies? excruciations?

She hesitates on the brink
Of speech, on, at, the bank
Of language. Is she driven?

In the city a car encumbers.
Into a helicopter would she hop
As from her roof it rose?
Or will she walk through the fumes
Of automobiles, of buses that start and stop,
Of smokers in exile from their rooms?
What a pity is age. She lumbers.
Will she go the way the elephant goes,
The antelope, buffalo, zebra goes?

What things go from a to b?
What things go from a to z?
Shall she designate as airships, blimps,
Or zeppelins these irritants on high,
Not high enough? Or will she try
Not to look and not to see?
Nevertheless does one quick glimpse
Unexpectedly belie
Her apprehension of each decibel
Remembered, dreaded, in the sky
As an increment of hell?

Is a blimp but a blot
Upon the blessedness of vision
Stripped of the blemish
Of the aforementioned hellish,
Of an unendingly unrepentent,
Unsound sound,
As though an innocent childhood's bright balloon
Grew too big, too brash,
Flew like a gasbag full of empty braggadocio?

Something is perceived, perceptible.
Must she query which it is or what?

Is this an aerodyne, an aerostat?
What airplane tilts and straightens, comes, will come?
What helicopter turns, turns, turns, returns?
What vast balloon floats captive or floats free?
Which airship or which dirigible,
Nonrigid, semirigid, rigid, fat
With hydrogen if not with helium,
Sails, obeys directions, burns?

Did she see the inflation of the ship?

Did she see more than the hulking hull
Of the high-class hotel in the heavens?
Did she see the affluent passengers rapt
At the view from their slanting, open windows
As they bent over the spires of New York City?
They could not be smoking at such a moment,
Sequestered in the special space below.
Of course, there was a smoking room although
A year before, when, clad in flowing alb
And ample airy chasuble and with
The maniple that bore its Latin cross
Hanging upon his arm like a remnant of wing,
The flying missionary, Father Schulte,
On the feast of Saint Michael the Archangel's Apparition,
Offered Mass above the North Atlantic,
The candles on the altar were not lit.

Father Paul Schulte now has said the first
Real High Mass, the American announcers punned.
Fulton J. Sheen, then still Monsignor Sheen,
When later he introduced the German Oblate
To the students of Catholic University
In Washington, asserted that Our Lord
And Savior Jesus Christ had celebrated
The first Holy Mass on land, and an Apostle,
Peter or Paul, the first Mass on the water,
And, only after nineteen hundred years,
The flying priest, the first Mass in the air.

Of Catholic Masses she knew nothing at all.
An atheist was she
And merely nearly three.
Of Christian crosses she knew nothing at all.

A crucifix must have hung above the altar,
No, must have stood before the tilted windows.

Did she guess at the fresh flowers,
The linen tablecloths, the silverware,
The shimmering wines from the wine cellar in the keel?
Prohibition had lost its powers
Three and a half — or nearly — years before.
Her parents drank no alcohol at all.

Did she see the few excrescences of the ship,
The small control car down at the bottom towards the bow,
And four more cars, nacelles, those gondolas,
Two on port side, two on starboard side,
For the engines with their roar and, at their rear,
The four four-bladed wooden propellers, or rather,
Behind each of these streamlined power cars,
The two two-bladed propellers fastened together,
And, abaft, the cruciform unit for the stern,
Two horizontal fins with elevators,
Two vertical fins with rudders and crooked crosses?

BY THE TREE

Did she see D-LZ one two nine
Inscribed above East Nineteenth Street?
Two weeks and three days hence she would turn three.
Officially she still was only two.
What counting or what reading could she do?
The story from the storybook hung suspended.
The history commenced. The mother lifted
Face, voice, and finger skyward. Then the child
Looked, and her gaze reached something. Did she see
The bent eight-cornered crosses over New York?

How from the fire escape a childish eye
Beheld a whale sail up in the sky
Before its flaming fall
She cannot recall.
Over Manhattan passed
The Hindenburg that Thursday afternoon
Early in May.
It had to take, cursed,
A course the same as that of the last
Year, the which lay
Across to Lakehurst.
It would berth there very soon.
New Jersey was not very far away
While it was cruising above East Nineteenth Street
In nineteen thirty-seven bound to meet
A Thursday evening's cheat.

It crossed. There is a blur.
Should she have called it her?

But there and then the burnt or broken bodies
And then the giant's crumpled skeleton
Testified. The cause is still in question.

Thus that was that. This thing is far from focal.
This flat, this garish, thing is not celestial,
Not tragic, not disastrous, is defeat
Of the quotidian kind, the unbearable kind
To be borne one day and then another day.

                                                  Which

Which is the name that names the one that thunders
Without a scripture read as rain or rainbow
Or script of lightning or enlightening,
The one that moans and mocks like a fallen angel
Back up in heaven malevolent and angry?

She will visit the Bibliothèque.
She will visit the Internet.
She will check and check and check.
She will get and get and get.
Words will turn to things and so
She will learn, will not not know.
Ah, but what of the words she learned and loved long long ago?
As the red glitter and glister and glisten and glint and glow
On heights, on depths, of endless blue is the tupelo,
And as the trusted truth of the tree
To druid, to dryad, has been, will be,
Is shelter, self, identity,
So the duramen, the discovery,
Of a high, deep, archaeology
Of a beam that leafs in a fiery glee
Of tongues is her core, is her heart, is she.

She means it all to mean so much
She pastures herds,
She manufactures curds,
She mines,
She refines,
She is a millionaire of words
Of which you must experience the touch
Of each as all advance in hordes,
And if you peep between the lines
To catch reverberations of some chords
Subtler than such
You will receive rewards.

Her journal turns epistolary. Who
On earth are you?

She runs a mint. From consonants and vowels
She issues sounds to treasure or to spend.
Will they be audible among the howls?
How will it all end?

Are her crossroads crucial, trivial?
Is she too cold? Is she too hot?
Will she find in fine a finial,
An anodyne, a thermostat?

The unrelenting plane or helicopter, near
Or far, is far too loud, too coarse.
She will never be heard. She cannot hear
Herself. She will not use force.

Up above her head flew meaningless noises,
The utterances of adults. Pearl Harbor. Choices.
Our war commenced when she was seven.
When it was over she was eleven.

She is a pacifist. She will not shoot
This pitiless plane or that or that or that.
Four roar, no, five, no, six, no, more, yes, eight.
Gratuitous pollution of this blue,
This graceless violation of the sky,
Must be unjustified, must not be right,
She thought, must not . . . But she is deaf, is mute.

She thought because she cannot think.
Is she on the brink?
Is her all in flux?
Is she about to reach the crux?

Does she mean to mean
In a place between?
Will she enter
A center
Where image
Or where mesoscale

Could

Could certainly avail
Without a scrimmage?
Ave atque vale. Hail, be hale.
After the reds let there again be green.

Quantitas materiae est,
He wrote, mensura ejusdem . . .
Newton's Latin is easy enough,
His mathematics very tough,
His physics quite a climb,
She thought, all out of breath, far from the crest,
Though motion is the same as rest.
As for the questions of her time,
Can she approach, not to say discuss, them,
Not to say, in rhyme?
Her macroscales are pitifully rough
And things much smaller than she could have guessed.

Who is standing there
Poised with a puny sling?
How can a vast, immense, enormous thing,
Gigantic, mammoth, rare,
Be a lightweight mass,
Be a big bag of gas,
Be a lot of hot air?

What is the meaning of the symphony?
Is the cathedral, is the Comedy,
Architecture or theology?

Is her fall free?
Is this her diary?
Why do I call her she?

Diary of Flora Baum

October 23

She hesitates on the edge.

Is the euonymus aflame?
She hesitates at the hedge.

Is the self the same?
I hesitate at the edge.

Diary of Flora Baum

Tuesday, November 7

Must you, O Tuesday, be the day of Mars,
Or are you Zeus's, Jove's, and Jupiter's?

Something must shine above the deodars.
Is it Diana? Is my journal hers?

Once I heard Willkie, Roosevelt, and Browder.
That sound is softer now. Must this be louder?

That is the first choice that my life remembers.
Now I must dial through sixteen Novembers.

Can earth be verdant still? The sky is azure.
The leaves are flickering. Must earth turn bronzer?

To benefit a kingdom of amassers
Must some estate accept a season's tonsures?

This diary must rise past sky, sun, star,
To Tiwaz and to Tiu and to Tyr.

Must this be light of day or night of war,
Choosing Buchanan, Nader, Bush, or Gore?

Diary of Flora Baum

Wednesday, November 8

How mercurial
The political

Can be I did not know
Twenty-four hours ago.

O my florid Florida, your fount
Of life is found. You count.

This our creed: One life, one vote,
All of us the witenagemot.

Will we not now abolish
The electoral college

While differences diminish
And the living image

Is of the sums that go on slowly mounting
As we keep recounting?

Mercury or Woden may connote
Paradigm or antidote.

Diary of Flora Baum

Thursday, November 9

It may be the day of Jove
Or may be the day of Thor
When the oaks glow bronze and gold
And the sky glints silver.
Or is it iron?
Or is it lead?
We feel the feel of effulgence
As we submit to hints of winter
Or at least of weather.

Diary of Flora Baum

Friday, November 10

What is the silver glint of May
To the silver glint of November?

What is the iris to the sky?

What is rain to my cheek
Or Latin to my tongue?

What today is venerable, what free?

Sweet is the falling of the golden leaf,
Sweet the unfolding of the golden rose.

Whose wish will win?

What friendly planet hides behind the cloud?
Which winsome goddess hides behind the word?

This is the fragrance of foliage, this of a flower.

Trees were filling. Trees are emptying.
Blooms came, come, come.

Was it the sacred name or hallowed function?

What appellation flashed in prayer?
What title blazed in sacrifice?

And what am I to blossom, beam, and heaven?

What if the son of Venus knew
That Julians are Jupiter's?

Diary of Flora Baum

September 11

Rome was not built in a day
Like New York.
Rome did not fall in a day
Like New York.
O my,
O my own old Rome,
O my own New York,
Is there something to say
In a day
On a day?
Is there something to sigh?
How long was I rooted in rock?
How long did I flame afire for the azury empire of sky?
In the dock
Can that be I,
O my own sweet home?

Diary of Flora Baum

October 11

Remember Pearl Harbor.
So close to childhood's evergreen arbor
Over my head
Grownup voices flew
Through December dark dropping
Words which like bombs
In my ears exploded.
Holly boughs bead red.
Can words be written up on leaves?
Have leaves been blown down streets of eves?
What did words once say?
What blew leaves away?
Have words been dropped?
Can bombs be stopped?
Beneath my feet
I feel a feeble cry.
Remember Versailles.

Diary of Flora Baum

October 25

Who unfurls sentences? Who hurls the stars?
Will the trees cease to breathe beneath the stars?
Why is the sugar maple sweet with gold?
Why is the honeylocust soft in gold?
I who have opened my mouth beneath the tree
Tasting both good and evil and have known
Neither, known nothing, stand with fruit in hand
And lips apart and stiff and still. And will
I cease to breathe if I must cease to speak?

Diary of Flora Baum

October 26

Why pose a question from a different year
As though to query from a different star?
Who may with uninfected breath endure
To ask, to tell, to be, what we once were?
Distant, familiar, does the silver moon
Above the golden needles of the pine
Growing reflect as goldenness goes down
How fall is spring and old gold is new green?

Diary of Flora Baum

October 29

Shall I admit, amidst the bronze and gold,
The world and I are wintry invalids,
Too long too sick, too blind, too early old?

It is yet summer in the golden rose,
Not yet November in the bronzy beech.
Shall I admit this story has been told?

Behold in me the nursling of the good.
Behold the handmaid of the true. Behold
The bride of beauty.

     Pink and white, the flower
Dazzles in delicacy. Before the rush
Downward of darkness, in a burst of spring
The mockingbird begins once more to sing.

Diary of Flora Baum

Halloween

When my work was play,
When I was dedicating every day,
Devoting every hour,
To the Fragments
Of Vulgar Things,
I learned the poet's seven words for arrow.
Out of a land, a world, of plague and war,
Through an amaritude of sweetest rhyme,
Each dart
Became a weapon that went flying
Into the heart.
Must the missiles of metaphor,
Must the arms of art,
Be blunter,
Carriers causes of less anguished crying,
Sources springs of less impassioned sorrow,
Than all these pointed shafts, appointed segments,
Which power
Through this late
Though no less bitter time
Shoots, slings,
In love, in hate,
So as to enter
Being's center?

Diary of Flora Baum

November 1
All Saints

Once we made it
It might have been better
If we had stayed up there
On the calm and cloudless moon.

Diary of Flora Baum

November 8
Mundus patet

The library is still open.
On the way some golden ovals are still golden up on the elms
And more lie down on the dark of the grass and of the path
And most have already been banished by the blowers.
I still can open the doors,
And the system is not down, and the shelves are full,
And still
I have rushed once again between this and that leaf
To gobble knowledge, never tasting truth.

Diary of Flora Baum

November 11

Some golden ghosts keep haunting chosen trees.
Felled multitudes lie dying in the streets.
Hosts blown clash, scatter, under man's machines
Or nature's blasts, with siffling or shrill shrieks.

Birthday Card

November 24
Joanna Maria Budenz Gallegos

Not in November's nebulosity
A sudden spacious space of azure in the sky,

Not in too sudden sundown
The flash of a gold on the Chrysler Building's spire,

Not lone golds of leaves lingering among the browns of the beech,
Not the last gold of the last gold rose glittering in the darkening park,

Not notes, bass or treble, of excitement
Articulate and intellectual

Within the constant calls of the weeping wind
Crying along long avenues of Manhattan,

Not only this, this, this,
Not only that,

But under dark long lashes
The baby's big blue gaze,

But on the child who dances
The golden ringlets gleaming, dancing too,

But from the roses of girlish lips sweet laughing
In Latin, Spanish, Portuguese, Italian,

Sweet breathing, babbling, chattering, sweet laughing,
Soft, subtle, sinewed, sensible, in French,

Laughter, language,
Earthy, urban,

That ripples up the streets, above the river,
Into the mists, and lightly over the clouds

Was what the first big sister saw with joy,
Heard with delight and pride.

Not in November's negativity
Another no was uttered but a new

Unawkward, gracious, golden, blue,
Resilient, smiling, saffron, sapphire oui.

Five

Diary of Flora Baum

May 15

Patient: I do not know what the prognostication is.
Doctor: The prognosis.

Am I not only words, yes, only words,
And not not only words but also something,
But words alone, since not is positive?

How can I then be Mrs. Malaprop?
Ms. Malaprog is what I am. I am
Miss Malaprognos. Must I miss or mix?

Prognosis glints of science, medicine,
Pure Greek, Hippocrates or Aristotle,
Newtonian. Hypotheses non fingo.

Prognostication hints at hybrid, hiss,
Hick, hit or miss, religion, divination,
Part Greek, part Latin. Fingo. Am I fiction?

Flora Urania Baum will I remain,
Linguistic mix upon a triple tongue,
True not to bloom, sky, tree, but to the song?

Diary of Flora Baum

May 23

But I, or rather my originator,
Must gasp aghast at maladies past language,
My origin and my original,
For she not only speaks but acts and is.
She is, for instance, the Miss Maladrop,
And in the instant of each instillation
Being is doing, doing is misdone.
Not only falsely filling syllables
But also, hitting ill as she instills
Little things, missing that big thing, that eye,
She must soon lie there not just dumb but blind.

Is only death more terrible than life?
Evidence is not requisite for proof.
Is only life more terrible than death?
Evidence is not necessary if
A tiny taste of knowledge yields enough.

Do purgatories open onto hells?
I grope through speech and deed and hope. I stop.
All things are not mistakes, debts, viruses.
Not all is killing. Not all is unkind.
The shield of seven hides gleams bronze on top.
Glancing from his grim countenance he smiles.
Thorns wound. The pink sweet scent heals — or consoles.
Strata of grand and petty build to one.
Not only does Jove thunder. Rain distills
A glisten through those smooth blue irises
And soon a blue reopens through the sky.

Diary of Flora Baum

May 25

Of things that were not whites or golds
Many, if not true blue
(Is there a tune of truth for things and words,
A tone of truth for nouns and adjectives?),
Were parity and purity
Of plumes of purple.

Diary of Flora Baum

June 13

Gray as cosmic coloration.

So much rain.
So much hating of the rain.
So much loving.

Like lovings pure and passionate
Great white clusters in bloom
Pendent and unfallen and unfalling

Among the great green skies of the virgilia
Under the greater fostering skies of gray
And the fostering fall of the rain.

The softly indigo iris standing strong
And soft and softly
Embracing rain, by rain embraced.

So many raindrops.
So many graves.
So many new graves dropped below the rain.

So many rosebuds red as lovely
Little kisses kissed by raindrops.
Above the grave the rosetree with its blossoms

Osculated into gold.

Diary of Flora Baum

June 15

Staring at the tulip tree
I quaff its cups of sun.
If I drink only with my sight
Will I be filled with light and light
And will my chalice run
Over? Is knowledge pledged to me?

Part Two

The Tree of Knowledge

It might be March.

I know how it feels to stand in front of the sun,
In front of the sun in the tree,
In front of the tree in the sun.
It feels like of and like in.
I know, too, that the front feels like knowing.

It may be April.

THE TREE OF KNOWLEDGE

All that I loved is lost or will be lost.
Earth will be left below. Already heaven
Has been dissolved. The simile alone
Survives, like ancient forest and cicada,
Like Helen's delicate and tender tears,
Like Helen's undimmed beauty in dim eyes
Of aged Trojan orators on towers
Of Ilium by very beauty doomed,
Like potent shock of sweetness of viburnum,
Like glimpse into the garden where, across
Vastness of grass, lawn green again, perfection
Of pink floats delicate and full, the weeping
Cherry afloat in laughter, in perfection
Of plenitude and tenuous demesne,
Until ascending I can enter azure.

Zeus. Wicked. Agamemnon names.
Zeus. More deadly. Menelaus moans.
Apollo. Most deadly. Achilles claims.
Aphrodite. Devilish. Helen groans.
Whom a god hates. Who a god blames.
Whom a god loves. Who a god owns.

Deus disintegrated. Saints dissolved.
The splinters and the drops lodged, lived, in me,
Growing as ghosts and goddesses and gods
That charmed my mind and that entranced my heart.

A bottle of the goldenmost Meursault,
A buffet or a banquet multicolored
On the white tablecloth, tender temptation
Even to one abstemious or lean,

Especially to one abstemious
Or lean, one's hunger hugely comforted
By gluttony and by extravagance
Or by the solace of a single sip.

Deus meus, quare me dereliquisti?
My God, is it that I abandoned you?
The dead elm was hacked down and dragged away.
Why do I see it on this empty sky?
It stood tall, reached out widely, and yet through
Green leafiness I grasped moon's white, noon's blue.
I saw it and I saw by it. It fell.
Is seeing what is not or is not seeing
More perilous? The peril is believing.
The tree, the truth, the trust are crossed, are crossed
Out, exed, ex. I know not what I do.
I know that you are not. I know no more.
No, more I know. There is more that I know.
I know that I know not. Betrothed to knowing,
Veiled in the bridal white of this weeping cherry
Gleaming in azure, sapphire, silver, gold,
I know not blossom, branchlet, bough, beam, beaming.
Abandoned, derelict, abandoning
The trust, the truth, I must, in sooth, in ruth,
Brush off the tears, wait gazing, step ahead.
I still will cross the field, I still will seek,
Seeking if necessary what is not,
Seeking if necessary what might be,
As misery flirts with pomposity,
As the elm stands gigantic, vanquished, vanished.
And was there ever an elm, ever a cherry,
Ever a weeping over a death? The present,
The past, the future fuse and fade and fail.
You were so long the now, the one, the all.
So long you beckoned. Long, so long, you tugged
And took. You ate my unreluctant heart.
Then was I heartless? Or was I infused
With purity of mere ethereal fire?
Then we were separated, separate,

So long

So long disjunct. Then how could you come back?
Ne nos inducas in tentationem.
My God, you are temptation. You are my
Temptation, you my tempter. You, my God,
Are not my God. You are not mine. You are
Not you. You are not. Flashes crack the oak.
So long. I am alone again. So long.
No longer dreaming you, I search out it.
Through this last desert I will seek the tree.
This is my loneliness. This is my trysting.

I did not die while I stared heavenward,
Glimpsing the infinite, forever yearning
To live eternally with the eternal.

I will die when the dying is a death.

The pear tree rises, white, spectacular,
Not specular. It shines towards azure, bright.
This flourish makes a minute worth existence.

The hours of mere survival
Are neither death nor life.
Must I then like Tithonus
Be nothing but a voice,

A voice that says the lilacs
Are barely opening
Yet with their first faint fragrance
Ratify the spring?

Someone Homeric might say to some other,
Orseo, orseu, orso: Rise! You know —
And here you must be I — I rise, I know
These forms, their variations, and their reasons,
Even if "rise" is not an apt translation
In many if not all of those twelve verses
Where one of these imperatives appears.
Is grammar nothing? Is morphology
The trivial at most? The trivium,
Or rather from its plenty one small path,
Must be the whole, the goal, the sole, my soul.
Is there glee when one tiny beech bloom blossoms,
Obscure and purplish on the great gray tree?

THE TREE OF KNOWLEDGE

Was it dualistic?
Was it a knowledge of God or the devil?
Was it solely the rich self's sweetest savor?
By sampling each of the plums she knew
That two fruits grew
And gleamed
On that golden bough of help
On this verdant tree of light.
Was she I?

Was it monolithic?
Was it a knowledge of good and of evil?
Was it purely the poor self's fullest flavor?
Was it a matter of life and death?
She tasted both.
It seemed
It was of grammar a gulp,
It was of beauty a bite.
I was she.

Thank you, I said. To whom?
To whom? To what?
To whatever came
Into my heart
For better, not for worse,
Out of the universe.
Thank you, I said, to some
Bright distant spot.

White dogwood bright by darkest purple beech
First as pure vision glimpsed will quickly reach
Deep consciousness and then burst into speech.

They were both standing, and the sword had shattered.
He dragged him by the beautiful plume of his helmet,
Luxurious sweep of a horse's gorgeous mane,
And under his chin as he was hauled along
The fine elaborate embroidered strap
Choked him drawn tight against his tender throat.
Strong was that band of leather from the hide
Not of an old ox ravaged by age and disease
But of the bull with forceful purpose slaughtered,
With violent deliberation killed.
Who broke that choking thong, who snapped that strap?
She of all beings the most beautiful
In all the universe of radiance.
A beauty saved a beauty for a beauty
Until the ultimate in ugliness
Had won. For now, the empty helmet hurled
By Menelaus in whose powerful hand
It hung for just an instant until swung
Slung flung from the measured space set for the duel
Into the gathered ranks of watching Greeks
It touched a bit of ground among his friends
Had come to comfort one side as bronze prize.
The trusty comrades picked it up. The goddess
Picked Paris up and hid him in thick mist,
Facilely carrying him, as gods can do,
Back to his scented bedroom and his Helen.

Go to him, he is shining with beauty, she said.
You would not guess he is just back from combat.
You would conjecture he is on his way to a dance.
And she herself despite her disguise was shining
With beauty. Though the Trojan women saw
An aged female slave from Sparta, Helen
Among them high on the wall where they watched the duel
Played on the plain discerned the elegant beauty
Of neck, observed the ravishing beauty of breast,
Perceived the radiant beauty of eye, and answered,
I will not go to him. You go to him.
You love him. Ache for Paris. Care for Paris.
What force was this? The goddess made her go.
What force of nature or divinity,
Compulsion of divinity or nature,
Made Helen go, with scorn, rebellion, dread,
To what the cosmos asked of her, his bed?

Robins. Lilacs. Trees
Tall, spreading, green.
Gentleness of song, of breeze.
Expansiveness of something seen.
Let me last a little longer, please.

THE TREE OF KNOWLEDGE

Three oaks standing. Shall I advance
To syntax? Three oaks stand.
Three boles stand in a line.
Three oaks rise in a row.
Three trunks wait in a queue.
These poles are simple, straight, severe.
Parataxis suits simplicity.
Shall I advance to hypotaxis?
If branches lift and arch and crest, if leaves,
Still new and fresh, float full and green,
If golden dangles linger or have left
The boughs to subtle futures as the spinnings,
As the weavings, as the stitchings, as the wearings
Of time, of space, of movement even in
Stillness of wind, even in quietude
Of action, interaction, thrust, reverse,
Reach, involution, intermingle, will
Simplicity be fitly understood,
Complexity complexly comprehended?

The biding bloom is small.
The silent tree is tall.
The distant sky is dark.
Asyndeton is stark.

Where is a conjunction?
What is the connection?

THE TREE OF KNOWLEDGE

Must the grammar of beauty
Include a grammar of loss?
These large, these lush, these luscious lustrous clusters
Of lilac droop in the rain.
These individuals, these little lovely
Multitudes of tetrapetalous blossoms
Of lilac rust in the rain.
Big green leaves last.

Is there, can there be, a grammar of lasting?
Is there, could there be, a grammar of gain?
How many commas, how many question marks,
Precede the period? Three periods
Parading make the spaced suspension points
Which march in space, which silently proclaim . . .
If large, if green, if leafy leaves of lilac last . . .
Summer has not yet begun.

What are these marks that mark the fading page,
What these sharp points playing against dull age?

They will march into space with a trumpeted proud proclamation . . .
They will be anapaests! Must they merely remain punctuation?

If little lovely multitudes of blossoms
Are lovely multitudes of little blossoms
Or multitudes of lovely little blossoms
Must multitudes become less lovely? Will
The little blossoms glint less multiple?

The little lilac blossoms like stars shine.
Can multiples gleam multitudinous?
Whence is the bright beam? Where the equal sign?
Can multitudes be multiplicitous?
Does summer rise or does the spring decline?

Are such the spaces of astronomy?
Where is a logic, music, mathematic?
To what grand duels does phonology
Utter its challenges so phonomanic
To grammar, rhetoric, or poetry?

If multitudes of blossoms
Are multitudes of blossom . . .

THE TREE OF KNOWLEDGE

The tree of knowledge grows in Paradise.
Does the tree die or live or fall or rise?

But, no, the tree of knowledge rose at Aulis.
Does knowledge win or lose or rise or fall?

Was the snake lying tempter or true sign?
Did he devour? Did he invite to dine?

And was the woman Helen? Was she Eve?
Was there a god we guessed or could believe?

Is the dream realized by sacrifice?
Did son or daughter pay the bloody price?

Is the tree bright or shrouded in a pall?
Can we see something? Do we know at all?

The disintegration is also,
Is equally, is especially,
Of the self. It is a kind
Of unselfing, even in the recognition
That one is not unselfish, not selfless,
Although the self itself crumbles
To crumbs, to dust,
Anticipating ash.
There is so little, yet what there is
Is a mess.

But this sky is so clean and blue
That all the laburnums start turning into gold
And the wide sugar maples above
And the blades of grass beneath
Are of that green of which freshness is so essential
It seems easily everlasting
Although only the moment
Matters, lasting long enough,
Briefly opening large enough,
To be whole.

THE TREE OF KNOWLEDGE

It is hard to imagine.
There are poets
Whose pages are published,
Whose publications are read.
Then there is the sort of poet
Or poetaster
Whose iris gardens of purple and gold
Are opened upon only by her own eyes.
This is her purification,
Perhaps a purgatory,
Possibly a hell,
Maybe the paradise
In which she exists like Adam
Before the arrival of Eve.

At times the measures measure out the times
Exactly, as the times and measures match
And new and old and old and new are one
In wonder. Thunder thunders. Azure answers
Over the verdant choruses of oaks.

Then there appear to be days when an irregular
Breathing births suddennesses
Of sobs, unexpectednesses
Of short laughs, necessitudinousnesses
Of holding one's breath.

Why have I failed?
Where are the flowers?
Why am I a failure?

Can it be fate?
Is it a flaw?
Is it my fault?

Is it the gods?
Is it my guilt?
Is it a garden?

Is it that first garden,
That first gift,
That great fall,

Or the first four gardens not forgiven?
The fifth garden is growing fitfully,
Still glimpsed, not given up, not fixed, not finished.

Something still glows. Is it a Troy in flames?
Is it one further Goetterdaemmerung?
Is it the sight of white azalea alight,
The recognition of red rhododendron afire,
A gasp, if even the last, at the azury aether ablaze?

Is sky the end? Now here on earth
The sweetness of the robin meets
The sweetness of the robinia. Now
Long, full, candid floats the blossom,
Long, full, canorous flows the song.
Night falls, as it must. Must sweet May end?

The metaphor becomes the simile.
The cloud of soldiers turns into the cloud
Seen from the mountain by the goatherd man
As it comes down the sea under westwind's blast
And to him far away black black like pitch
Appears as it moves down the sea and brings the big stormwind.
Seeing he shudders and takes his flock under a cave.
Not like the man, not like the animals,
Were the massed warriors, but like the weather.
Is this the story or is this the song?
The Ajax duo armed. Their soldiers marched.
King Agamemnon seeing them waxed glad.

Who were the fighters? They were lusty youths
Nurtured by nature's God, by azure's Zeus.

Whether the roses were the weather or
A time of year, whether they were the world
Or merely a weeping in the rain or merely
A waiting for the rosy-fingered dawn
Ask the roses if you have a moment.

To visit the virgilias one goes
On pilgrimage and, reverent, lifts one's eyes
To grand and whitely lustrous pendencies
Stately, stilled, billowing, filled, on their fresh green seas,
And, no less reverent, sensitive, lifts one's nose
To exhalations strange and sweet that rise
And condescend to sense. The same charm frees
The heart imprisoned in its miseries,
Enchants and elevates. The same wind blows
As topmost blossoms toss upon blue skies.

What is a failure? Such a simple thing.
A failure is a break within the ring.

To fail is not to do what one must do.
To fail is not to be what one must be.

One must deduce for any tree a life.
One must infer for any bloom a time.
One must imagine for the self a self.
One must accomplish for the rhyme a rhyme.

Is this not easy? Must this not be true?
Shun complication. Ban complexity.

A subtle blending of bole, blossom, sky
Must be success, complexity be I.

Here is some sun and some blue after days of grays and rain.
Here is the mighty beech arising high into glory.
Here is the gentle tree. Can might be gentleness?
Can gentleness be might? Can darkness be such light?
The blackest purple is the whitest silver shining
In all the gleaming leaves, the gleaming of a million
Shimmering leaves. Can they be fragile? With the power
Of the titanic trunk are they to be contrasted
Or is the contemplation of the whole a joy
Sober, subtle, rational, ecstatic, total?

Olden-time, old-fashioned,
Intimately plush,
Innocently plain,
Exquisitely pale,
Delicately pink,
Not without folds of deeper rosiness
And secrets of some subtler singleness
Amid the greenness of their wreaths of leaves
Along the whiteness of their picket fence,
Are these breathing roses
As sweet, so sweet, as they are
Because in their brief season,
Entangled and relaxed,
They blossom only once?

Then must the future be forgotten and forgone
Before it is the past
Or are that darkness and that dream
The fair fields of the flashlight's beam
Whether or not they last
While little minutes go on ticking
And little footfalls go on clicking
On towards that knowledge, vast
And waiting, that could glimmer in dim hints of dawn?

Is the smile of the roses
The reflection of my smile
Or is mine a reflection
Of theirs?

Is the sob of the robin
My sob or his
Song?

The linden is immense and old.
The innumerable blooms are very small and very new.
Could they be deliciously sweet
To the linden? They are to me.

THE TREE OF KNOWLEDGE

Well, dear old self,
Yes, my own self,
Well, Flora Baum,
Even in June,
Well, yes, Flora Urania Baum,
Even in June in Cambridge, Massachusetts,
Know thyself,
Well, yes, know thyself.

Yet remember.

And coming home
From nature, from the cosmos, from the whole,
To the rented apartment, to some
Normal disaster, to some
Ordinary catastrophe, remember

To remember.

Facing the absolute
One chooses all or nothing.
Like Therese of the roses
I said: I choose all.

She said, and went away
To the land of the roses.
She rose to the realms
Of everlasting bloom.
She flew to the absolute
And dwells in that domain.

I said: I choose all.
What else could I say?
What less could I do?
My feet could walk
Among the perishable roses,
My heart could run

Towards an imperishable rest
In the deathless ecstasy of all.
It was a dying. Now here I am living.
Here now must I say: I choose nothing?

The trouble was
That it was such a love.
It was such a love
And it was such a choice
And such a being chosen.
It did not matter
That I was never worthy.
It did not matter,
For it was such a passion.

If this is a poem
There must be an image,
There must be a music.
It was beyond all music,
Above all images.
I suppose it was ineffable.
This, too, is a passion.
Must it matter
If its words cannot be worthy?

Not yet the night.
Not yet the silence.

The tulip tree huge harp
To play before the sky.

Its tulips golden notes
To read for melody.

The score and instrument as one,
Reading and playing as the same.

What else is there? Traverse five gardens.
Is there before and is there after?
Count five gardens. Is there more?
Is there a past that plants the seed of life?
Remember depths.
Count five gardens and before and after.

Is God the first?
Is Death the last?
Before the Garden of Life
Is there the sky?
After the Garden of Knowledge
Is there the text?

If in unwavering depths I can remember
The time of the sky,
The time of the sighted unclimbed heights of sky,
Even in trembling abysses I foretell
The time of the text,
The time of the offered sturdy words of text.

Count five gardens and discover seven.
Foretell and tremble.
Is there a future that bears the fruit of knowledge?
Count five gardens and discover five.
Sky and text are everything and
Everywhere. Traverse five gardens.

Is it not unfeeling,
Is it not unseemly,
To see blooms
And to be briers,
To know roses
And to grow thorns?

As it becomes more difficult to live
Does it become much easier to leave?

This great domed oak that gleams with June's green life
Relinquishes to winter each last leaf.

June's great green life is gleaming. Does this give
To my thin wintry leaf its slim reprieve?

The noisy sea
Was like the silent soldiers.

The sea kept coming on and on
Swelling and sounding, roaring, thunderous.

The troops kept coming on and on
As though their breasts possessed no breath of voice.

The silent God
Was noisy in my heart.

Can I face this day?
Can I bear one hour?

I will live with the linden
In an ecstasy of June,

Or is it an escape?
It is not an exaggeration.

As long as the waves of fragrance keep coming on and on
Under the breaths of the breeze,

As the waves of the sea kept coming on and on
Under the breaths of the zephyr,

My breaths in my breast like the breaths of the breeze,
My breaths in the world like advancing battalions,

Not martial regiments of Mars, of Ares,
But irenic legions of Venus, of Aphrodite,

Garlanded phalanxes of Flora, of Thalia,
Harmonious ranks of Carmenta, of Camena, of Calliope, of Musa,

Keep coming on and on
Until the end comes on and on.

Why does she remember with horror
What she once experienced with joy?
What has been lost?

Nothing is lost
Except the prison
Of the delusion of being loved.

Nothing is lost
Except the darkness
Of the unreasoning of belief.

Nothing is lost
Except the torture
Of the slaughtering of the self.

Nothing is lost.
The ideal even gains in greatness
By all its purity as abstract,

For higher, more sublime, than dear I-Thou
Is bright I-It, bright, brilliant, glistering
With a grace and with a gleam as of aglaia.

The loss was the beginning, not the finish.
It was fifty years ago that she lost all
To slavery, to blindness, and to death.

It was the day after Independence Day.
Were the catalpas blooming big white bells of blossom
As in big white ritual spells of benediction?

It was nineteen fifty-six, the fifth of July.
She stepped from the apartment in Manhattan.
She stepped into the train that ran north along the river.

It was nineteen hundred fifty-six.
She was wearing those elegant slender slim blue heels
And that elegant linen suit of powder blue

Or was it that elegant linen suit of beige
And those slim high heels of matching brown?
She stepped into the taxi that ran along the country road.

She stepped into the dim enclosure.
She stripped herself of every stitch.
She tied the big black oxfords. She was robed, caped, veiled in black.

It was fifty years ago.
It was summer among the rural fields
And the wooded hills above the river.

It was summer. The black veil was a net.
The short black cape and the long black sleeves
And the long black skirts were all black wool.

It was hymned as a gift.
It was praised as a vocation.
It was called a call.

Was it ineffable?
It was unspeakable.
Now can she speak, now seek

A final minute of feeling free,
A subtle second of struggling to see,
An unclocked beat as she begins to be?

The picture fills.
The shepherd from his hills
Hears in the distance from far other mountains
What had been little rills
With wintry torrents' flood
From their first fountains
Go flowing,
Go rushing
From those high springs down to their deep ravines.

Spear bangs on spear and shield on shield
And breath meets breath
And death meets death
And groans and boasts of killers and of killed
Meet as the blood
Over the summery field
Goes flowing,
Goes rushing
Among the similes and through the scenes.

These torrents merely flow from the bathroom ceiling.
The plumbers are unable or unwilling
To specify a cause.
There is no heroism in this hurt,
But lots of water, lots of dirt,
And very little pause.

We know well that there are
The bang and the whimper,
The big bang and the little whimper.
Do we know as well that there are
The little bang and the big whimper?

Homer, too, is it
Or, similarly, they.
He is more than just a bit
Better, greater, just that way.

If Flora Baum is I
Julia must be she.
Thus when Julia comes to die
She can leave the field to me.

As the water came down through the ceiling
So the music comes up through the floor.

They moved in below me.
They called it music.

They call it music.
Do they consider me a mystery?

I do consider it a misery.
I call it miasma.

It pumps through heel and sole.
It pounds through, pummels, every pulse.

As before the descending water naiads fled
So before the ascending music muses tremble.

The oaks are standing free, not subject to these indignities.
The oaks are standing fortunate, far across the street.
The oaks stand as a threesome, beyond Massachusetts Avenue.

They feel no fatigue. They stand straight, sturdy, strong as Atlas.
They stand there like lords, like kings, regal in the majesty of Zeus.
They stand there like girls, like maidens, lovely as their resident dryads.

Are they a triunity, the good, the true, the beautiful?
Their nymphs keep trust, know oakness, breathe sweetly glees of
    treeness.
I could move there and live there, I think. I think I could live there, too.

The lace-cap hydrangeas
Bloom blue and bluer,
Ever pure, ever sensuous, ever essential.

Here is a sufficient ratio
For delight.

Here is the sufficient reason
For delirium.

This bloom is serenity.
This blossoming is subtlety.
This florescence, this floraison, is superabundance.

Even on days of cloud
There are domes of sky blue on the earth.

Even on days of rain
There are arches, are vaults, of lapis lazuli to sparkle.

On days when azure is alone and all
There are the million little brilliancies
Of bluest mirroring and multiplication.

The day is heavy.
My step is heavy.

The path is pang.
My pace is pain.

Is the last catalpa
Beyond the path

Heavy
With whiteness

Rising
With lightness

An alleviation
Or like alleviation?

Does each of the white bells
Blossoming on the boughs

Ring with a sweet sound
As through its largeness and its largess

Of leafage of green the tree
Sings with a sweet song

Lingual with languages
A catalpa cannot know

Even though they are sung
With a tongue of gold

Sweet with speech
Sensed ascending and descending

Around the questioner
Above the question

Blending
With the ending?

She entered twenty-two and blonde,
Exited thirty-one and gray.
Escaping black and white she donned
Color again. Ahead life lay
Open again. Dark ugly scars
Might turn into dim or glittering truths as of stars,
Might burn into a beauty as of stars.

Shall I recount the miles and hours of distance
Which countless fates created in resistance?
For the first time in fifty years they gather,
All four and in one single place, together,
Julia and Jo and Justine and Joanna,
From twenty-two, nineteen, thirteen, and nine
Crossing each crack, surpassing every line,
Traversing desert, mountain, thicket, river,
To this grand goal, to this resplendent end,
Beyond the toasts, the photographs, the dinner,
Tasting in happiness this gladsome manna,
Happy as sister, sister, sister, sister,
And happiest as friend, friend, friend, and friend.

The lilies are not trees. They are too small.
They stand here sturdy, slender, straight, and tall.

Raising their trumpets lusty, lovely, long, and bright,
They signal how their gravitas on them is light.

They gleam. They glisten.
They dream. They listen.

Their sweetness is profound and obvious and rare,
For what they deeply hold they liberally share.

The lilies are not swans. They do not glide
Smoothly across a lake. These swans abide.

The tree fell like a wounded warrior.
The slayer stripped it of its shining armor.
The pulverizer was its blazing pyre.
The sawdust was its ashes.

My mind became the mound
Remembering the beauty of its body.
Its spirit haunts the hades of my heart.
Beyond this knowledge is there yet a knowledge?

Which tree was this? There were so many trees.
There are so many trees, known and unknown.
Will a new Homer still sing an Achilles?

Even in Homer levees do not hold.
The waters surge above them or the waters
Batter them down. The river rushes out.
The river rushes in, come suddenly
As far as walls of gardens. Soon the blooming,
The fruitful, gardens lie awash, trash, ruin,
As heaven's rain rests heavy on the earth.
This is what war is like in Homer even.

THE TREE OF KNOWLEDGE

Is this the lore:
A simile,
A metaphor,
Metonymy,
And further four,
Phonology,
Which is the core,
Morphology,
Which is the floor,
And number three,
Syntax, the door,
And fenced and free,
Lexicon's store
From a to z,
And maybe more,
The quantity
Of sounds that pour,
The quality
Of sounds that soar,
The harmony
Of script and score,
And in a key
Wrong to ignore,
Society
Of rich and poor,
The family,
The world of war,
The history
Of years of yore,
Cosmology,
The grand decor,
Biology,
The grand rapport,
Astronomy,

Ambassador

Ambassador
From point d'appui
On farthest shore
Of spaceless sea
With soundless roar,
Philosophy
Of either-or,
Both-and, I-we,
Ever-encore?
Can beauty be
Celestial ore
And truth of tree?

THE TREE OF KNOWLEDGE

Is beauty hoar,
The dinosaur?

I dedicate a later part
To straighter science, greater art.

I proffer promises and rhyme.
I will touch timelessness and time.

Instead of scope
I offer hope.

In my soul there is a lack.
In my mind there is a crack.

Am I ever the adorer?
Am I ever the explorer?

In my mind there is a break.
In my soul there is an ache.

Through my core I feel a borer.
Through my cor I know a horror.

Please come down from the chariot and pull
The bitter arrow from my stricken shoulder.
Come down. His aorist imperative
Is both sigmatic and thematic, mixed.
Extracting the desiderative, I sieve
Future, imperfect, present, as I mull.
Must grammar make his heroism bolder?
Must he stand patient, waiting there, transfixed?
My eyes, my ears, my mind, my heart are full.

Poring over the poem of obituaries
I am not like the old men daily
Squinting over the columns of their New York Times
To watch the ranks of contemporaries
Passing, processing,
Before them slowly out of the world.
These reports of Greeks
And of Trojans and of allies
Are notices of the young,
With anxious fathers and mothers in their homes
And sometimes just-married wives,
Brief biographies of brief lives,
Not the long histories of the old
Living a life that is not
Killing and being killed.

Blue the skies.
Green the trees.

The roses gold red, brick red, rose red.

Even in the heat
The blossoms sweet.

Even in the humidity
The little breezes levity.

The roses red white, rose white, white white.

White bloom in the blue sky.
Green dome on the green tree.

The root is what I know.
For now this can blow.

The tree is what is true.
For now this must do.

If the autumn anemones were nameless
Their fair and fresh pale purple petals
As their sepals seem to be in the absence of petals
Beginning to bloom at the beginning
Of August would not be the beginning
Of autumn, which is the beginning
Of the end. The beginning of August
Is far from the end of autumn
Unless less of flower and more of fruit
Signals the beginning of the end
As the pears still filling the pear tree,
As the pears still filling on the pear tree,
Ever in the form of those initial tears
That flowed from the slow cessation
Of the bright smiles of the blossoms
Incessantly advance towards the fulfillment of that form
In tier upon tier up the tree upon the tree.

The autumn anemones are blossoms.
They smile as smiling Aphrodite smiles.
Carried to Olympus in the borrowed car of Ares,
Smile-loving Aphrodite weeps in heaven.
She is the daughter of Zeus and Dione.
The daughter collapses onto the mother's lap.
The mother clasps the daughter in her arms.
Bear it, my child, hold up,
No matter how hard it is,
No matter how bad you feel,
For many of us gods have suffered at human hands
While we have been bent on hurting one another,
Have been intent on thwarting one another.
The father smiles: My child, make love not war.
Wounded by a mortal, Aphrodite does not die.
Love does not die.
Wounded

Wounded by a mortal, Ares does not die.
War does not die.
Wounded by a mortal, Hades does not die.
Death does not die.
Wounded by mortals, Gaius Julius Caesar
Has perished.

A month and a half have passed since the Ides of March.
It is April twenty-sixth,
Forty-four B.C.E.
The eternal wordsmith is engaged in composing an epistle.
We are too old for war, claims Cicero.
Cicero is writing a letter
To Atticus, his dearest friend.
With some validity I could say
To you and you to me:
My child, make words not war.
His missive is pretty long, but he encloses
A copy of a recent letter from Mark Antony to him
And a copy of his reply.
And what about August in that same year?
What about August, a month
Of confusion and complication,
Of journeys, reversals, returns, by land and by sea?
On the nineteenth Cicero writes to Atticus of Brutus:
What distressed him most was my absence
From the Senate on the Kalends of Sextile.
What day is that? That which will be
The Kalends of August. It is August first.
At Rome in the Senate could Cicero have waged
Not war but words?
On the last day of August he reenters Rome.
On the second of September he speaks at length in the Senate.
And thus the great orator's last great war of words
Can and does begin.
Will the words, too, die?
Soon Cicero, too, will die,
Like Caesar killed, killed, killed.

For

For these two thousand years his words have lived.
More than two thousand years these words have lived.
Too soon will the words, too, die?

The windflowers live. They live on still
In a light late summer wind.
Are they still ignorant of winter?
Are they unwitting within the distant winds of war?
The anemones breathe the evening breeze.
It is yet day.
Soft days persist in seeming, in being, long.
Fall rustiness has not yet touched green leaves.
The hurricane season has hardly yet begun.
Rough animosities are yet far off.
The anemones have held their sepals well.

These are our shields.
Can I stand like Ajax, speed like Diomedes?
Must a mist still hinder vision?
Does a haze, a fog, a cloud, blind eyes, blind mind?
How much can one know?
Can one distinguish man and god,
Woman and man,
Weak and strong?
Apollo as a god of war is strong.
Athena as a god of war is strong.
Aphrodite is weak.
Ares is ambiguous.
Is war itself ambiguous?
Is winning losing?
Existence is itself a victory
Even if one is zealous to avoid, to void,
The vocabulary of conflict.
We cannot speak of peace, explains the statesman.
We only speak of conflict resolution.
The anemones seem at peace.
The anemones seem as yet victorious.

The blossoming
Of five well-fitted white-edged lavender sepals
Which in the absence of petals seem like petals
Both light and light about the central golden
Coronet about the very center
Of soft small verdant boss
Is fresh as yet, renewed, renewable.
Are any flowers falling?
Will many fruits fall rotting?
Is the month Sextile?
Is the term autumn?
Is the name August?

THE TREE OF KNOWLEDGE

In September
As we number
Hours of night
And hours of day
We await
Equality
Of the amber
And the somber.

An azure
This October
Is embodied on the tree,
Is embedded in the tree
If one can think of this position
On the twiglets among the leaves
As in.
Some of the lustrous leaves are still deep forest green,
Others, more, many, most, are already deep blood red.
The little fruits, these beads of blue, appear
As they appeared when from their summer green they emerged
In their true color.
These are an azure
Deepening into evening.
This is the tupelo
Ascending into autumn.
Can the blue beads, blue berries, blue fruits, blue drupes
Darken: drops of sky,
Wholly cerulean,
Turning nightlike?
Do I know them?
Can they be blue-black?
Can they be bluish?
Can they stay, as for me they stay, aspects of azure?
No, no, do I not know that they are nocturnal
Bits amid all this glister and glitter of glory?
Nevertheless is not night mother?
The azure of August is the augury of August,
The celestial azure of September,
And, above the blazing blazon of the tree,
Over the maternity mature upon the boughs,
The archangelic azure of the arch of October,
In fine in the sky the height and the depth
Of the almost undeniably divine.

                                               And,

And, oh, how the wide, wide, widening air
Seems to favor, seems to care,
Seems not to need to seem, being so clearly fair and fair.
No, I grovel, apologetic, pathetic, bathetic.
Yes, that is, no, I know nothing. Even in trope I know nothing.
All the azured assonance,
The aleatory altitudes of all the alliteration,
Cannot fuel the red or blue music of understanding.
Some comfort of causality has caused,
Must have cleverly or crudely engineered,
The fruition of the bloom, the first blue drupe,
Sent up from the earnest earth
And down from these gleaming gorgeous haughty heavens
Hearing, hovering, not watching, not listening,
Towards which the brilliant bluejays cry.
To confess may not be fitly to be forgiven
Lack of the love distinguished from the distance of desire.
I linger. I linger. I cannot let it go.
I gaze at the great, the glinting, tupelo.

Is this all? Is this gracious gleam the end
Or the sufficient pattern? Are this fit
Designer bark, the accents of the leaves,
The jeweled fruits a dressiness that weaves
Or that is woven in the perfect blend
Before fresh fashioning? Must that be it?

Do you hold as holy the golden glow of October?
Announce the news of the novelty of November,
Declare the details of discovery of December,
The manifestation of the metaphor,
The knowledge of the truth told in the tree,
The oldest story, the latest revelation,
The barest tale, the simplest multiplex,
The trunk and the branches, the one and the many, becoming
And being. Can biology, can physics,
And can linguistics stand imagined here?
Poetry grasps analogy as valid.
And science? Will the sun stop at the solstice?
My mind must climb the branchiness of time.

Bereft of brightenings of blue, green, red,
The tupelo can climb into December.
What if I freeze or shiver as I stare?
What if I study enchiridia?
What if the real cannot reconcile
All opposites and every contradiction?
What of the specimens with rounded crowns?
What of cylindrical and flat-topped heads?
What of the straight sharp trunk and conic flare?
What if the habit is pyramidal?
What if unnumbered boughs are horizontal?
What of the zigzags in the laddered branches?
What of the branches sloping slanting downwards?
                                        What if

THE TREE OF KNOWLEDGE

What if the name is nyssa, pepperidge,
Blackgum or sourgum, hornpipe, even snagtree?
What if the tree is not lit red and green
For Christmas? Is it less a Christmas gift?

This one near Garden Street is seasonal.
This ornamental has no ornament
Of luminosities and colorations
Yet is a welcome presence, pleasant present,
Sane restful entertainment for December.
This tree is signal in its treeishness.
The dome is classic, and the domiciles
Below are two enormous empty rentals,
Or ample vacant condominiums,
Once home to infants, testimony now
To strength and freedom and maturity.
The trunk divides in two and then divides
In two, just like my mind; just like my mind,
Some boughs rise skyward, some are parallel
To the horizon, some descend, some cross.
The low, the lowering, sun pats highest branches
On one side; on the other side, above,
The growing moon peers pale through highest branches.
Look at me, silver moon; warm me, gold sun.
You fill a vacancy in azure sky.
You gild a ramifying on tan tree.
These are dimensions of a winter's day.

This tupelo, this space, is space in time.

Is this a tree? the tree? Is this the tree?
Is this the whole? Is it a total loss?
Is this a particle, a truth, a beauty?
Is this not knowing? Is this not not knowing?

The scientist may see at last a truth.
The humanist may hear at least a word.
Poet, you taste a truth that from a tree
Glows in a gold. You whisper in a wind
A word that flowers fragrant maybe maybe.

What rose still blossomed in the early dusk
Of late December? Was my mind too cold
For images? What sliver shone above
Half curved on unadulterated blue?
Is there philosophy that is too brusque?
Can there be poetry that is too old?
Will the agnostic feel these deeps as love,
The atheist admire this height as true?

Must I conserve chronology, preserve
The moons that are the measure of the month,
Count up from one to ten? May I reserve
Remembrance if the countdown is a logic
Or metaphor or scent that slips from something
Rounding towards Ides to something nearing zero
Back when the calendar began a truth?
Ides were once Jupiter's and plenilune's.
Jupiter once was truth's fiduciary.
Verity was fidelity of Jove.
Kalends commenced with Janus, who was facing
Backwards and forwards. Is this truly true?

The poet's truths are merely dreams of truths.
The poet's words are only plays with words.
Dream on. The day of dreaming must be brief.
Play on. The price for playing must be steep.
Down rush the nightmares. Up the deadlines rise.
The roses in the hedge fluff full and fresh
In play of dusk. In truth of noon they wither.
The Cretan said: All Cretans always lie.
The Muses said: We know that we can tell
A lie like truth; we know that we can tell,
If this is what we wish, the truth as truth.
I said: I know I know I do not know.
Is my name Ariadne? Daedalus?
Pasiphae or Icarus or Theseus?
Is my name Hesiod? Is it Odysseus?
                                    Circe?

THE TREE OF KNOWLEDGE

Circe? Calypso? or Nausicaa?
Is the name Eros, or can it be Cupid?
Is it Odysseus? Or is it Ulysses?
Or Flora and Urania and Baum?
Or Baum or Flora or Urania?
Am I in air, at sea, or on an island?
Am I an island? Am I on the island?
Is the December sun too far away?
Is it too near as I fare far afar?
Does my ship speed by rocket on in space?
Does my ship speed by wing or speed by sail,
Of white, of black? Or does it speed by oar?
And does it speed, or is it old and slow?
Row on until the river meets the sea,
For life is but a dream and thought is play.
Row, row your boat until it feels the ocean.
The world goes round. The round goes round and round.

Merrily, merrily. Eat, drink, merrily.
The tree bears fruit. The fruit is good for eating.
Put forth your hand and open up your mouth.
Know that the fruit is gold, that it is good.
The golden apples, sweet between my teeth,
Are sweet to memory and to desire,
To aftertaste and to anticipation.
I will traverse a sea to seize this fruit.
I will support a sky to find these apples.

What genes, what memes, are these? What centuries
And what millennia unfold themselves
Into my brain and then out of my brain
Into my mouth and now out of my mouth
Into my hand and soon out of my hand
Onto my page, this patient passionate
Page of the past, production of the present,
Pledge, plan, and plea that fumbles for the future?

The premise

The premise that endures the centuries,
The promise that survives millennia,
May be still fittest or be dead at birth.
I may be fit or one that never lived.
Could I live in this instant till I fall
Into abysses out of which I rose?
Could I know in some moment till I close
Eyes blinking blinded by bits of some all?

THE TREE OF KNOWLEDGE

This posthumous existence
May also be the adventure
In which I reach the height
Of Purgatory where Virgil
Gave up his guidance of Dante
And left alone for Limbo.

He brought her back.
Song is that strong.
And he was neither dumb nor dumb.

Up from the land of lack
Together they did come.
We see her on his arm.
We feel her through his charm.
We hear her in his song.

Song is that long.
Art is not harm.
This is not rhyme of Jill and Jack.

THE TREE OF KNOWLEDGE

But what is how
And how that rod,
That magic wand,
Is of a god,
God's arm and hand,
Olympian bough,
Jupiter's brow,
Jupiter's nod,

Divinity
In Virgil the tree,
Virgil the word,
Unsounded, not surd,
Virgil the tone,
Loved, not unknown,
What in the urn
Lived, did not burn.

Homer, Virgil,
Dante, Tasso,
Milton make and are

The epic as the word, the many words,
The epoch of the god, the many gods.

And what is fellowship, and what is folly,
What understanding, what insomnia?

With Walt, with Wallace, I watch,
In our west, for white of dawn.

The supreme fiction
Is supremely loved.

The final paramour
Is finally enough.

The whole is of harmonium.
And what is literature, and what is life?
What makes theology, and what makes thought?

THE TREE OF KNOWLEDGE

Did I recognize
Why the tree might rise?

How can I explain
That she was Julia the Apostate?
I sagely pressed her to read
For her sake and for mine
Daniel Clement Dennett.
I wisely advised her to read
For my sake and for hers
Titus Lucretius Carus.

Was she, to my ken,
First atheistic, then
Monotheistic, then
Atheistic, then
Polytheistic, then
A-, poly-, mono-, then
All atheist again
As ending, end, -en, en-?
What is all this patter?
What is all that clatter?
What is all such chatter?
Does knowing truly matter,
Matter, matter, matter?

How did I explain
The not that was the it,
The it that was the not,
The not that was the all,
The all that was the all?
This all was auld lang syne.
The tree was pretty plain.
The tree was very tall.
The tree was surely fine.
                    And was

And was this all psychosis?
What is reductive? What
Is simply accurate?
Dendrophily may not
Be pathological.
Which garden has a wall?
Which is an open plot?
Shall we untie the knot
Or designate it null?
The tree was not alone.
But was the tree unknown?
The tree was plainly pretty.
But was the garden gritty?
How did I explain
An Eve within a bone,
An Eve without a fall,
The Adam lacking pain,
The druid missing gnosis?

Was I, from her pen,
Monotheistic, then
Atheistic, then
Polytheistic, then
Polytheistic, then
Atheistic, then
Atheistic then?
Or was it truly then
Agnosticism, yen,
A taste of madeleine,
A touch of La Fontaine,
Ainsi soit-il, amen,
Amen, amen, amen?

THE TREE OF KNOWLEDGE

How can I explain
That I was something ancient,
Perhaps an ancient daughter,
Perhaps an ancient dryad,
Perhaps an ancient dragon,
Maybe an ancient oak tree,
Maybe an ancient acorn,
Maybe an ancient atom?

Is gray cognition far
From green deodar?

Oh . . .
Ooh . . .

Know . . .
True . . .

Gno . . .
Dru . . .

Lo . . .
Clue . . .

No . . .
Too . . .

THE TREE OF KNOWLEDGE

Is this enough? Can that have been enough?
Will being the agnostic be enough?
Archangel Dawkins stands there beckoning
Back to the paradise where knowledge blossoms
And atheism is the fleshy fruit,
Edible, ripe, digestible, nutritious.

This is December. Will it soon be March?
Beyond this clarity the sun descends.
Beyond clear air the sun has just gone down.
The bare black boughs and boles are beauty on
The beauty of the dimming azure heaven,
The beauty of the darkling blue of sky.

The minute mysteries of winter buds
Under chilly January's less impatient suns
Are the miracles of red blooming on the maples of March
And the miracles of green blossoming on the maples of April.
Consider then the Junoesque mystique of aceraceous June.
Of such moon's suns what can be the patience and the passion?
What are the august mythologies of August?

Part Three

Knowledge

Section One

The Margaret-Ghost

No. 1

Cambridge, July 19

Dear Margaret Fuller, Marchesa Ossoli:

Can it be still July? Will August come?
Will August ever come? It is July.

Close to the American shore your ship goes down.
A whole ocean has been traversed. So close to the shore.

You, the American woman go down. This makes the news.
Your Roman husband, your Roman baby, go down,

Your Roman book goes down. So close to the shore.
Shall I speak of sadness? It is tragic. How I wish I could
   have helped you.

I seem to see it. Even your manuscript drowned.
The universe still rises all around.

Sincerely yours,
Julia Budenz

No. 2

Cambridge, May 23

Dear Leila Saint of Knowledge:

I am reflecting upon two birthdays, your Margaret's and my Julia's, both on Wednesday, May 23. Identical calendars mark the years 1810 and 1934: May 23 is Wednesday, June 13 Wednesday, July 4 Wednesday, August 1 Wednesday, September 26 Wednesday, October 3 Wednesday. Were you born on a day, in a week, in a month, in a year? Was I? On a day, in a week, in a month, in a year will we die? In two centuries will we live? For ten millennia can we breathe?

Sincerely yours,
Flora Urania Baum

No. 3

Cambridge, February 23
TERMINALIA

Dear Leila,

There is nothing more.
There is nothing but white and blue.

The sky glitters, a surface dazzling, a deep,
Wholly azure, without the cloud
Even of angelic wing.

The earth is what is white,
From the cloaks, the togas, of aspiring trees

To the calm comforter, the thick blank blanket
Spread to where the snowdrops shyly glance
From the coverlet's edge.

Consciousness is everything.
There is nothing more.

Love,
Flora

No. 4

                              Cambridge, February 24
                              REGIFUGIUM

Dear Margaret,

Too long, too long. You understand. Too long. Too short.

                                        Love,
                                        Julia

No. 5

> Cambridge, March 15
> Feriae Annae Perennae

Dear Leila,

White, yellow, red, blue, white. A year. Forever. And ever.

> Love,
> Flora

No. 6

Cambridge, March 20

Dear Leila,

Orange, violet, green. Growing a longer light.
A crocus.

Love,
Flora

No. 7

Cambridge, March 20

Dear Margaret,

Too soon, too late, calls love. Love laughs, laments, Sinks, lingers.

Love,
Julia

No. 8

Cambridge, March 25

Dear Margaret,

Love is goodbye and dear hello. Then hail, Farewell.

Love,
Julia

No. 9

Cambridge, July 20

Dear Margaret,

Wings of an eagle. Wings of the dove. Not wings. Winds, waves.

Love,
Julia

No. 10

Cambridge, July 21

Dear Leila,

Myth. Symbol. Image. Syntax. Diction. Rhythm. Sound. Sounding.

Love,
Flora

No. 11

Cambridge, July 22

Dear Leila,

Virgilian, Homeric, let the sound
Resound.

Love,
Flora

No. 12

> Cambridge, July 23
> NEPTUNALIA

Dear Margaret,

You say that what is limitless is alone divine.
I listen. Let us long long

> Love,
> Julia

No. 13

> Cambridge, July 25
> FURRINALIA

Dear Margaret,

Do we write of
The eagle with the broken wing,
The eagle chained below the falls,
The fallen feathers of the fallen brave,
Using the quill that once went soaring?
Do we rise to
The high and higher heights of the sublime?

> Love,
> Julia

No. 14

> Cambridge, July 30
> Fortunae Huiusce Diei

Dear Margaret,

Do we write of limit
Or do we spell out the unlimited?
Are ghosts, like angels, winged?
Are angels winged?
Are wider skies entirely of azure?
Are white clouds loves?
Is there a poem without a picture?
Is there a day without a date?
Are there ghosts?
Can we write of ghosts?
Can we write?
Is there a reading missing a misreading?
Is there a writing minus a miswriting?
Is there a question with no other question?
Is today's templed time fixed now and here
Or is it everywhere and every year?

> Love,
> Julia

No. 15

Cambridge, July 31

Dear Margaret,

The boat is battered.
The ship is shattered.

I sit on a splinter.
This is disintegration.

White lilies wilt, wither.
Black oaks creak, crack.

They ask: Sibyl, what do you wish?
Still, Sibyl's will,

Odorous as lily,
Roboreous as oak,

Is like a filament,
Is like a limb,

Is like a ventilation,
Is like an undulation.

This wind is death.
That wave is death.

I hear the wind.
I feel the wave.

Love,
Julia

No. 16

Cambridge, May 23

Dear Margaret,

If this is spirit it is lifted on the wind
Into its extinction.

If that is matter it is sunk under the wave
Unto its deconstruction.

Taste all these sweet birthday cakes.
Blow all those bright birthday candles.

Happy anniversary! Last, return!
Buon compleanno! Be, complete!

Love,
Julia

No. 17

Cambridge, May 22

Dear Leila,

Can you and I be simpler
Than your Margaret and my Julia,
Or are we in our fabric more complex?
Are we more superficial,
Or are we more profound?
Can we in our own substance be profound?
Is my multicolored robe
More multicolored than Julia's robe,
Woven of wizard web as by a Helen,
As by a Hector's wife waiting within the wall,
As by a swift Minerva who has flashed into the sky?
Is your black robe nocturnal
With a far deeper black
Than Margaret's, stellar with more spangled white,
Ebon as Hecat, argent as Diana,
Pearly as Phoebe reigning chaste, serene,
Diamonded as by a million Pleiads
Distant throughout the limits of the heavens
And through blue whispers of infinitudes?
Do our robes flow, our arms extend?
Do we stand straighter, walk on longer,
Run with greater quickening, sit in greater repose?
Does the Sphinx work wing
As well as voice and eye?
Do we fly higher than Margaret and Julia?
Do we know how to fly?

Love,
Flora

No. 18

Cambridge, May 22

Dear Margaret,

Must there be Leila and Leila
As there are Flora and Flora:
The Flora of the cosmos
And the Flora of the self?

Where there are two are there three:
As middle, you and I?
Have we called out to the all?
Have we plunged in to the one?

Who is speaking, who the word?
Who is singing, who the lay?
Who is mother, spouse, or daughter,
Who ghastly ghost, who lasting guest?

Who is speaking, who is spoken?
Who is weaving, who is woven?
Who is writing, who is written?
Who is sung, and who is singing?

Who is weaving, who the web?
Who is forging, who the form?
Flora wears a fragrant garland,
Leila a brilliant diadem.

The gems are red.
The blooms are blue.
The psalm is sweet.
Can love be, too?

If the book is drowned
The jewel must be lost unfound.
If the song is snuffed
The budding blossom will be crushed.

Will nature wonder?
Will culture blunder?
Will all go under?
Is one asunder?

                                                    Love,
                                                    Julia

No. 19

Cambridge, July 18

Dear Leila,

What all supplies loss of the all?
What one redeems death of the one?

What rescued mind shines diamond?
What gardened universe turns paradise?

Love,
Flora

No. 20

Cambridge, March 25

Dear Leila,

Desire. This is the song
Of the purple sheen
Of the lowly crocus
From the sod of March.

Is it merely April
Or the feel of April
Or the ancient wait for April
Or the maiden haste towards April
That is the desideratum
Or that is the desideration?
Is it not the exultation,
Is it not the exaltation,
Of the canticle that magnifies
The wildest ruby- and the vastest azure-fire,
The highest of all the highest of all the highest of all the heights,
The chant of lowliness,
Laughter of pasts and futures,
Rapture of purpureal sublime?

Aspire. This is the psalm
Of the dark-gleaming sheen
Of the dark-purple crocus
From the soil of March.

Love,
Flora

No. 21

Cambridge, April 1

Dear Leila,

Knowledge is red,
Beauty is blue,
Seeking is sweet,
Gaze savors hue.

Love,
Flora

No. 22

                                                                                Cambridge, April 30

Dear Leila,

If it is the greenest tree I watch
Will it be the reddest fruit I catch?
When it is the orangest dawn I find
Can the bluest day be far behind?

                                                                                                       Love,
                                                                                                       Flora

No. 23

                                                                      Cambridge, May 1

Dear Leila,

The virgin mother's fashioned gown,
First richest red, went dearest blue.
Does, as the rainbowed ages run,
The beautiful replace the true?

                                                                           Love,
                                                                          Flora

No. 24

                                      Cambridge, May 23
                                      Feriae Volcano

Dear Margaret,

Is it the moth now rushing, crashing
Into reddest flame with reddest fling?

Is it the butterfly fluttering, flashing
With the reddest flick the reddest wing?

Is it dying?
Is it trying?

Is it sighing?
Is it flying?

Who is this bearer, this beater, this eater of rubicund fire?
What is this waste, this haste, this taste? I savor, I devour, I desire.

                                        Love,
                                        Julia

No. 25

Cambridge, April 2

Dear Margaret,

The sky today was that unbroken blue
That is one whole note pure sustained sheer strong
Enough to be a measure for these hours
Broken by one great break. To spreading time
That break was one, to me triune, to time
Little, to me of magnitude surpassing
The million minutes of the wind that filled
This April day as once invincible
Achilles filled a windy Ilium,
Matching his swiftness with his matchless strength,
His fury with his force. If that grand blast
Is great Achilles, I must be his Hector
Lying all broken on the battlefield.
Felled in my duel with the warrior wind
That like a hostile god pushed, slapped, me down,
I lay on Massachusetts Avenue.
Facts of the fractured elbow, pelvis, thigh
Shall not demean my narrative. I cry
With Hector, Let me live before I die,
Laboring to accomplish something great
And monumentalize with fame my fate.
Sibyl, what do you will? Now much too late
I wish for death, she whispered with voice too dry.

Love,
Julia

No. 26

Cambridge, April 11

Dear Margaret,

 Am I Flora writing to Leila, or am I Julia writing to you? Am I some sage — Oedipus or Emerson perhaps — cleverly writing to the Sphinx? Am I some churchperson — not Waldo, I would judge, but Julia, I conclude — who suddenly wanted and begged the suddenly appearing Holy Communion rejected by each of these many years before as the mind of each forced a rejection of the church? This particular version or relict or relic or symbol of ancient custom or belief manifested itself in the hands of the gentle pious woman from St. Barbara's as she opened the gleaming pyxis like a gleaming compact holding its mirror and its puff of powder. From St. Barbara's, did she say? I moved from Mount Auburn to Woburn on the noon of April ninth. To Woburn? I told the movers I thought Woburn was the moon. It's only a drive of twenty minutes, Ruby exclaimed when she phoned from her home in Cambridge. The movers, Adam the First Man and Geoffrey the First Crusader, floated over the potholes of Massachusetts.

 From Mount Auburn? Am I then a ghost? Was I visiting your cenotaph among the grand boney trees as they struggled out of winter? Was I lying on the cold intimations of grass as I perused your poem written about the Sphinx, or shall I call it the letter of the Sphinx written to you about herself? Or was it not on but beneath the chilly hints of grass that I was lying?

 It was under white sheets that I was lying. It was upon white sheets that I was lying. My body was boney, but it was a breathing, eating body, eager for air, greedy for food, yearning for corporeal and spiritual nutrition, wanting nourishment both of flesh and of mind. It had lain on the white sheets of the hospital called Mount Auburn. It had lain on the white

sheets

sheets of the ambulance transporting it to Woburn. It was lying on the white sheets of the hospital denominated by the vernal promise of that substantive serving as an adjective: Rehabilitation. Into this space of April came the white-haired white-faced woman holding the white moon of food, the white disk of bread. Muriel, she said to the mother of thirteen children who was lying couched on the other side of the room, I am Barbara from St. Barbara's, and I have brought you Holy Communion. Excuse me, I called across as she began to depart, Can you give Holy Communion to me? Compressing into a sound bite my whole religious history, known well to the students of Flora Baum, I concluded with the elucidation that although I was no longer a believer I deeply respected the Ideal. Soon I was chewing the white plenilunium, the panem angelicum, the accident of the white bread that was the substance of a body, the substance of a god. I was not a believer, I was an unbeliever, but I chewed a meaning and hungered for a knowledge and tasted a beauty.

I chew the white sheep, the Sphinx wrote in her letter addressed to me. I am the lion who speeds on four feet through the wheatfields. I leap the wall and chew the big white sheep. I chew and chew. I devour. I am the lion who lies down with the lamb. I am the woman who climbs down from the tree and strides on two feet across and across the grass. I am the winged one, the winging one, the poet of the winged words of reddest red, of bluest blue, of brightest fullest whitest white. Or am I Flora, your word of words?

Do you, Julia, she continued, need Flora as your word because her name is fragrant with flowers? Does your friend Margaret need Leila as her word because Leila in ancient tongues means night, because Margaret's Leila, ancient and young, displays the starry black of blackest night? Are these my riddles still? Maybe they now are yours. Maybe the black night of Leila and the many-colored flowers of Flora are merely cloaks.

Something else the Sphinx said in her letter: Every answer is another question.

Did I receive this epistle on April tenth? Later on the tenth I found myself whizzing from Woburn to Mount Auburn, transported once again past those gray graves, past those white, those whited, sepulchers, glancing once again from jostling ambulance to resting garden, entering then a world of emergency and emergence. Late that night — that is, late last night — my new physician and I, as we met and exchanged names, were conversing very briefly in and of the German tongue. And is your primary language German, I inquired. It is Hebrew, she replied with a little smile as over her beautiful white countenance fell her beautiful black tresses. And how do you wish to say good night, she asked as she was leaving. In German? No, please say it to me in Hebrew. Leila tov, she said.

                                        Love,
                                        Julia

No. 27

> Woburn, April 16–30

Dear Margaret,

Was it lack? Was it loss?
Was it rack? Was it rope?
Was it Auburn, was it Woburn, was it Tyburn?
Was it that piercing, that penetrating, pain?
Was it this numbness all along the length of the left little finger?
The ulnar nerve reaches that far.
How far does cognition reach?
Was it cognition?
Was it the questioning of cognition?
Was it the self?
Was it the encounter of self and self?
Was it the questioning of self?
Was it the assault on the self?
Was it the stapling or was it the unstapling of the skin?
Was it the stitching or was it the unstitching of the mind?
When the mind was relinquishing God, was it finding the self?
When truth refuses both,
How does truth stand?
What can I stand?
What can I stand until
Nothing can stand?

In this extreme of uncertainty
Am I forfeiting the poem?
My letter belongs to the poem,
To Flora's bright garden, to Leila's bright night,
In all exuberance of burgeoning,
In all extravagance of glistering.
Forgive me, since regret
Rhymes with Margaret.

> Restore

Restore me, since, as night
Brings out the light
Of stars, so sorrow brings
The truth that rings
High in the highest sky
Or down here where I lie
Hearing the tinkle,
Watching the twinkle.
I adopt, I adapt, your words, your own and those you borrow,
On rhyme, regret, night, stars, truth, sorrow.
But after such nocturnal clarity will day be clear?
Behold the handmaid of the golden breeze.

This gold is not the yellow of the good.
Just as in the painting,
Above, beyond, the yellow, red, and blue,
The gold leaf gleams,
So, outside one ordering
Of real and of ideal,
The aura aurea must blow, must glow.
I will rise and breathe and wander.
I will even see.

The painting
Contains the infinite fire of red
That burns the yearning into flame
Which does not kill but must forever call.
The painting
Contains the blaze of absolute blue
That fills the gaze. Where has it gone?
Or does it stay, and in the loss of all
Is it the all?
The structure of the universe
I do not know.
The structure of my knowing
I do not know.
Is the book of knowledge
The book of beauty?
Is the tree of knowledge

The tree

The tree of beauty?
Is the whole one, two, three, four, or five,
Or countless wafting winds and breathing breezes?

Here borne by the hands of the good
Come the yellow red-touched tulips
In the vase where the bear grass waves
Green bands of slender splendor
To the flowerless hospital room.
Here springing beyond the gray patio
With its walkers leaning on walkers
Sing white cherry trees, sing purple azaleas,
Through all the gold of the golden breeze
To all the blue of the azure air.
What have we found?
What can we find?
What have we lost?
The woman in the wheelchair across the room
Says her rosary three times a day.
She lost her treasure, her only son.
He died a year ago at fifty-eight.
Richard kept on smoking.
Frances will be ninety in October.

How old am I? I am a baby. I cry, I wail,
I scream. I do not walk. I am in pain.
Last night my roommate prayed an extra rosary for me.
She heard my crying. I am a baby. But I cannot crawl.

I can stand. I am a biped. I can stand
With infinite and terrified exertion.
I scooch to the edge of the chair one thigh at a time,
Using the word and the movement taught to me,
Lean forward into fear, in fear push up
Into impossibility, employing
The right arm only, following my orders,
Forbidding the fractured left to try to assist,
Lean forward, forward, straightening two legs,
Two unaccustomed legs that cannot stand,
                                        Two legs

Two legs that I can stand on as I grasp
In unbelief the handle of the walker.
I must trust one leg and then the other.
I am not taking giant steps.
I am almost human.

I am far from human at night.
Or is pain close to human?
If night is pain, what are the stars?
Or are there stars?
Or is the night of pain the night of clouds,
Rolling across the ceiling,
Descending to the seething air mattress of the bed,
Tossing heavily, out of control, with the blankets?
If night is pain, can pain replace the sorrow?
If clouds replace the stars, where are the truths?
Are your truths stellar? Mine are very cloudy.
If night is pain, my truths are nebulous.
My night is very long. My April sinks
Into December. I sink into dark dolor.
I do not sink. I strain against black pain.
I am drawn and quartered. Woburn could be Tyburn.
Where is the handmaid of the golden breeze?
My roommate across the room
Says that my bed is hers
And that hers is mine.

Tonight my nurse is the one
Who is most incompetent, most lazy,
Most careless, most uncaring.
Tonight her aide is the one
Who is meanest, roughest, most resentful,
Whose tone, with all her gestures, with her whole bearing,
Declares: I hate my job,
Announces: I hate you.
She makes me hopeless.
Her name is Hope.
What self is hers?
What self is mine?

What night

What night is this?
This is not Leila's night.
This is not Flora's April.

What made my April?
What meets me here?
Neuropsychology,
Neurophilosophy,
Emerged from earth,
Autochthonous,
Ballooned from air,
Spaceshipping down,
And towards me strode.
Have they arrived?
Or does experience
Escape analysis,
Await analysis?
Gods, God, must go.
Selves, self, may come.
Must self, too, go?
I can now stand.
Does truth, too, stand?
Is April pain?
The golden breeze . . .
Am I that self?
Am I loss, lack?
The letter lags.
The poem sags.
Dear Margaret,
Accept regret.

                                        Love,
                                        Julia

No. 28

> Woburn, May 2
> Floralia V

Dear Leila,

I do not mind saying
That you are Margaret's alter ego.
I hate to say
That I am Julia's.
Both could be said,
And saying them is rational.
Can something be too rational?
I think it is too rational.
I dare not think it is too rational.
I know it is prosaic.
It is reductive.
It is easy.
It is even not entirely true.
And how I want the truth!
And it is not merely prosaic.
It is prose.
But you are Margaret's poem,
And I am Julia's.

We can be glimpsed
Darting or dawdling
Through the streets of Cambridge, Massachusetts,
Searching for blood-red, fire-red,
Rubies, tulips,
Glowing along our eager routes,
While Margaret lies in agony with
Days and days of headache stabbing
The body, robbing the mind,
While Julia lies in agony between

> Sacral

Sacral decubitus and fractured femur,
Shiftless shoulder that refuses to help
And elbow that will not straighten or bend.
The vacuum dressing begins to beep.
It must itself be sick.
When it is well it croaks like a frog.
But why do I go croaking on?

Beyond Margaret and Julia,
Beyond even you and even me,
Gleams and glimmers and sparkles and dazzles
Another image which the poem loves,
A metaphor, an etymology,
A bit of history, a bit of myth,
A glint of culture, a glint of personal ideal,
Oh, this is prose, that image is part of the poem,
A hint of divinity, a sign of the divine,
Oh, no, there is no god, there are no gods,
Yet there is Flora, there is Leila, there is each,
An aspect of sacred space, of sacred time,
On earth, out through the cosmos, within the poem,
A frequentation, a celebration,
Leila, Flora, a meditation,
A depth, a height, a gasp, a gladness, a goddess.

Love,
Flora

No. 29

> Woburn, May 3
> Floralia VI

Dear Margaret,

For this you will hate me more
The more you know me:
I am all words.
I am nothing but words.
My thoughts are words.
My deeds are words.
My works are nothing but words.

All my goodness is in my mouth and pen
Repeating thank you, thank you, thank you, thank you.

All my knowledge is either in my mouth
Like saltimbocca in Roman restaurants
Leaping between my lips from the dish, from the page of a book,
But barely tasted, wholly undigested,
Or in my pen rushing across my page
With words preceding, words succeeding, words,
Loud starlings flying like determined migrants
Yet going nowhere and achieving nothing.

But all my beauty shines into my eyes
And sings into my ears and scents my nostrils
And moves my hands above the smoothest marble
And pulses from the pulsing of my heart,
Filling my being. Then I devoutly hope
That from without and from most deep within,
From that without and that most deep within,
Of that without and of that deep within,
My mouth and pen will make it all anew.

The fragrant hyacinth unfolds profound its indigo hues.
The ruddy robin above unfolds serene its azure intonations.
O Flora, word of my word, I begged of my own Flora,
Unfold your words, my words, if there are some, of beauty.

Love,
Julia

No. 30

Woburn, May 5

Dear Leila Saint of Knowledge,

    I am addressing you by the title given to you by your Margaret because I hope you can help me to help my Julia. In her heart swells a huge conflagration with its spiring twofold flame, two fiery swords, one blue, one red. The blue is the desire for beauty, ever fulfilled and ever renewed, ever serenely appeased and ever arising once again. The red is the passion for truth, that is, for knowledge, the precious knowledge about which I have written over and over, which will be yearningly, diligently, sought, searched for, over and over, which entices and excites, which eludes and evades, which is glimpsed and is grasped and is tasted and is dropped and is lost, which is discovered with delight and rediscovered with rejoicing, which calls and calls and calls over and over.

    Julia is eager to keep walking along the ways of knowing, the routes to knowing, even in her present state of wounded, fractured body and distracted, inadequate mind. Help me, Leila, to help her as you helped the erudite, passionate, incomparable Margaret. By you, by Margaret, the carbuncle is found. Maybe through you, through her, it will be found by me, by Julia.

Love,
Flora

No. 31

Arlington, May 7–11

Dear Leila and Margaret,

Our desperation demands a twofold voice.
Julia and Flora must write to Margaret and Leila.
And our epistle must be Menippean
Even within one page of correspondence.
Please do not mind if verse shifts into prose,
Prose into verse. As for the poetry,
Alas, alas, although the poem is all
It sinks to nothingness. This is the fall.

Why did we expect the carbuncle, garnet, ruby, the red tulip, the red red rose, the red fruit gleaming on the ancient, sturdy, fertile apple bough? The poem must know as well as be. Can it know truth and beauty? Must it know good and evil? Must it know evil? Can it gaze upon the day of reddest dawn and bluest noon? Must it endure the blackest night, the pain, here, here, here, here, the pitiless stares and ruthless hands of the staff? I, Flora, am the inarticulate cry. I, Julia, am Iphigenia. The aides with stony faces stand above me. The aides with steely faces stand above me. They do not need a knife for the sacrifice. Plenty of knives are already inside my body. Plenty of knives are already inside my mind. Are there knives in my Flora, in my poem?

For me, that is, for Julia, plenty of red turns up: a bowl of sliced beets at dinner, the red button to push for the nurse, the sore red blemishes along my arms, the blood from my lips on my teeth. At night they will not let me brush my teeth. They want only to plop me into bed. Bed is the place of pain. I must lie on my side. I cannot turn myself. The enormous wound on my back is being vacuum-cleaned. I am chained to the cleaner. It is plugged into the wall. I try to keep hold

of

of my pen. I cannot write poetry. I can barely be said to be writing prose. Flora, the letter asks itself, will you disintegrate if I cannot write the poem? Will you be vacuumed away? The letter asks, will you die before me? Sibyl, what do you wish? Flora cannot wish to die, but Julia may.

How can we handle these things? How do we cure the languishing poem? How do we reach the vanishing cosmos? How do we bear the famishing lack of the fruit of the tree?

With apologies the activities director asked the questions posed by the part of the form concerned with residents' spirituality. The first question: Do you believe in God? Answer: No. The second question: Is religion important to you? Answer: Yes. But we, Julia and Flora, do not pray. We are tempted to pray. But we must not pray. Once it was good to pray. Now it is evil. Maybe it will some day, some night, be good again. We remember the great splendid gracious transcendent Thou, utterly beyond us, profoundly within us. We remember Janus. Surely he might glance this way again. We remember radiant Flora. Surely she will walk among the roses. We remember beneficent Fortuna. Surely she will return us to the heart of the poem. How did we become so pagan when we had long since renounced the living God?

But now if we are faithful to what he was we must if necessary renounce him again and again. We must follow our bit of knowledge, our glimpse of truth, in all weathers. We must not fall like a tree, like a fruit from a tree, like a leaf of a tree. And if we are blown down by the wind, we must struggle to walk once more. We must struggle to walk on the paths of knowing. Will we see both ways? Will we discover the red rose in blossom? Will we return along the route of our own red blood, with the heat and light of our mind's reddest fire? Will we advance to new rhodedactyl visions, to new rubrous treasures of sight and insight, hitherto unguessed, unknown? Will we remember to acknowledge the good we have felt and seen and not keep looking at the evil? What of the inimitable sisters? What of the incredible friends? What

of

of the devoted doctors? What of the cheerful, competent, caring nurses and nurses' assistants? What of the nights when they let me, wretched Julia, even brush my teeth, when they are willing to offer gentle and effectual help as I manfully strive to lie as ordered on my side? But this is the crybaby Julia's pitiful prose. Will we in the night think backwards and forwards to a big yellow sunshiny sun? Will we perceive the lemon yellow of goodness, the pineapple yellow of the good? Will we apprehend the bluejay blue, the tupelo blue, the pools of squills in bloom of blue, that are beauty? Will we comprehend the high-perched gleaming red cardinal's high-pitched gleaming red exclamations? Will we, like you, dear Margaret, dear Leila, announce truly: The carbuncle is found?

> Love,
> from both of us,
> from us as two,
> from us as one

No. 32

Arlington, May 12

Dear Leila or Margaret,

Why do I care so much if they don't care?
Why could I bear so much if they could spare
The slightest sign of human fellowship,
The dimmest hint of smile upon a lip?
You know already how those nurses' aides
And nurses fail, fail me. My outrage fades.

Did I care that the High God cared for me, that the cosmos itself was thus beneficent, that even my fault could be fortunate, that good could be counted on to come out of evil, that my pain could serve as my purification, that in my profoundest suffering I could trust that I was loved?

Or was it rather that I cared for him, that I loved, that I worshipped, that I adored, and that he was to me the infinitely lovable, the supremely precious, the absolutely worthy of adoration? Before the All I was pulled to renounce all else, called to abandon all. He was the eternally excellent to whom I was the fervent, the burning, sacrifice.

I write these plain basic facts in simple sober prose.

I write these truths as I am falling asleep, yet they were dawns as well as dreams, they gleamed and glittered and sparkled as stars and drew me into the hearts of stars, they consumed me night and day in the universal fires, and hell was heaven, and the All was All.

Yet are these truly truths? Did I live many minutes amid distraction? Did I feel guilty? Did I feel afraid? Oh, the All was All.

My paper slips and slides. My pen will, if I am not cautious, drop irretrievably to the floor. I am writing while I lie in bed on my side. Will I be the devout and devoted offering as I enter upon the night of pain?

Or will I endure like the severed worm, like the trampled ant? Or will I sensibly choose to make, instead of the worst, the best of it?

I bear the night attendants who do not care.
Each brutal pair of hands, each cruel stare
Serves to declare: This bosom which no prayer
Can ever penetrate is marked: Beware.
In dark, in glare, the foul is never fair.
Despair, despair, despair, despair, despair.

Love,
Flora or Julia

No. 33

> Arlington, May 15
> The Ides of May

Dear Margaret,

If it is not mysticism
Is it poetry?
Instead of being the universe
Can it be the poem?
In lieu of a kind of knowledge
Could it be a kind of beauty?

Suddenly I seem to see it:
The poem must be the offering.
As once the self was sacrificed,
Was given, was devoted,
With joy and fervor to the Absolute,
So now the poem, the other self,
Is offered to what it may be offered to,
Even if this is an emptiness,
Even if this is the nothingness,
Even if the poem is null and void.

Forgive me, Margaret, for my prose
Pretending to be the verse of the poem.
Forgive me, Flora, other and self.
You are the sacrificial offering.
You are the offering. You are the gift.
You should not be abstract, abstraction.
You should be the gorgeous purple orchid
Planted, rising, winging,
Not quite dark and not quite bright,
Subtle and yet extravagant,
Softly shining and softly soft.
Flora, you are the offering, the sacrifice, the victim,
Flower

Flower or flame,
Milk or wine,
Bull or lamb,
Tree or spring,
Desert or jungle,
Flush with being or full
Of negativity.
Here is a kind of meaning
Even in meaninglessness:
The poem as the gift,
The poem as the tribute
To the possibles,
Here to the slim green blade of grass,
There to the round orange ball of fruit,
There to the violet hour before the dark,
Here to the violet bloom beside the path
Of grayness to impossibility.

Flora, do you read over my shoulder?
Flora, do you feel the flux of my pen?
You are less you than I, less other than self.

Margaret, it is you whom I address.
The envelope will be inscribed to you.
Will you respond, and how will you reply?

The daughter of Linnaeus
Over the red lily
Discerned the red flame
Which was the spirit of the flower,
Or like which was the spirit of the flower,
You reported
That she reported.
Looking steadfastly at the lily
She saw above it hovering
The red exhalation.
She could see the red flame.

Do I report?
Do I distort?
What I deplore
Do I, Julia, do,
Must Flora do, too?
Do I fail in devotion to knowing
Just as the many, too many,
Whose practice I contemn,
Whose practice I condemn,
Fail when they mix
Quotation and paraphrase,
Fail when they miss
The meeting of the ways.

Will you judge
My indignation
Unwarranted, surprising?
Does such laxness matter?
Does exactness matter?
Accuracy must matter.
Yet how easy it is to fault.
Yet how easy it is to fail.

I approximate what you, Margaret Fuller, said
The daughter of Linnaeus said she saw.
I relay at least the flower and the flaming and the redness.

Was this the red essence of a knowledge?
What was the golden breeze?
Where was the white of the holy?
Was there a beautiful blue?

I was the multicolored.
Was I like the divine Flora?
Did my soul resemble the self
Of the patroness of my Flora?

For ten years I knew nothing of religion.
I was still, on my tenth birthday, The Atheist.
At twelve I felt the stirring of my spirit
To hope, to strive, to pray, to be made The Mystic.
At thirty-one I confirmed myself as The Scholar.
At thirty-five I began to write The Poem.

These are my religions
Save that throughout them all
There ever blazed and blaze the azure skies
Stretching before my enamored azure eyes.

These are my religions.
I have not chosen them,
For they have chosen me. Should I not choose?
If I reject their choice, what do I lose?

Though I feel deep dedication, yet I am delinquent.
Though I feel the heat of burning, yet I am lukewarm.
Though I commit myself sincerely, yet I am mere words.
Here is the atheist, the mystic, scholar, poet.
Here is the ignorant, incompetent, dull, weak.
O God, O gods, why can I never forget you?
O universe, why can I never be free?

Will I never never know?
How red is red?
Will I ever offer the poem?
How blue is blue?
Can white be white? How many
Are the colors of flowers?

Margaret, please excuse my journal jottings.
Excuse apostrophes, apologies.
Excuse expressions of perplexities.
In stillness will I listen to the cosmos?
In stillness will I listen for a minute?
Will there be oneness or duality
Or Janus Quadrifrons? Will there be number?
Will there be time or everlastingness?
What is this letter in eternity?
What is the poem in the universe?
Must my choice be the world or be the work?
Nothing matters. Maybe something can
Matter for a moment or a life.
Hector and Sibyl speak for us to death.
The phoenix and the amaranth may shine
Like the rhodora or the fitful lantern.
Achilles strides across the asphodel.

                                          Love,
                                          Julia

No. 34

Arlington, May 18

Dear Margaret,

Hector and Sibyl speak to us of death,
Hector, the hero, the man,
Sibyl, the woman, the wise,
He whose life was far too short,
She whose life was much too long.
Which yours was I know.
Which is mine?

In five days you will be forty
There in a fragile sailing ship on a sea
With the treasures of your life:
Husband, baby, written pages.
The pages are your deeds.
The pages are your victories.
You are the heroine.
You are Hector.

In five days I will be seventy-four
Here in a cramped double room of a nursing home
Struggling to guard and multiply
My treasure. The scribbled pages slant
Constantly towards the dirty floor.
The pages are my leaves.
The pages are my prophecies.
I reach out a boney arm.
I try to reach out a numb little finger.
From my back I am attached
To the heavy vacuum machine
Which is plugged in to the wall.
I am not sibylline.
I am Sibyl.

The orchid shines and rises still.
The pages yet for good or ill
Like clouds or fountains fill and fill.

Five minutes may remain
Of battle and of pain,
Of glory yet to gain.

Is it not best to die
Between the hostile sky
And the earth that cares not why?

When as I sit in my wheelchair
With its special roho cushion
Aides drain the narrow leg bag,
The urine tends to spill out onto the floor.
The soles of my sneakers squeak.
Are the laces wet, too?

At four in the morning the nurse
Emptied the big wide catheter bag,
Leaving it open below, unsecured at the base.
Three or four hours of pee (as they say)
Puddled the linoleum beside the bed.

When this had been mopped with the dirty mop
Plopped again and again into the black waters
Of the big black bucket and squeezed through the big black wringer,
The toilet in our bathroom shared by two double rooms
Overflowed abundantly with the paper, pee, and poop (as they say)
Of someone from the room adjoining mine
And pooled all over my room,
From the bathroom's threshold
To the spot where my wheelchair sits
And around and under my bed,
Over to my roommate's bed towards the window and the view.
The dirty mop returned to swish the site
Over and over with dark undulating waters.

Under dark seething waters you will go,
Swished and sucked and utterly claimed.
In five days you will be forty.
In two months you will be gone.

In five days you will be one hundred ninety-eight.
I am still grieving deeply for your, for Hector's, fate.
But rejoice, heroic ones, for you are great.
Yet he was granted burial. His mound
Rose on the shore. Your corpse was never found.
Close to the shore you drowned.

Sibyl wished to die.
I wish . . . I cry . . .
I could forever lie . . .

I am just learning to walk again.

Love,
Julia

No. 35

Arlington, May 20

Dear Margaret,

Some things should never be said.
If I were not lying in bed
On my side in a place
Which as I face
The night I can barely bear
I would not dare
Say what I sense I shall say
As day turns into eve, eve into day.

I wanted you to be an atheist.
I did not want to be an atheist
Though I have been one more or less
For over fifty years, I guess.
I needed to deny I was a theist.
I wanted to deny you were a theist
As lengthy study had affirmed
You, unlike Emerson, remained.
A source should be named.
This I had learned
From Capper's recent big biography.
My books and Harvard's are now far from me.

I wanted your comfort if I could not sip
A consolation from the transcendent guest.
I wanted the comfort of your fellowship
In the courage of a truly godless breast.

What weakness makes me taste
His sweetness of the past?
The savor will be gone with haste.
There is no knowledge here to last.
Let me turn off the light.
Let me turn on the pain.
He feels so close again.
Soon I will know the night.

Now for an instant
Here is eternal day.
Here is the distant
As a present yea.

Love,
Julia

No. 36

Arlington, May 21

Dear Leila,

This is perhaps strange. This is perhaps true. I think that it is true. I fear that it is also tedious, for you and for others. Yet I suspect that it is true.

It was while she was a child, a naive and innocent atheist, maybe rather to be deemed a proto-atheist, knowing nothing of atheism, knowing nothing of religion, that Julia gradually and secretly and perhaps intermittently (how hard it is to recall those early years) began to be what might be termed religious, what I will for the moment term religious. Insofar as she became religious, she entered upon this state all by herself, so to speak, without strong, or without clear, human influence from without. Was the influence God or nature or the self or a fact, a factor, a matter to be studied and solved by science? Was it *The Wizard of Oz* and *The Song of Bernadette*? Will there be a determination, a definition?

Will there be some logic here? Will some reasoning show how her religion can coexist, perhaps must coexist, with atheism? Or is the logic not necessary? Is it even logic?

The religiousness may be her self. Maybe her true self is that being which is both atheistic and religious.

What religion was that, is that? Does it matter? It is surely a dualism longing for, striving for, unity, for union. There is surely transcendence and intimacy. There is surely a sort of ecstasy. There is something like an aspiring tree in green. There is something like a vibrant mind on fire. There is something like a breathtaking breathgiving bloom in gold. There is something like a deeply beating heart. There is something like an endless sapphire sky.

Love,
Flora

No. 37

> Arlington, May 23

Dear Margaret,

Where is the magnificent copper beech
Solidly lightly spreading soaring
Out and up into May air?

Where are the enchanting lilac lilacs
Freshly sweetly breathing blowing
Out and forth into May breeze?

Where are we on this day of our birth?
Are we nowhere now?
Will we ever get anywhere, somewhere, home?

> Love,
> Julia

No. 38

Arlington, May 25

Dear Margaret,

Just two days after ours
Gleams golden Waldo's day of birth.
We celebrate his gentle purple powers,
His forceful presence on this verdant earth.
The sky today is very blue.
But are you certain it is true
That his serenity, so calm, so high,
Is — that he is — too much of clear blue sky?
How, what, are you? How, what, am I?

Love,
Julia

No. 39

                                      Arlington, May 27

Dear Margaret,

Flora dreamed of drowning in the Tiber,
Her father's river, black and glittering,
As from the bridge she peered into its stream,
Her father's life, her mother's death, her own
Conception in mortality and eros.
The Charles might do for you and me. The ocean
Did for you. The birth of Aphrodite,
That birth of beauty from a foaming sea,
The rippling of a little pool, the dripping
Of willows, images of elegance,
Down towards the pond and upwards from the pond,
Since elegance must elegantly drip
If salix is elegantissima,
And up and down, not tamely similar,
May be the same for willows by the waters
Beneath the sun or underneath the moon,
The moon that moves in liquid, and the sun
Igniting waves that sweep in from the deep,
Rushing upon the rocks and undulating
Around the crevices and sucked below,
Create an aqueous life or aqueous death.
The ambulance returning from Mount Auburn
Back to the nursing home beneath a cloudburst
Splashed through the swirling river of the road.
Save ship, crew, pilot, but the passenger,
The patient, jostle out into the flood,
I prayed, or almost prayed, for orison
Is not permitted by my will. Permit
My quick escape from home that is not home,
Deliverance from life that is not life.

                                                    Love,
                                                    Julia

No. 40

Arlington, May 29

Dear Margaret,

For a wishable watery end
One would with no hesitation select
This most illustrious, most difficult, exemplum:
When all the rest was dead and gone,
The famous sailing of the head alone,
Not yet bereft, perhaps never bereft,
Of knowledge and of beauty, nothing less,
A knowledge streaming through the gleaming eyes,
A beauty ringing from the singing lips.
If we must perish wretchedly, miserably,
If we must each be cut from our own trunk,
If we must lose our every severed limb,
Or if we somehow die as mortals die,
Could my, if not your, conscious pate perdure,
And might the light of Leila's eyes live on,
And might the flower of Flora's lips stay fresh,
Might, in these, deeply see and sweetly sound —
O life, O dying,
O good, O evil,
O love, O knowledge,
O truth, O beauty,
O golden rose, O golden tone,
O golden song, O golden sun —
Something splendid like the very head
Most glorious of Orpheus?

Love,
Julia

No.41

Arlington, May 30

Dear Margaret,

Does May have to end
Without my being a part of it?
It is out there somewhere.
Somewhere there are the usual things of May.
Perhaps I can remember just a few:
The fresh full green of leaves on trees,
The soft magenta gleam of blossoms on bushes,
The dazzling alluring blue serene of sky on sky.
This is the May of Flora Urania Baum.
This is my May.
This was mine.

Does life have to end
Without my playing my part in it?
Is this a part in life:
To fit into the rehab center?
Is this a part of life:
This piddling world of the nursing home?

In this small universe
Is the small patient never right?
Is it only little I who ever err?
If purgatory endures forever
Must it not be actually hell?
What spot in possible cosmoi multiplied
Does this speck occupy all by its little self?

Is the patient never right? Is it only I?

I saw you walking in the hall.
Why can't you turn in your bed?

Your left shoulder is too high.
Why can't you sit up straight?

You talk like an English teacher.
Why can't you say, Do this, without complication?

You declare, I'm sorry, and, Thank you, much too much.
Why can't you stop sounding insincere?

Here I am always denigrated.
Here I am always wrong.
Here I am always being lectured.
Here I am always being bossed.
I am the youngest resident.
I feel I am not senile.
I guess I am not demented.
Do I believe I have a brain?
Do I regret I have two ears?
Here the television sets
Blast day and night from room and room and room.
Except for me
Is everyone deaf?

Is this a loud life within a little place?
Is this a far vision within a little space?
Can I get out
Before I cannot hear or see or breathe?
Can I get out
Before, in short,
I die?

Yet if this is not hell but purgatory
Should I not first be penitent, repenting
Of sins committed by a willed omission?
Can I forget, no, I do not forget,
I only focus on the bad, that bad,
I never will forget the good, such good:

The dressing

The dressing of the huge and horrid wound,
The dressing of the awkward sagging body,
The bringing of the breakfast, lunch, and dinner,
The bringing of the dozen potent pills,
The bringing of the johnny and the diaper,
The changing of the dirty for the clean,
The making and unmaking of the bed,
The making and remaking of my strength
Through slow, skilled, wrenched, inventive therapies
That leave me almost human once again,
Almost like someone meant to be erect
And walk, not wobble, with two legs and feet,
A subject for an anthropology
Or for redemption through and from a hell.

Margaret, forgive this metrical confession,
This unpoetic versified short list.
Must I repent? Must I eschew despair?
Is there not something which I must get out of?
Is there not less of living than of dying?

Can I escape
From this death
Into life?

Can I escape
From this life
Into death?

Can I escape
From this death
Into death?

Does the poem have to end
Without my reaching the end of it?

> Love,
> Julia

No. 42

> Arlington, May 31

Dear Leila,

Julia, tired of feeling blamed,
Can in turn disparage me.
Imagination, your very life, she imagines,
Addressing me, accusing me, has seeped away
Like blood, like ichor, whatever flows through your veins.
You seem anemic, or are you hemorrhaging?
O flower, thou art frail, O rose, thou art sick, she opines,
Murmuring, muttering, thus, although she does not know
If the earliest shy enticing roses of Cambridge,
Visited with delight by us together
Throughout her previous, preposthumous, existence,
Have started to enter upon their own full life,
Which I should now be sharing, should be showing,
As May is closed, June opened, by those roses,
Those white ones, say, of that hedge on Walker Street,
Or, in Longfellow's garden, those varied delicate ones,
Authentic selections from the nineteenth century,
Relics of roses which Margaret kissed with passion.
If Julia gives me a little kiss on the cheek
Maybe I will come to full life again,
Or if you, Leila, conduct to eyes and ears
The dances of the stars and the music of the spheres.

> Love,
> Flora

No. 43

Arlington, May 31

Dear Margaret,

An Orphic moment
Interrupted
By a wavering of green leaves
Or by the black blast of the hurricane
May be recovered
I suspect
If it is deep and radiant enough.

Even if Orpheus
Does not descend to help
Will his Eurydice, will I myself,
Now call for him, help him?

Shall I like Orpheus shade my eyes
Gazing bravely at what I still must do?

Shall I like Orpheus sailing by the cliffs
Outsing the Sirens?

Margaret, though I am now a woman
Of two centuries later than yours,

I do not feel ready to effect a rescue,
I do not feel eager to peer ahead,
I do not feel so strong in song
That I will not soon plunge from the ship
And decorate the rocks with my bare bones.

Margaret, maybe not too late
I will gain an Orphic courage,
I will regain an Orphic commitment,
Partly from your writing,
Partly from your life.

Love,
Julia

No. 44

                              Arlington, June 3

Dear Margaret,

Can I still perceive the sounds which the ear does not hear?
Can I listen to the lilies of the valley in that direction
Where the little white bells in their churches with the low green roofs
Keep ringing silently sounding in the silent breeze?
Can I hear the enormous organ of the Norway spruce
Across the way in the great gold cathedral of the air
Playing pulsing subtly splendidly deep
And high and light and long and multivalent
In eternal green or what seems everlasting
In the soundless breeze that seems a beginning of summer?

I fear I cannot hear. There is only tension.
I fear. I cannot hear. There is only terror
Before behind around me everywhere.

                                      Love,
                                      Julia

No. 45

Arlington, June 4

Dear Leila,

Hector and Achilles both lie low
At last. They lie in glory. Margaret lies
How many fathoms deep? The monument
Erected in Mount Auburn cannot hold
Her corpse but holds up, holds out, holds forth honor.
The lowliness of Mary Virgin Mother
By the Most High is lifted high forever.

June's trees are drooping drearily in rain.
I wonder if wet heaviness can threaten
Even the splendor of the rhododendrons
In their extravagance of greens and purples.
Can I climb greening hills of history
Or mount the purpled mountainsides of myth
While Julia lies here low inglorious?

Love,
Flora

No. 46

Arlington, June 5

Dear Margaret,

   A corporeal story. I'll skip most of it, though. A few hints may be sufficient to intimate, however indirectly, a few answers to contrasting questions. In whatever position I am found, how low do I have to lower myself to lie low, to be lying low? In whatever situation I am found, how high do I have to raise myself to rise high, to be rising high?

   At five this morning the summoned aide brusquely pulled the door, angrily asking: "Why you do go to bathroom so soon?" With equal anger she added: "I hope you not go again." I had already gone at one and at three during my first sleep without the catheter since its insertion on that antagonistic second day of April. Well, this aide would have left by seven o'clock, when I could anticipate standing in the same place waiting for someone from the next shift to bring me a clean diaper. Not, I must note, that I am incontinent, as the aides suspect, but the problem is one which I find it difficult to explain to them and which I will not impose upon you. I am lucky and happy just to be able to get out of bed and to function somewhat like a normal human being. Thus my body once more begins to become my own. Is it to be compared with the corpse of Orpheus and the ever-knowing ever-composing head of the man of intellect and art, of prophecy and poetry, of musing and music? What do I see or sing as I stand and wait? What truth and beauty do I serve? What goes through my head as I imitate an undiapered baby up on two wobbly legs? Is my head, too, infantile? Or is it moribund? Is it thinking or unthinking? Is it composing or decomposing? Is it connected to or disconnected from my neck and my trunk and my arms and my legs?

Last night, possessing to a certain extent all of my limbs, I walked up and down the halls at about nine o'clock without my cane. The door of the elevator slid open, discharging a calm businesslike middle-aged man in suit and tie pushing a stretcher furnished with a coarse brown cloth. I guessed the cause. I swerved abruptly. But wanting very badly my anthropic exercise, I soon returned. From one of the double rooms emerged the stretcher with its brown cover wrapped around the form of a human body. No opening for the head. A corpse, of course.

           Love,
           Julia

No. 47

Arlington, June 7

Dear Leila,

    She was about five. She heard the song. She knew that it was the music of her own heart. Somewhere over the rainbow, far far away . . . There pulsed reality. To this she was summoned.

    She was about nine. She saw the vision. She knew that it was the insight of her own mind. The lady, the immaculate conception . . . There stood reality. To this she was invited.

    These were incidents, almost accidents, which perhaps confirmed the tones of the mother's voice as she recited poems and sang lieder, looking lovingly out of enormous azure eyes, and which certainly confirmed what was of supreme significance: from above the vertical city the everlasting quintessential substance of the incomparably, immeasurably, enormous azure skies. Were all these events and phenomena, then, aspects of social and natural encounters? These were her heart and mind discovering her own being and the being of the other that was of herself and not of herself, that was more serious than her childish intimations and that was more lasting than her childhood experiences.

    How trivial, how common, all this seems, except for Julia herself, except for her descent into the profundities of her little single soul, except for her ascent into the expansiveness of the immensities and multiplicities of the universe. How secular, how unreligious, all this seems, except for its burgeoning into the eternal blossom, the cosmic tree, the desirable and desired infinite dazzling splendor, infinite darling friend.

Later the call became more and more clear and complex and the response more and more concrete and complete. Still later everything changed. No, nothing changed. Everything changed except what was everything, a secret depth and an aspiring height, vaguer but even greater, in desire and intention, if not, alas, in attention and execution, than all that preceded.

Will you object that my depictions become too wordy? These are merely words about Julia uttered by Julia's word.

Love,
Flora

No. 48

Arlington, June 8

Dear Margaret,

I sing of purple and I sing of gold.
These are two systems of reality,
If of reality they are. Of song
They are or will be if my singing sings
Itself into reality. But if
My worded music or my musicked word
Fails to be real, the purple and the gold
Will have no dwelling in the universe
Of discourse or in that of that which is.

I sing for Julia and I sing for Flora,
And which is which and which is both you know.
If I am Julia, Julia is myself
And Flora of my mind and of my tongue.
Flora, my Orpheus, floats down the stream,
All golden, of her Roman father Tiber
And mother Roman Canens who dissolved
In song as she conceived her in that river
Of golden love beneath an azure sky
And sighed her way along a golden breeze
Of life and death in breathing forth her singing.

Flora the daughter sees and sings and floats
Along the azure stream, the golden river,
Up up the golden breeze and azure sky,
Down down dark rivers underneath the earth
With currents purplest black and blackest purple
In surge or slack to where Eurydice
Waits sighing, singing, for her Orpheus
And calls for him at last. How can she call
For Orpheus and he not call for her

If she

If she is yet below and he above?
Who dies, who lives? What is the history,
What is the myth, what is the linear,
What is the cyclical, what is and now
Is not, what is and then is not, what is
And/or is not, what was and then was not,
What was and now is not, what is and is?
Is death the ending of this history?
Loving not death but life that may be lived,
Not loving life that is but living death,
Not loving death that is but dying life,
I can half hope to live, half hope to die.
Loving not non-existence but existence
That is existence, must I make my choice?
Is not existence, if there is existence,
The better choice for Orpheus, for Flora,
And for Eurydice the higher hope?

Existence is for me the nursing home.
Turning my back upon the bingo players
And air-conditioned room in which they played
On this hot humid afternoon in June
I pressed the plate for opening the door
And tapped my cane along the large gray slabs
That pave the patio. Beyond the border,
The gray stone wall and rusting chain-link fence,
Extend some edges and some sections of
Reality more real: the real homes
Adjacent, houses, gardens, parents, children,
Big clapboard houses, large green grassy gardens,
Men mowing lawns, sons splashing in wading pools,
Splashed daughters laughing (if in all this distance
I make deductions), mothers cooking dinner
(If in their absence I may make conjectures).
Lo, over there, in distance, not in absence,
Not in deduction, nor imagination,
But in existence if there is existence
Beyond dubiety or cogitation,
In a large garden, standing in a row,
                                        Could

Could be discerned the purple and the gold
Of irises, arising from long greens,
Bearing the rainbow's name, raising the colors
Of my own history and my hope. Those rainbows
Shone far away. That coloration called.

Plunge, plunge, into that purple. Let me plunge
Into that merged and melded red and blue.
Thus my heart spoke. Thus my lips almost sang.
From the red cardinal burst red exultation
As the notes splashed from high green exaltation.
Flew two blue bluejays darting in sheer joy
As the wings flashed by mirroring a sky
Paler than they but likewise blue with white,
Substance of blue with accidents of white,
Soft pillows of caressing clouds of white
Or clouds held gently by this heaven of blue.
Pursue that blue and red, plunge into purple
Opening to your heart your heart's desire.
Thus my heart spoke and thus my mind repeated.
Thus my heart sang and thus my mind responded.

Some irises were purple, some were gold.
Go, glow unto that gold, my being cried,
Go with the wings of golden butterfly,
Go on the golden wings of golden breeze,
Go to the wings of golden irises.
The breeze was hot and humid but it blew.
Today it was not silent since it made
Physical, audible, music, real, true, sweet.
Today the breeze sang with a leafy sound
All through the full green leaves of Norway maples
Which wait and wave along the wall and fence.
The butterfly was gleaming on the breeze.
The breeze was gleaming to the gleaming earth.
The earth was gleaming with the irises.
I hovered just above their golden wings
And in their aura found my golden flight
And with their gold began my gold ascent.

Deep in a purple world I heard a singing.
Out in a golden universe I sang.

Would I were worthy. Would the song I feel
Were truth and beauty. Would my song were real.

Love,
Julia

No. 49

                         Arlington, June 11
                         Fortunae Reduci, Matri Matutae

Dear Leila and/or Margaret,

Shall I say I, or will we speak as we?
Shall we say you, or will I speak to thee?

We are not goddesses, yet on the margin
We stand as two or one before the day

Of two or one who stand between the out
And in, the yes and no, the is, is not,

Departure and return, city and garden,
Dual and singular. We yearn to pray

For blessings large or little, for a death
To liberate our flesh or for a breath

Of freshness near the entrance to our prison
While the beneficent grand beech holds sway

Over the borderland between this home
And the wide world where dead and living roam.

We — no, let me here speak as I — did not yield to the temptation to pray either for permanent release or for temporary relief, but out of the blue — why not say out of that azure heaven of this sunny, breezy, hot June afternoon, of this festival of Luck and Dawn, why not say out of a dawn of luck, a birth of return to that to which I am summoned — out of the blue of the afternoon, without petition to persons or powers divine or human, immortal or mortal, dawned luck: the chance of stepping outside to tap my cane on the cement and asphalt, to breathe real air under unobstructed sky, to contemplate the comfort and the splendor and the grandeur
                                                           of the

of the great copper beech. I even dared to ascend, hesitantly and unsteadily, a tiny incline forming a minor stretch of the palpable rise of the drive, in order to enter the fringes of the great fagaceal shade from which the dazzling brightness of beech, sky, afternoon might undazzlingly brighten eyes and mind and being. The celestial immensity of blue that was so true, that was so calm and so vibrant both, gleamed above the sturdiness and flutter of the responding terrestrial immensity of the beech. Just as the sky was both pure and alluring, both serene and exciting, so the beech rose up in its gray stability, that smooth solidity, and spread out in its incessantly shifting glitter both brilliant and dark.

Was the breeze becoming wind? Did I play the hero and lean upon my cane as upon a sword or a spear? Was dying still perhaps desired? Was breathing now perhaps inspired? Must I fear a fall and dread a death, or might I quicken and deepen my grateful breath? Thus I spoke to the day of the double goddesses. Thus perhaps I may speak to you.

                Love,
                from the border

No. 50

> Arlington, June 11
> Fortunae Reduci

Dear Margaret,

Shall I attempt to live,
Which is to endure,
Not so much for Flora's sake
As for that which she and I
Feel called to do?
I softly said
To Fortune of the glorious return.

Shall I attempt to give
An offering so pure
That it will transform the ache
Which we suffer for the sky,
For call of blue,
And care of red,
Into that warmth and light for which we burn?

> Love,
> Julia

No. 51

> Arlington, June 13
> The Birth of Margaret Rodgers Budenz

Dear Margaret,

How is the pearl discovered or recovered?
What are the waters into which we dive?
What are the waters into which we die?

My mother like your mother was a Margaret.
How can this high light festival of birth
Find me down, dark, distracted by her death?

The curling cardinal, blaring bluejay, rang
The bells of noon that celebrated June:
Strong sun and wavering shade and subtle breeze.
Rectangles, long and green, the flower boxes,
And circles, big and red, the flower pots,
Along the margin of the patio
Beside the nursing home hold leaves and blossoms.
The marigolds are gold or gold and red
And the petunias purple various
In tint and shade or purple very pale
In stripes that alternate with white in patterns
Strict or free. This seems significant.
If it is this, is it significant
For life or poetry? Shall I not ask
The master? Will he prove it is for both?
Is it philosophy: the one, the many,
The same, the different, the up, the down?
Is it perhaps significant for dying?

Is it a pattern for my celebration?

My mother's pattern was both strict and free,
Her life both one and ever opening
Into new musics, into new fusing hues.
She was a pearl. Her price was great. She gleamed.
She was the stone that shone, the precious gem
Both hard and soft, the real and the ideal.
I will not sing again what I have sung.
She lived for life, lived life. She chose to live
Until that moment when she chose to die,
Knowing the dying time. She did not act,
She who had always acted, but at last,
Not acting, satisfied the final act,
The final fact, achieved the final passing
Within a same from same to different.

I dive down to that difference profound,
The pearl beneath blue waters, and I rise
Up to the same blue skies, same clouds of pearl,
Remembering how Flora's mother sighed
Dissolving disappearing singing sighing
Down blue-gold currents up to blue-gold heavens
And how my mother nurtured tenderly
My Flora, and my mother was our mother.

      Love,
      Julia

No. 52

Arlington, June 15

Dear Miranda,

I know what you told Margaret. Would you tell it also to Julia? I hear her saying, swaying a little as she stands without walker or cane far from the heavy iron tables and chairs, in a space like space but grave with gravitation: I do not want to fall. I do not ever want to fall again. And, reflecting upon the syntax: I do not want ever to fall again. And, altering the modification: I do not want to fall ever again.

What do you want, I murmured, abruptly but sympathetically.

Shall I only lie down on the patio's flat gray squares, never again to get up?

She certainly could not ever get up. But, behold, is she standing on the flat gray squares of that bridge? I seem to be hearing her as she seems to be peering there over the stones of the wall: I am not able to leap.

What do you wish, I whispered, urgently though softly.

Shall I merely stretch out on the river's swift gray current? It runs and rushes and wrests, and at last it rescues and rests.

This is what she uttered as she muttered or seemed to have screamed as she dreamed.

Was she not capable still of a fire of desire, of a flight to light? Was all only gray, or was there yet the lure of the glorious red, the delight of the irresistible blue, the subtlety and splendor of the whole arching rainbow, the first and final entirety of white? Was all only whimpering and whinnying, or was there yet the chant, the lyre, the violin, the harp, the immense elaborating simplifying symphony? Was there not still the flower, the tree, the sky, the pulse of the universe, the feel of infinity?

Miranda, bear witness now to Julia of the testimony you gave to Margaret long ago, speaking with deepest seriousness, about that with which, if I judge correctly, you were glossing religion, or one of two essential components of religion: a sense that what the soul is capable to ask it must attain.

Of what is Julia capable? What will she ask? What will she attain?

Love,
Florinda

No. 53

> Arlington, June 16

Dear Margaret,

Is there a way
To pray?

Pray for me, my sister Jo just said.
Don't only think of me instead,

But, I say,
Really pray.

How easy that should be
For one like me.

Any day
I might start to pray.

What would be the norm?
What could be the form?

My mind and heart are gray.
Shall I begin to pray?

My sister is the splendent yellow rose.
Just as she ever grows

Even lovelier, stronger, may
She ever grow, I pray.

Fullness of yellow, red, and blue we might
Attain. Might we reach white?

White of infinitude, now and forever play
About, within, before us. Thus I now pray.

> Love,
> Julia

No. 54

Arlington, June 17

Dear Margaret,

The Norway spruce is a prayer.

It curves upward in petition.
It stretches outward in recognition.
It possesses itself and is possessed in union.

The Norway spruce is a green prayer.

Up and up it reaches in seeking.
Out and out it extends in adoration.
And still it fills and fills in intimacy.

You know how I am a failing, a fading, a grayness.

I barely beg, although I am a beggar.
I hardly acknowledge, although I am an admirer.
I scarcely exist

Either in communion or even in myself alone.

My gluey tongue,
My gravelly voice,
Should surely now keep still.

Maybe that tall, full, vibrant spruce will pray for me.

Should we not pray?
That is, we should pray.
That is, we should not pray.

Is there a should for the firm and flexible verdurous grandeur
   of the tree?

Love,
Julia

No. 55

>Arlington, June 24
>Forti Fortunae trans Tiberim

Dear Margaret,

Shall I travel through
All the modal auxiliaries

As I trail by train
Or as I float by boat

With the lovely lively young
Frenchwoman archaeologist in pink sneakers

Or with the festive Romans of every age
Of every age in boots, in heels, in sandals,

Or as the waters waft me,
Or as the river ripples me,

Alone to seek my fortune
Along a turbid Tiber

On Fors Fortuna's day
In Fors Fortuna's fane?

Shall I step into the deep greenness of the grove
And rest to ask my veritable questions

Of the very fortune that I seek?
Is it death or is it life?

Must I decide?
Can I decide?

Should I resolve?
Could I resolve?

Might I decide to die?
Will I resolve to live?

May I find the sibylline unsibylline
Will and still omit the million years,

Shrinking, shrinking,
Living, living,

Wishing, wishing,
All that wisdom withered, withering?

Will I imitate the will and can I skip
The bitter mixture: gift and dire omission?

Might I find the sibylline?
Shall I treasure in my breast

The heart of Hector
Ready in the seconds of the end

To make his death, for all its failure and its pain,
The hero's act, grand fact, great fame?

Shall I cross my heart and hope to die,
Willing victim of my fault and fate?

Will I, brave between the blows,
Commit myself to the other, dearer, victim,

Garlanded with irises, with roses,
Clothed in the many-colored rainbow cloak,

The sacrifice, the offering, the word,
The form, the feel, the music, and the meaning?

Would I refuse the hard, high, holy route?
Will I commit myself to live for this?

Can I be hero on this battlefield?
Can I be priestess in this sanctuary?

Must I run round and round on mud, in dust?
Might my triumphant monument soon rust?

I hold up high my offering, the work.
Is this for me to shoulder or to shirk?

Must this be too imperfect, too uncertain?
Is this the shrine? Is this the curtain?

Love,
Julia

No. 56

>Arlington, June 24
>The Birth of Saint John the Baptist

Dear Margaret,

Will I listen to the crows
Crowing from the lofty boughs?

Shall I, dear Margaret, rant and rant and rant?
Shall I abandon, Margaret dear, my cant?

If the raindrops were the syllables of the sky
The sky was eloquent. Then why

Was, when the blue resumed, the river's word
Of light and life not heard?

>Love,
>Julia

No. 57

Arlington, June 25

Dear Leila,

How was it when the god came to the sibyl?
How was it when the sibyl came to the god?

Gold shone in azure and the heat of the bright rays
Reached the whiteness of the brightening lily widening,
Fragrant, in whiteness, fully fragrant, fully lovely,
Full of love.

        Immortal youth was his.
She, mortal, elegant, bloomed in her youthful bloom.
He filled her with his words, with radiant words.
She told his truths. She spoke his radiant truth
To any seeker. She wrote his burning words.

It was only for herself that she erred, failing
To say everything that she could have said,
To ask everything that she should have asked.

Love,
Flora

No. 58

Arlington, June 27

Dear Margaret,

This would seem obvious.
This must appear daunting.

If the offering, if the sacrifice, is the poem
The poem must be a poem.

What if the priestess,
What if the poetess,

Fails, falls,
Sinks, sins,

Hobbles along a false path,
Stumbles adown the facile descent,

Grovels among the huge hogs,
Lies low with the little pigs?

How must one grade the gluttony of the supper,
Gulp the great gluey double-sized chocolate brownie,
Gobble the big beige wedge of chewy pecan pie?

How can one assess the data of the dinner,
The white of the rice pilaf,
The orange of the glazed carrots,

The brown of the bread of the roll,
The browner brown of the coffee,
The smooth pale tint of yellow that was the custard's,

The satisfaction of the salmon
Poached to the perfection
Of pink delicacy?

The sacrificial banquet must feed and please
Apart from the training of the baker,
Apart from the merits of the chef.

Bake it with the bread of exodus.
Make it by the magic of the muse.
Take it from the psalmody of the robin.

This solemn sacrament
Works ex opere operato.
Consider the lilies of the field.

But there must become,
Still there must exist,
Work, a work, the work.

In my heavy hands the hoe
Could do something here,
Should do something now.

The daylilies live their golden day
In the green of lengthening leaves,
In the gray of descending rain.

Love,
Julia

No. 59

                                        Arlington, June 28

Dear Margaret,

There is no poetry here.
This is the home of hopelessness.

This is the place of pain.
This is the land of counterpain.
This is the country of waiting.

Bordering the gray patio,
From the brown earth emerging
Above the largeness of the leaves in their amplitude of green,
The largeness of their big green hearts,
The bits of palest purple
Of the hosta just budding
Attempt to contradict me.

                                                    Love,
                                                    Julia

No. 60

Arlington, June 28

Dear Leila,

The fronds, the fringes, the fillets, of the Norway spruce
Seem to droop from those lifting, spreading, boughs
Encountering no answering eye
Among all that chance to glance across.

See the tree,
Foolish Julia tries from time to time.

This is the kingdom of indifference.
This is the domain of negation.
Here there is no room for you and me.
Here we cannot exist.

Love,
Flora

No. 61

Arlington, June 29
Saints Peter and Paul

Dear Margaret,

 The vestments are red. The vestments for this festival are red. You will remember them from Rome. I remember them from many years of Latin. That was all long ago, but today I saw them glowing in splendor on the huge television screen of the big common room with the red carpet in the red brick building where at present I reside or, shall I say, where I am confined. The images were so large and clear that for a moment as I watched it ascending from the thurible up, up, through the glory of the basilica I smelled the incense.

 Is today's red the red of knowledge? Is it the blood of martyrs? Is it the fire of witness? Is it the red of the road to Rome, Caesar's, Peter's, yours, mine? Along the road rides the crimsoned imperator. Along the road rides the crimsoned Jove. Is the crimson guilt? Is the crimson victory? Is the crimson triumph?

 Do the red bricks of this facility hold knowledge in or do they keep it out? Can I still recall the red bricks of the Cambridge apartment building which contains my home with its shelves of books and chairs of books and tray tables of books, with its files of papers and piles of papers and plastic bags of papers? Can I remember the red bricks of the library for which I long, for which I yearn, for which I mourn? My body wants to pass through those walls, my feet want to scurry through the stacks, my hands want to reach greedily, gleefully, for the books, my eyes want to gaze gravely, lazily, sagely, upon the pages.

Is there knowledge within the regular red walls of my present domicile? Nursing homes resemble hospitals, convents, prisons. The person suffers. Regulation operates from without. Pathei mathos functions from within. Here rule also the dreadful distractions of the double rooms, the medications in the middle of the night, the junk music piped incessantly through the halls, the television sets shouting constantly from every doorway. Shall I think of the guardian beech as gleaming with dark red leaves? Here the tree of the knowledge of good and evil feeds me chiefly the knowledge of evil. To me, at least, it seems so. Does this feeling reveal the evil deep within me? Am I Eve?

Did that other tree, the tree of the cross, reverse this evil? Did the blessed fruit of Mary's womb hang on its bough? Did Eva shift to Ave?

The blood of martyrs is the seed of the tree. Is the tree the tree of Eden with its bright red fruit? Is the tree the tree of Calvary with its bright red blood? The red apple is dangling down. Shall I eat it? The red blood is dripping down. Shall I drink it? From the blood grows the tree. From the tree grows the fruit.

The martyrs are the witnesses. The witnesses speak with tongues of fire. But if the tree die, if the fruit perish, if the martyrs be slain, if the witnesses be killed, may they rise from pyres like Heracles, like the phoenix. May the carbuncle tongues of ruby red utter their burning words. Must the fire and the blood be one?

Does knowledge demand blood? Does knowledge produce fire? Must I be ready to bleed as a martyr? Will I be willing to flame as a witness? Must I be the martyr to knowledge? Will I be the witness to knowledge? Oh, how I love that gleaming tree. Must I suffer? May I partake? Can I share?

Love,
Julia

No. 62

Arlington, July 5

Dear Margaret,

Was it a call to woman?
Was it a call to women?
Was it a call to a woman?

Was it a call to the all?
The leaving all for the god?
The finding all in the books?
The gaining all from the goddess?

This was a day of the call.
This was a day of the calls.
Is this the day?

The sky on the eve was striped with red and blue.
I, too, am striped
When I am not gray.
I, too, am striped with two, with red and blue,
When I am not rainbowed, redolent, in many colors,
Colors of divine Iris, colors of immortal Flora.

Of the many what do I the gardener glean?
For the many what do I the painter plan?
At the one how do I the mystic gaze?
On the one and the many how do I the philosopher ponder?
Re the all how do I the physicist reason?
About the two what shall I say?
In two do I dwell?

My room is denominated double, but it is not two.
It is half a room, numbered two-two-two, side a.
Thus I live, if it is living, on the second floor.
The second floor has my room and the patio.

The third

The third floor has a porch set over a portion
Of that patio, which I know so well below it.
From the head nurse and a therapist I obtained
Permission to take the elevator alone
From the second floor to the third floor all alone
And to walk out on the porch all all alone.
From there I beheld a garden.

This grace was not glimpsed when I walked below.
Up here I could seek and I could be sought.
Up here I could find and I could be found.
Up here what was far could be also near.
Up here I could reach that unreachable garden.
Here I could be reached by the reach of the garden.

From the midst of verdurous green
My two colors called to me.
There leapt a fiery red
Like the red of a dancing flame.
There rested ethereal blue
Like the blue of a morning sky.
The red was tending towards orange
Yet it was really red.
The blue was tending towards purple
But it was truly blue.
Each large and shining lily opened up red in depth
Like a talented diligent student receiving, a knowledge received.
Each light lace-cap hydrangea opened out blue in display
Like a splendid tender tenor giving, a beauty given.

Is this, on the day of the call, another call?

You remember Fishkill Landing, where you responded
To your special call to do your work as a woman
For woman and for women. I responded
There to a special call to me, to a woman.
You know my history, begun there, as a nun.
I will not write again what many know.

You remember Harvard Library, where you accomplished
The feat of reading in the reading room
Although a woman, thus the very first
Permitted access there to precious volumes.
I responded there to a special subtle call.
You know the story of my Harvard library card.

You know the myth of Flora and Minerva,
The third call of this mythic ritual day.
I will not write again what I have written,
What you know well. I will not write again
What you have written of the wise Minerva,
What wise Minerva's wisdom says to you.

Do I hear, on a feast of the call, a clearer call?
Will a woman have the strength to listen and to respond?
Will a woman have the courage to be an Orpheus,
Seeing and singing? Will Eurydice arise,
Ascend, transcend? Where is Eurydice?
Am I part of the narrative, the song?

Will I leap into flame like the big smooth gleaming lilies
Opening to knowing,
Reddening receptive down to their red depths?

Will I spread into serenity like the wide lace-cap hydrangeas
Resting in the beauty
Extended in their blue giving, as their blue gift?

Is this still the call?
Will there be an answer on this day?
Shall I once more choose the all?
Shall I lay me down in gray?

Oh, over this gray ocean of my troubles
Let me blow the multicolored bubbles.

Oh, on that far horizon, red and blue
Both summon, ever old and ever new.

                                      Love,
                                      Julia

No. 63

Arlington, July 8

Dear Margaret,

I do not have this at home.

From the porch, the evening breeze,
From beneath, the evening green,
Seem the evening dream
Yet seem to dream reality.
Can anything as evening falls be real?

Out in front, the feet of the beech
Look ready to set forth in some direction
Selected from, say, seven possible
As they point here, there, out into the evening.
Will they tread the long path on to the land of giants?

Following them the foot of the book goes hopping.

Love,
Julia

No. 64

Arlington, July 9

Dear Margaret,

My evening paradise of porch and garden
Has now gone up in smoke.

The Orpheus who tries to sing this missive
Sings at the noise of the sirens.

Seeking this humid afternoon's green breeze
I found a nurse and staff assistant smoking.
The space was small. The breeze could not prevail.

Seeking the succor of my double room
I found my roommate's television shouting.
The space is small. My song cannot prevail.

I flee the wheezed out breezes of today
Blighting fresh green happiness.

I fly the strident sirens of today
Enticing to loud ugliness.

Love,
Julia

No. 65

Arlington, July 10

Dear Leila,

Anthe called the porch a ship.
Holding the black iron railing
We stood looking out over the green sea of the garden.
The whitecaps were blue, the bluecaps
Of the lace-cap hydrangeas opening petal by petal.
Green waters deeply still or freshly moving
Were verdurous as greens of grass and leafage,
Verdant originals of that marine.
The breeze blew over sea and ship.
The ship kept sailing into thought.
I do not think that Anthe thought of drowning.

Love,
Flora

No. 66

                                      Arlington, July 13
                                      Apollini

Dear Margaret,

Although it is July there is a breeze
Blowing the morning in,
Blowing in the morning.
Shall I pretend the leaves are laurel leaves?
They are more flexible. They lack the scent,
That fragrance of Apollo's breath. Shall I pretend
The breeze is sweet Apollo's breath? Shall I pretend
The day is his? The day is his. His is the wind
Of wish. I plead to breeze, to morning, Come.
I plead to breeze, to morning, Really come.
Is this a recognition of the god?
What breeze of breath breathes on me, into me?
Come sweetly, strongly, come, physician, heal me.
Come strongly, sweetly, come, musician, free me
With breath of genuine song for breath of genuine song.

                                                Love,
                                                Julia

No. 67

> Arlington, July 15
> EIDUS

Dear Leila,

Gleam, eagle, lifting to the throne of Jove.
Linger here, lily, living, Junoesque.

Thus I petition. But why do I pray?
Thus I keep speaking. But what do I say?

> Love,
> Flora

No. 68

Arlington, July 17

Dear Margaret,

It is not the particular place.
It is not the particular persons.
It is not perhaps the particular pain.

It is not so much these which constitute my prison.

It is the generic.
It is the general.
It is the joke of existence.

It is rather these of which I am the victim.

Here the sun is setting slowly gold.
Here the moon is rising swiftly silver.
To the special particulars, silver and gold, I am grateful.

My honor roll is posted starry on the night.

Love,
Julia

No. 69

Arlington, July 18

Dear Margaret,

I have flashed my message to the heavens.

I am grateful for the graces of the place.
I am grateful for the goodness of the persons.
Did I say that I am grateful for the pain?

Would I dissolve or would I solve the problem?

In its bitter stinging orange,
In its pricking probing purple,
In its sickly sickening green,

The pain is to be thanked

If dear clear yellow and red and blue
Are not yet utterly muddied,
Have maybe now and then been clarified.

I cry my clarification to the whiteness.

Love,
Julia

No. 70

Arlington, July 18

Dear Margaret,

These two great loves: Call them Apollo and Eros.
These two great loves: Call them Flora and Anthe.

To me they are like the bright yellow petals
Brightening, brightening yellowest sunflowers.

For me they ray from a higher, brighter, bloom,
The bold blossom of the gold sun.

Love,
Julia

No. 71

Arlington, July 18

Dear Leila,

Easy the descent to hell.
Hard the ascent to heaven.

Facile the discourse of Pluto, of Lucifer.
Difficult the labored language learned from the angels.

Love,
Flora

No. 72

                                        Arlington, July 19

Dear Margaret,

Which way are the sunflowers staring?

Never again chez nous?
Not in New York?
Not in old Rome?
Not in old Newtowne,
Our new old Cambridge, Massachusetts?
From the hateful house of Hades will we see
No emerald meadows sprinkled joyous with all the festive colors of
    flowers,
No ebony heavens scattered delighted with all the whitest vigils of stars?
Will we hear the young queen weeping?
Will we listen as the daughter laughs?
The waves of annihilation rise to greet us.
The waters of nothingness rush to hug us tight.

I hold a bottle for my letter at the last.

                                            Love,
                                            Julia

No. 73

Arlington, July 19

Dear Leila,

No, none of the earth's green fields,
No, none of the world's black skies,

For them. For us the tides
Of life, the golden breeze.

But long and perilous the roads,
And faint the constellations, frail the rose.

Love,
Flora

No. 74

Arlington, July 19

Dear Leila,

If there are undulations
They are not felt.
From the deck of the porch ship
Nothing exists but green and black.
If there are flowers,
If there are stars,
They are not seen.
If there are songs
They are sung by the bugs.
If there are words
They are stifled by the heat.
If there is construction
The voice is inclined towards the passive.
If there is condition
To be is inclined towards the hypothetical.
If there is expression
I am writing in the dark.

Love,
Flora

No. 75

Arlington, July 19

Dear Margaret,

August is forgotten.
There is only July.
There is only so much of July.
Aeneas will never reach Rome.
Augustus will never triumph thrice.
August will never be August.
From the altars swift incense
Will never ascend to the gods.
From Olympus swift divinity
Will never descend to the city that is,
That will be, that once was.
Then it once was?
Once there was June.
Maybe there was May.
Maybe we once were born.

Love,
Julia

No. 76

Arlington, May 23

Dear Margaret,

    I have been in the house in which you were born. I have been in the room in which you were born. I think it was the bedroom with the fireplace on the second floor of your parents' home on Cherry Street. It was a plain house on a plain street in a plain part of Cambridge known as Cambridgeport. No port developed there. But your birth honors the plain place. And your life brightens the dull spot.

    I was not born at home but in Knickerbocker Hospital. When the water broke, my mother took the subway uptown and crosstown from the small apartment at Lexington Avenue and Twenty-ninth Street. The obstetrician was Dr. Stix. Not being Minerva, I did not know how to spell. In any case, the name sounds ominous. And it suited aspects of the ambience. There were plenty of passages under the ground. There were plenty of waterways all around. The place was also a port, the port of New York. I am not aware of any luster cast upon the site by my birth or by my life.

    I must write much more. I defer further writing. For now I remark that we, you and I, were born. We were born somewhere once on a Wednesday the twenty-third of May. We were born and we lived. We have lived.

Love,
Julia

No. 77

Arlington, July 23

Dear Margaret,

Your first memory was a death, the death of your baby sister Julia. You were three years old. My first memory was a place, the island near the shore of which you died. I was three years old.

I could have said that your first memory was a death and my first memory a place of death. But I eschew the rhetoric because you knew at first hand Julia's death while I knew nothing of yours. What we both knew was the feeling of being very small and looking up at someone very tall.

You looked up into the weeping face of your nursemaid, who took your hand and led you to visit your dead sister. Later you were lifted into a chair and gently held there in order to listen to the minister. You gained the vision of a beauty, the beauty of death. You lost the presence of a companion, the companion of life.

I looked up into the vigorous and cheery face of one of the firemen whom I went to see every day during our brief vacation on Fire Island. I took it for granted that the place was named for the exciting enormous fire engines into which two strong arms lifted me during each visit. Many years afterward, when I reported my distinct recollections of grandeur, I was told that the gleaming red trucks were only small carts and that no motorized vehicles were permitted on the island. But I had sat in a magnificent chariot. I had been treated as a princess, as a queen.

And thus we remembered what we both remembered. We remembered being three years old. We remembered being very little. We remembered something very big. I remember still. Do you?

Love,
Julia

No. 78

>Arlington, July 25
>FURRINALIA

Dear Margaret,

Do you walk in Furrina's Roman grove?
Will the goddess of the sacred spring
Spring into my desiccated heart?
I know only evil.
I am only evil.
I know I am only evil.
The sentry of my red brick prison,
The tree of knowledge and recall,
The huge elephantine beech,
Has seen good and evil,
Remembers evil and good,
Wrestles with the evil,
Rests in the good.
The strong gray trunk
Is muscular,
Is motionless.
The leaves laugh happily.
The sun laughs through, above, around, within them.
The blue sky smiles.
May the beech guard the good
That can laugh into my ears,
That might smile into my eyes.
The same sky smiles upon Furrina's spring.
The slope is grassy, is very green.
Above it I have walked wonderingly along
Little Viale Margaret Ossoli Fuller.
Where have you walked?
Will you walk there?
Will you walk on the Roman path officially named for you?
>Will

Will you see my evil?
Will you lead me to the good?
Will the goddess spring up into my evil heart?
Will the goodness spring up into my evil heart?
Will the beech know my evil?
Will the beech know the evil of my heart?
Will the beech know the goodness of the nurses' hearts?
Will the beech know the goodness of the nurses' hands?
Will I remember forever
The goodness of the nurses' hands?
Will my repugnant repulsive sore, my wound,
Be healed by the nurses' hands?
Healed will I walk in the ways of the good?
Will the feet of the beech walk all the way to Rome?
Will my feet walk once more on the roads to Rome, of Rome?
Once more will I walk wonderingly along
Little Viale Margaret Ossoli Fuller?
Will my evil be healed?
Will I walk in the good?
I must ramble in my walking.
I must ramble in my talking.
The good must reach to me.
I will never reach the good.
Will I reach the spring in the green of the Roman grove?
Will the spring reach to me?
Will the spring of the goddess bubble in my heart?
Will I walk up the slope, up the grass, up the green?
Will I walk up to your path in the green of the Roman grove?
Will you, too, be walking there?

                                            Love,
                                            Julia

No. 79

Arlington, July 27

Dear Margaret,

Shall I recant
The recantation?

How did I become
The inhabitant of an insane asylum?

How did I become
The resident of a den of torture?

Shall I begin the long tale?
Shall I commence the many stories?

If I should tell, there would be worse to tell.
You know we do not dare to tell the worst

About the convent, nursing home, rehab center,
Hospital, prison, madhouse, torture chamber.

Let me not tell.
Let me forget.

Let me forget until I dare to tell.
Let me remember when I need to tell.

Your grand Goethe
Perhaps will understand.

Your great Torquato Tasso
Maybe will understand.

You, the newspaperwoman,
The columnist, will understand.

From the black and white tribune your star
Revealed what needed to be told.

From the black and red porch I have not glimpsed
The points of light light in the night sky.

Here I have heard the cicadas.
Here I have never seen a star.

The rain rains through the open window
Onto the windowsill, onto the floor.

I shall not now
Recant the recantation.

Love,
Julia

No. 80

Arlington, July 30
Fortunae Huiusce Diei

Dear Margaret,

The fortune of this day. This day. What is this day in a small room in which memory fails? When memory fails, time itself fails.

My room is very small. I should say our room, for we are two, with two beds, two bedside tables, two sets of furniture. At three o'clock this morning I woke up and reached for my watch on my bedside table, which stands between our two beds. Nothing met my outreached hand. Nothing met my eyes when I pulled the cord for the light, when I moved the writing pads, the little box of tissues, the table itself, when I investigated the tangled bedclothes, when I bent down precariously to scan the floor and peer as far as I could under the bed. Nothing. That is, not what I sought. Nothing: that is, not my watch. I pulled myself up cautiously and squinted at the big round electric clock on the wall. My roommate was awake and very sympathetic. On my return from the bathroom she stretched out her left arm. Is this your watch? Oh, yes, it is. She took it off. Yet she was dubious. If this is not my watch, where is mine? I wear my watch all night. My watch is just like this. Nevertheless, she handed it to me. We searched for hers but found nothing. And where is my ring? I wear my ring all night. We searched for it but found nothing. She was what is called philosophical. We can't do any more at three o'clock in the morning. By then it was closer to four.

It was thus that we began this day. Fortunately we are both good sleepers, and we both lost consciousness again until six or seven o'clock. As for the excitement and confusion surrounding our definitive awakening, I will not describe them here. I am not a storyteller. In any case, I should be accustomed to my roommate's propensities. I have found her wearing not just my watch but my socks and my slippers. I have observed her sipping water from my
half-filled

half-filled cup in the middle of the night. I have heard her claiming as hers my tissues and tabletops and bureau drawers. How many times have I told her — I sound like the impatient mother — which cord belongs to the call button, where the call button is on her bed, how it works, what she pushed it for? If I list all the losses of memory I will exhaust and exasperate you just as I myself am exasperated and exhausted. I do not want to remember all this. She luckily does not have to.

What can be the cause of her innocent and inadvertent behavior? Is it the weight of ninety-four years fallen upon her? Is it the bulging red-and-black bump on her forehead resulting from her nocturnal fall on the floor? We converse at seven, at nine, at noon. The conversation is intellectual, witty, vivid. It is the same conversation each time.

Must there be progression in time? Is there time when there is no memory? Without memory is there a present? Is there a past? Is there a future? If I write about this day am I making it a memory? Am I making it a fixed point in time?

I may write about this day, but may I write about a woman whom I have come to respect and admire, of whom I have become very fond, whose beautiful smile and whose play of mind and whose strength of body and of will have impressed and delighted me, whose sensibility is eerily similar to mine? We have been forced to live intimately together. What is she and what am I? Am I writing about my tenseness, my anxiety, my distraction, my wickedness? Could I remember if I did not write? Should I continue to compose letters to you without style, without insight, without compassion, without anything except my own desperation and despair? I hoped for knowledge. I know only hopelessness. Shall I play at knowing? Shall I play at living? Am I killing time?

I look at my watch. It is on my arm. What time is it? Shall I write another time?

I look at my calendar. It is lying on my bed beside the cushioned wheelchair in which I sit. What day is it? Shall I write some other day? What fortune will be ours some other day?

Love,
Julia

No. 81

>Arlington, July 30
>Fortunae Huiusce Diei

Dear Leila,

The great guardian beech
Watches over the smooth green slope of the lawn
And the elegant regularity
Of the red brick building.
The gray trunk of the beech is old and strong and still.
The green and purple leaves, yet young, are summery
And flicker in the sun and in the breeze.
They did so today.
The sun was a golden sun.
The breeze was a golden breeze.

From up the ascending avenue gold beckoned.
Sunflowers were unclasping their golden rays.
Sunflowers beamed their unclasped rays of gold.
Golden butterflies flitted and glittered all about them.
Gold-tinged insects lunched at the plates of golden pollen
Presented by the flourishing.
Gold-and-black goldfinches dined at the platters of black seeds
Offered by the moribund.
Beneath the big blue of the sky
The breeze blew. It was the golden breeze.
Ecce ancilla aurae aureae.

The great gray guardian beech
Resembles an elephant
Not only in body but in memory.
I could feel when I could see
How long it had been standing there
How much it must have seen,
How much it must have come to know,

>How much

How much it held the knowledge of this day.
The winging singing beech
Was a flock of little green and purple birds
Summering in the sun and in the breeze,
Something of this day,
Of the luck, the fortune, of this day.

                                        Love,
                                        Flora

No. 82

                                      Arlington, August 5
                                      Saluti

Dear Margaret,

Health, safety, salvation: what will it be?
Oh, the sunflowers. Oh, the sun.

How the sunflowers stand and shine.
How the sun sinks but does not fall

But rises again. How the wind rises.
Fear of falling. Wincing at the wind.

How the sunflowers do not fall
But gleam with gold. They save the bees,

They save the goldfinches. Me they save.
They save me in the rays of gold,

Resisting wind. Could the wind fell
The handmaid of the golden breeze?

Does the breeze call? Could the wind kill
Her whom the golden breeze can heal?

                                              Love,
                                              Julia

No. 83

> Cambridge, August 6
> Transfiguration

Dear Margaret,

Though not transfigured
I am transported

With the assistance of three friends,
Two cars, and a donut cushion.

I am dining in silence.
I watch for words of quietude.

I delight in the darkness.
I await illumination.

> Love,
> Julia

No. 84

                                                    Cambridge, August 7

Dear Margaret,

I guess August came.
I came to Cambridge.

You are there too,
On Ellery Street

Where last night
'Twas so sweet and still,

Where 'tis sweet and still.
Here last night,

Here on Mass Ave,
'Twas still and sweet.

I want to walk out
And find the roses

Behind the white pickets,
Purpureal roses

So still and so sweet.
Are they blooming there?

Can I walk that far?
Will they meet me there?

How long will they last?
Can I walk through August?

I sit and wait,
I stand and wait,

For the visiting nurse.
How long this will last,

How long I will last,
I cannot guess.

>Love,
>Julia

No. 85

> Cambridge, August 7

Dear Leila,

There might be meaning without music.
There might be music without meaning.

Between the pickets the purple roses
Might sweetly peer.

Behind the white fence the purple roses
Might rise with shining faces,

Might open their mouths, might sing a meaning,
Might be singing a purple song.

I might be hearing the roses peering
Between the pickets of the bright white fence.

Then might I listen as roses glisten
Behind the white, above the pickets.

A purpling gleam may fill me with
Fragrant illuminations, fragrant tunes,

As I inhale, may fill me with
The music of meaning, the meaning of music. Oh,

No, I am empty. I speak without
Meaning. I sing without music.

> Love,
> Flora

No. 86

                              Cambridge, August 13
                              Florae ad Circum Maximum

Dear Margaret,

What some regret and some condemn
I envy:

Your vigorous learning of Latin grammar
When you were only six,

Your rigorous summer program of study
When you were just fifteen,

When I was a dreamy child,
When I was a childish dreamer,

When I played away the days,
When I lazed away the days.

What you could write about yourself
And others write of you

I could not write about myself
Nor others write of me.

What you could write to Miss Prescott
On July 11, 1825,

I could not write to Mother Grace
On July 11, 1949.

What could I do? What then?
What can I do? What now?

I walked to Widener today
Lured through a golden breeze

Taking a sturdy friend
Against a silver wind.

I walked to Widener today
Tapping a new black cane.

My friend carried my bag
Of books. Was that the end

Of all I could have learned?
My knowledge blew away.

My temple's stairs I climbed
Slowly. To know must I pray?

The marble columns gleamed.
My mind was dullest gray.

What I regret and I condemn
I am.

                                                Love,
                                                Julia

No. 87

> Cambridge, August 14
> Vigil of the Assumption

Dear Margaret,

Now I will be the ghost and I will live
Lives not my own as though they were my own.

> Love,
> Julia

No. 88

                                      Cambridge, August 14
                                      Vigil of the Assumption

Dear Leila,

Living the lives of ghosts,
Dying the deaths of gods.

                                      Love,
                                      Flora

No. 89

                                        Cambridge, August 15
                                        The Assumption

Dear Leila,

I dwelt with azure sky, I lived with God,
I lived with ghosts and gods, and now I dwell
With guests and grandeur, now I dwell with friends
And fortune, now I live with selves and splendor,
With grace and fragrance and a spaciousness,
With guides and founders, smiths and scouts and seers.
Sometimes the skies stay blue, the letters black.
Sometimes the texts and heavens stay legible.
I dwell among the dead, I live with life.

                                                Love,
                                                Flora

No. 90

> Cambridge, August 15
> The Assumption

Dear Margaret,

Can you hear me? Are you listening?

I dwelt with gods and ghosts. How long. How long.

The gods became philosophies. The ghosts became biographies. The gods and ghosts became mythologies.

Were they thoughts? Were they loves? Were they words?

I was words.

Hurry. Hurry. The words are calling.

No. Wait. Let the words have worth.

Are you listening? Can you hear me?

> Love,
> Julia

No. 91

Cambridge, August 16

Dear Margaret,

Will you find this list of interest?

>Cessation
>Consecration
>Conflagration
>Concentration
>Conversation
>Contemplation
>Creation

Shall I find that plan of value?

Love,
Julia

No. 92

>Cambridge, August 24
>Mundus patet

Dear Leila,

Like Margaret, like Julia, and certainly like you,
I know that ghosts have spoken very lifelike
To me who understand the language of Hades.

The entrance to the underworld,
The entrance to the otherworld,
On this August day
With the lifting of the lid
In Rome was open.

Through this exit from the earth
Ghosts could step forth every year
On three occasions: on November eighth,
October fifth, and August twenty-fourth.

At least, that is what some believe,
At most, that is what I have known,
About this structure in the Roman soil,
About this structure on the Roman soil.

From it I have watched emerging
Many a Julia.
From it I have glimpsed emerging
Never a Margaret.

I do not deny that I, like Henry James,
Encountered Margaret Fuller's ghost in Rome,
Was haunted by Margaret Fuller's ghost in Rome,
But the date was not the twenty-fourth of August
And the place was not related by location.

What about in or near
This Cambridge, Massachusetts,
Prodigal like Rome of ghosts?
There must be a local municipal mundus,
Perhaps in the noted Old Burying Ground,
Maybe in the marvelous Mount Auburn.

Here it is. Here it is. It must be here
In this delightful bit of yard between
Harvard Hall, Hollis Hall, and Holden Chapel.
Here is a door of Hell, a gate of Hades,
A box top that might pop wide towards a Heaven,
Towards overarching deeps of blue serene,
Towards heights of azure, large and pure yet marked
At times with white wisps, drifts, and puffs of cloud
Enhancing not detracting from the blue
Calm above fresh breaths of golden breeze,
Fullness of fresh green leaves still green on trees
Where elms once were and larches are, and sleek
Richness of green grass green between the red
Brick buildings trimmed with wood of cleanest white
And framing five short dark-gray crossing paths
That meet where concrete square of lighter gray
Itself frames centered iron grate of black.

Among the blacks, whites, grays, greens, reds, and golds
Beneath the beloved blue of Julia's sky

And shadowed, Leila, by red-brick Lionel Hall,
Fourth, newest, limb of the margin of this yard,

Hall home to Julia when she first was part of Harvard
As Margaret never was, could never be,

Though she dwelt within reach of the clang of the college bell,
Her intellect respected by male siblings

And male friends who themselves belonged to Harvard
As Julia later did, did even then

During those first eight weeks as a student there
Registered not as Julia M. Budenz

But as Mother Miriam, clothed in great black folds
Of veil and thick voluminous black robes of serge

Despite the heat of hot July and August,
Through all the heat of hot July and August,

Through her studious Aeschylean summer while
American elms still lived here, graceful and green,

As they do no longer although the space stays verdant
On, even on, this August afternoon,

I stood with my back turned towards the sunny west
Near the sturdy rough-trunked fine-leaved honeylocust.

The cement square opened
Like the lid of a big box.

It lifted like a hinged lid rising
High, then bending back.

I was looking east. I could feel shade, warmth, soft breeze.
I watched the box top as it opened slowly.

A human form might easily step forth
Onto the path, over the grass, and stride

Towards one habituated to the sight of spirits,
Towards one who comprehended the speech of Hades.

Did I stare?
I did see clearly
Margaret come up, come out.
Did I blink?
Did I see dimly
Julia go in, go down?

                                              Love,
                                              Flora

No. 93

Cambridge, August 27
Saint Caesarius of Arles

Dear Margaret,

Why
Do I
Desire
To die?

Will
The wish
To live
Still thrill?

Who makes the choice?
Who casts the dice?
Who breaks the ice?
Who has the voice?

Can I bid adieu
To a sky this blue?

Love,
Julia

No. 94

>Cambridge, September 1
>Iunoni Reginae in Aventino

Dear Leila,

Blue is the sky and golden is the breeze.
The queen is seated on the Roman hill,
Warlike, enthroned upon the peaceful hill.
She chose this temple in victorious Rome.
She loves this shrine in her triumphant Rome.
Once I was there with her. How far am I.
Gold is the breeze and azure is the sky.

>Love,
>Flora

No. 95

>Cambridge, September 1
>Iunoni Reginae

Dear Margaret,

Juno was angry: Incedo regina.
How was your father, watching as you walked
Along the garden avenue between
The tall white lilies and the apple tree?
He said, admiring: Incedo regina.
Incedo regina. How were you?

>Love,
>Julia

No. 96

                        Cambridge, September 1
                        Iunoni

Dear Margaret,

Margaret, my Waldo, do not sneer. Pretend
That I am in your conversation course
Sitting with Anna, Caroline, Sophia,
Seeking the level of pure intellect,
Rising to heights of coldest azure sky,
Seeking the deepest reach of warmest feeling,
Finding the human whole, the woman's part,
The soft unfolding of the reddest rose,
The sharp precision of the whitest diamond,
The most superlative superlative.

                                 Love,
                                 Julia

No. 97

> Cambridge, September 1

Dear Margaret,

Did August really come? And has it gone?
Did Hercules, Aeneas, and Augustus
Come and go? Can they have passed away?
And have my rational, my passionate,
Ideals, too, passed away? I sit inert,
Neither in motion nor at rest. September,
October, will for you be diamonded,
Will mean for you the carbuncle is found,
Will mean you are at home, no more below,
The Vestal, Virgin, Mother of the Child,
Devoted with a nun-like dedication,
Ready for golden sands, for flowery meadows,
For darkest forests, for untrodden mountains,
Ready for winter, ready for gentlest May.

> Love,
> Julia

No. 98

Cambridge, September [1?]

Dear Margaret,

Margaret, I listen to you. I hear
The history of the apple tree,
The whisperings of flowers.

Margaret, I listen. I do not fear
Approaches of the grimly ghost,
Endurances of hours.

Margaret, I listen to you. Come near.
I am your sister. I am your Julia.
My name holds subtle powers.

Love,
Julia

No. 99

                    Cambridge, September 2

Dear Margaret,

Let me be clear. Let me be insistent.
Let me be your lost sister.
Let me be your lost Julia.
Am I not dear? Am I not your student?

Do not refuse, mock, scorn.
I am a Julia, yours.

                      Love,
                      Julia Mairin Toledo Budenz,

                      thinking of
                      Julia Maria Allen Channing
                      (Mrs. William Henry Channing),
                      1813–1889,

                      and especially of
                      Julia Adelaide Fuller,
                      1812–1813.

No. 100

                              Cambridge, September 3

Dear Margaret,

Can you hear me? Will you listen to me?
Is it literature or is it life?
Is it rhetoric or is it death?
Is it parole or is it poesy?
The blossoms whispered with the sweetest breath.
What is that knife
That cut the branches from the apple tree?

                                      Love,
                                      Julia

No. 101

                                Cambridge, September 4

Dear Leila,

The genuine Julia is Flora Urania Baum.
For the true Julia look for the rose in bloom,
Look on the flowering of the flowering bough,
Look up at the sky that blossoms into blue.
What is this leaf untimely turning brown?
What this unbudding? What this unheavenly brune?

                                         Love,
                                         Flora

No. 102

                                          Cambridge, September 4

Dear Margaret,

Forgive the jingles, bear the jaunty rhyme,
Regard the dangers of the perilous game,
And comprehend the heaven-haunted gnome.

                                          Love,
                                          Julia

No. 103

Cambridge, September 4

Dear Leila Saint of Knowledge,

Is poet not a person but a plea,
Not maker but creation of the cry?
Spell out red rose for Julia, read green tree,
Peruse the blue that blossoms through the sky.

Love,
Flora Urania Baum

No. 104

> Cambridge, September 5

Dear Margaret,

The golden bud is nearly ready now
To be the golden rose where I walk now
Close enough to home to be home now
And stroll where golden roses are most gold,
Snapdragons deepest ruby, precious gems
And precious metals set along the borders,
Not hard, sharp, glittery, but soft, alive,
Bright choirs of color, orchestras of light,
Neighborhood friends, familiars of this site.
Although my hand aches as I grasp my cane
When gentle breeze hints of ungentle wind,
Although my heart aches as I clasp my pain
When consciousness hints thinly I have sinned,
If budding seems so sweet can I believe
That this return is merely a reprieve?

> Love,
> Julia

No. 105

>Cambridge, September 5
>Iovi Statori

Dear Leila,

Snapdragons standing here on Follen Street
Snap up red knowledge with their ruby lips.
Red lions roar truths from their ruddy mouths
Opened to utterance then once more closed
Upon new food to gobble and to chew.
Jupiter Stator, stop here my retreat,
I plead. Let me become again a Roman.

>Love,
>Flora

No. 106

                          Cambridge, September 8
                          Nativitas Mariae

Dear Leila,

The birthday of the Blessed Virgin Mary
Is what dim myths and rituals today
Call us to celebrate.

What calls us to await
As months lurch towards the twenty-third of May
Nativities that are not legendary?

                          Love,
                          Flora

No. 107

> Cambridge, September 9
> Ludi Romani

Dear Leila,

Will the tale
Stay told?

Will the gold
Grow pale?

> Love,
> Flora

No. 108

                              Cambridge, September 9
                              Ludi

Dear Leila,

I vowed
To smile.
The cloud
Must cry.

I chose
To dial.
The rose
Must die.

                              Love,
                              Flora

No. 109

                                Cambridge, September 9

Dear Leila,

Will I remember the blackness swooping
Upon the very light of noon?

Will I remember the stormblast lashing
The trembling flesh too soon?

I will remember the ruby, dark
And brilliant, deep and glimmering.

I will remember the gentle yellow
Rose yet summering.

                                        Love,
                                        Flora

No. 110

Cambridge, September 10

Dear Leila,

Yet in September
The purple of the clematis

Says all to the eyes,
Is all to the eyes.

Still will there be more?
Is the end an end?

The purple becomes an entire intense garden.
The purple bespeaks a whole high deep wide seeding world.

Here must surely spread the yellow harvest,
Mingle blue and red a single purple universe.

Love,
Flora

No. 111

Cambridge, September 10

Dear Margaret,

Telescopes, accelerators,
Microscopes, colliders,

Particles, dark matter, mass,
Black holes, bangs, strings, gravity,

Simplicity, consistency, complexity, dimensions,
Testing, theory, science, likelihood,

Learning, answers,
Asking, questions . . .

> Love,
> Julia

No. 112

>Cambridge, September 12
>Nomen Mariae

Dear Leila,

If I can name
Can I not know?

Round is the church in Rome
Found on this very day.

To Carthage then I came.
To Rome again I go.

Is Cambridge home?
Is Mary May?

>Love,
>Flora

No. 113

Cambridge, September 13
Iovi Epulum

Dear Margaret,

Reflecting
I said

I must banquet
On kashi

And prune juice.
Jupiter,

I shall feast
On pork, lamb, beef

With bread and wine
When I can climb

The hallowed hill,
The Capitol,

I promised.
Who knocked?

It was, in her ruby dress, dear Ruby
Bearing in her caring hand a huge

And holy cookie
From the high bold lookout

Of splendent latter-day temple.
With that I held festival.

Love,
Julia

No. 114

> Cambridge, September 13
> Iovi, Iunoni, Minervae Epulum

Dear Margaret,

The telephone was jangling as it rang,
But Alice brought a sumptuous wonderland

Up for a second Roman feast:
The dared enormous peach-pink peach,

The plum pulled out to purplest taste,
The jovial vermilion grape.

From high upon the file's gray steel
Mums' yellow rays sunned evening's meal.

Blueberry muffins must conclude the while
When frowning tearful life produced a smile.

> Love,
> Julia

No. 115

> Cambridge, September 15
> Dolores Mariae

Dear Leila,

Mild and bright the round moon sliding
Out into the black and back
Within the moon-tinged mystery
Of jagged masses on the murk

Might sing the sorrowful
Virgin Mother, Mary Mild,
Might sing the suffering,
The slain, the sacred weight of child,

Might sing you, Leila. Margaret's tears
Of pearl kept falling. Margaret's heart
Of pearl kept singing. Sorrow sang
The heart of ruby, Leila, night.

> Love,
> Flora

No. 116

> Cambridge, September 17
> Ludi

Dear Margaret,

I will lie
Down and die
Before my cry

Is overheard
And my word
Declared absurd,

I pledged. I lay
Down but day
Had a say.

> Love,
> Julia

No. 117

>Cambridge, September 19
>Saint Januarius

Dear Margaret,

Some went much too soon
Through the great dark door:

Virgil, Tasso, Keats,
You, and many more.

As blooded each ghost greets,
I speeded loss deplore.

But is the loss too soon
If I am seventy-four?

>Love,
>Julia

No. 118

>Cambridge, September 19
>Ludi Romani

Dear Leila,

Neighbor Alexis offers flowers.
Red they are up on
The simple gray of the file.

Neighbor Margaret offers hours.
Read they are deep down
The black and white of The Dial.

Matter and spirit offer powers.
Red they are if known.
Known they are through trial.

>Love,
>Flora

No. 119

>Cambridge, September 21
>The Death of Virgil

Dear Margaret,

Death, be proud.
The trees drip blood.

Go on to Thrace.
Do not retrace

The road to Rome.
You can't go home.

Thus I wept.
The poet slept.

>Love,
>Julia

No. 120

        Cambridge, September 29
        Saints Michael, Gabriel, and Raphael,
              Archangels

Dear Leila,

The sweet feast that autumn offers
Begins to be offered
As eyes begin to dine
Upon the varied various golds
Of sugar maples, of honey locusts,
And, it must be added, of the ashes,

Golds we can devour and digest and delight in,
Sweet as sugar, dulcet as honey,
Lasting longer than they last,
Lasting past the ashes,
Lasting as we greet the gold of the beeches in November,
Thankful to eat when the beech becomes the feast.

But must we not now dine with angels?
Are archangels now all gold?

              Love,
              Flora

No. 121

                                        Cambridge, September 30

Dear Margaret,

Only a rose
Can console
For certain woes
Of the soul.

Only that figure,
Only that color,
Only that texture,
Can soothe that dolor.

This is sooth,
This is light.
This is truth,
This delight.

                                                  Love,
                                                Julia

No. 122

                                              Cambridge, October 1

Dear Margaret,

In Rome the roses
Last into January,
Make their return as May
Is about to emerge from April.

In Massachusetts
One must be loudly thankful
If snows do not cloak the roses
Until after Thanksgiving.

We both have known
These notes.
We both have felt
These facts.

                                                           Love,
                                                           Julia

No. 123

Cambridge, October 2
Guardian Angels

Dear Leila,

Angelina, Emerson called,
When she was almost Anna Ward,
The dazzling Anna Barker safe at home.

Emerson was dismayed, appalled,
Emerson had been caught off guard,
When, finding Rome, she found the Church of Rome.

Love,
Flora

No. 124

> Cambridge, October 3
> Samuel Gray Ward
> Nativitas et Nuptiae

Dear Margaret,

What befell your Raffaello?
Did he fall or did he fly?

This is the birthday,
This is the wedding day,
This is the saint's day
Made holy by your homage, by your love

Of him the beautiful,
Of him of the beautiful
The knower and the maker,
Of him the lover of the bride,
The beauty and the blessing.

Who did not love Anna Hazard Barker?
Who could not love Anna Hazard Barker?
He alone won Anna Hazard Barker.

She was as good as she was beautiful.
He was as wise as he was sensitive.

You had looked deep into her deep blue eyes.
You had looked long into the play of his mind.
You had looked well into the work of his hands.

This day holds the holy, the celestial, hour,
This day is an era on the earth,
Union of red cross knight and spotless maid,
The birthday of the fair child of your hopes,
Son of the gods within the mother's heart,
The marriage of the maker of your dreams,
That first day of divine October beauty,
Ideal now nearest as the earthly real,
Poetry, music, deep, high, mystical.

He had bent over the canvas.
He must bend over the ledger.

In the end he paid the price.
In the end it was clear. In the end
Only the banker could have and hold
Anna Hazard Barker.

Friends may conjecture.
Scholars may scoff.
Strangers may gape.
Study may judge.
I may prize from my own mind the sighs
Of you who had peered into and with his gaze.

What befell your Raffaello?
He was the fallen archangel.
He was the fallen artist.

                                                Love,
                                                Julia

No. 125

Cambridge, October 4

Dear Leila,

Is not subtly turned or turning purple
That which is not grown or growing gold?

The ashes are our standards, our examples.

What of the prince of the purple island, Sam,
The clematis gaze of Anna, natural queen?

Waldo and Margaret know these in their temples.

Love,
Flora

No. 126

Cambridge, October 4

Dear Margaret,

Down down down
Lower than leaves blown
From trees I lie prone
Where we all will soon lie brown.

Love,
Julia

No. 127

> Cambridge, October 5
> Mundus patet

Dear Leila,

Live, spirit, live.
Give, ghost, give.
Thus I cried.
You have not died.

> Love,
> Flora

No. 128

>Cambridge, October 5
>Mundus patet

Dear Margaret,

Why do I hate
To go to sleep?

Why are so late
The hours I keep?

Is it not worse
To stay awake,

Incur the curse,
Endure the ache?

>Love,
>Julia

No. 129

                                                Cambridge, October 5
                                                Mundus patet

Dear Leila,

In these days so dark
The morning glories bloom
Into the afternoon
Late within them lurk
Blues of celestial rapture,
Paradises of azure.

                                                Love,
                                               Flora

No. 130

>Cambridge, October 6
>The Death of Margaret Rodgers Budenz

Dear Margaret,

Your Orpheus must to the depths descend,
Like Bacon's Orpheus outsing the Sirens,
Like Crawford's raise his hand to shade his eyes
From all still to be done, still to be sung.

Shading my eyes I strain to see three Margarets,
My mother, talented, passionate, at the piano,
Your mother, gifted, patient, in the garden,
You, learned, pensive, pondering by the window
In Cambridge, in Manhattan, and in Rome.

My Orpheus must still bring back, sing back,
Margaret, a Margaret, my mother, your mother, you.

>Love,
>Julia

No. 131

>Cambridge, October 7
>Iovi Fulguri

Dear Margaret,

How very odd.
There is no God.

My mind is old.
My heart is cold.

Skies black and blue
Guard pastures new,

Worlds yet to lose,
Worlds yet to choose.

>Love,
>Julia

No. 132

> Cambridge, October 7
> Iunoni Quiriti

Dear Leila,

Emerson had the last word. He spoke of Fuller
When all that eloquence was drowned in death.
We can last longer. As we do not live
We do not die. We are ourselves our words.

> Love,
> Flora

No. 133

Cambridge, October 8

Dear Margaret,

No poetry is in my pen,
No fiction in my fingers,
No knowledge in my nob. A yen
Nevertheless yet lingers.

I glimpse the yellows, reds, and blues
On earth and high above
And listening I hear the muse
Whisper to laugh, learn, love.

Love,
Julia

No. 134

> Cambridge, October 9
> Faustae Felicitati

Dear Margaret,

The house on Ellery Street
Is owned by others now.
They have restored your home
So far as they know how.

But when that home was yours
And when that house was new
Sam paid the first visit.
Now mine is overdue.

You sit there at the window.
If you push open the pane
As you watch the apple tree
I'll toss this letter in.

> Love,
> Julia

No. 135

Cambridge, October 10

Dear Leila,

Yesterday, as I was standing in the road, Margaret came down and opened the door. Samuel went in. One or two hours afterward they emerged. Despite the quiet of the Sunday they did not notice me even though I followed them to Mrs. Farrar's on Kirkland Street and then much later trailed them back to Ellery Street through what Margaret described as the damp Southwind night, fragrant with the autumn leaves. They seemed deeply in communion like old friends. Margaret had once told Sam that she would grieve to be a ghost to him. Now they both are ghosts to me.

Love,
Flora

No. 136

> Cambridge, October 10
> Iunoni Monetae

Dear Leila,

I cannot stop thinking about the house on Ellery Street, Margaret Fuller's last residence in Cambridge, the side-hall Greek Revival little card house. Does Margaret dwell there as a ghost for me? Or am I the ghost to Margaret and her friends? Or may Julia be Margaret's shade?

> Love,
> Flora

No. 137

Cambridge, October 11
MEDITRINALIA

Dear Leila,

Do not despise my simple style. Prize my prose. My rose will rise. The rose of October may bloom in Cambridge as in Rome. New buds, dark red, open and lighten. Are they like a wine? Are they like a cure? Of new and old I drink. Of new and old I am healed. The learned Varro helps me to interpret many words.

Love,
Flora

No. 138

> Cambridge, October 11
> Maternitas Mariae

Dear Margaret,

My little tunes
Do not demean.
My rudest runes
Construct. They mean.

> Love,
> Julia

No. 139

                                        Cambridge, October 13
                                        FONTINALIA

Dear Margaret,

Die rhymes
With cry.
Sieve chimes
With live.
The fountains flow.
Where do the waters go?

                                                  Love,
                                                  Julia

No. 140

                                          Cambridge, October 14
                                          Penatibus

Dear Margaret,

I live in Limbo,
Land of the Unbelievers.
Can I complete my web
Where Tully and Maro are weavers?

                                          Love,
                                          Julia

No. 141

> Cambridge, October 14
> Penatibus in Velia

Dear Leila,

The full rose,
Red amid green,

The full moon,
Silver in azure,

The moment of wholeness,
The instant of fulfillment . . .

> Love,
> Flora

No. 142

>Cambridge, October 15
>The Birth of Virgil

Dear Margaret,

What of earth, what of sky,
Is nigh?

What of farm, what of Rome,
Is home?

What of father, what of mother,
Is kin, is other?

What of speech, what of muse,
Is fuse?

What of chance, what of doom,
Is bloom?

What of sky, what of earth,
Is in this birth?

>Love,
>Julia

No. 143

>Cambridge, October 16
>Famam extendere factis

Dear Margaret,

The ghost of Virgil spoke to me last night
And said what Jove had said to Hercules
Who wept because young Pallas was to die
At the expert hand of his determined foe:
For every mortal is the day of death
Established; brief and unrecoverable
Must be for each the time of life; the work
Of virtue is to stretch out that by which
Men are and will be known, through what they do
And what they make. Beneath the walls of Troy
Fell many sons of gods, fell my own son
Sarpedon. Soon it will be Turnus' turn.
Thus to Alcides Jove spoke pithily,
Averting from the battlefield his eyes.
Thus Virgil's spirit spoke Jove's words to me.

>Love,
>Julia

No. 144

>Cambridge, October 16
>Iouem cum dicimus Salutarem

Dear Leila,

Was it great Jove who saved me from the rain
As he had often rescued me in Rome?
Or was it fate or fortune or my mind
Assessing risk and possibility
Or passion pushing me on towards the stacks
Of Widener for the book for which I yearned
Or sugar maples burning yet not burned?

>Love,
>Flora

No. 145

Cambridge, October 20

Dear Margaret,

Sweet on the chilly air the purple rose
Is not a pledge, is not a promise, is.

Love,
Julia

No. 146

Cambridge, October 20

Dear Leila,

The rose is violet, lilac, lavender.
That is the tint.
The rose rests known. The rose is rose is rose.
This is the scent.

Love,
Flora

No. 147

Cambridge, October 21
Ss. Ursula et Undecim M. Virg.

Dear Margaret,

We climbed the mountain over Fishkill Landing.
In gold the tale began. What was the ending?

Thousands of virgins through the golden fall
Ascended. I was one. I am one still.

Love,
Julia

No. 148

Cambridge, October 22

Dear Margaret,

Why as the rains fall
From those skies of gray
And as the leaves fall
From these trees of gold
Should I through blameless autumn fall
And all my vaunted gold
Turn shameful shameless gray?

Love,
Julia

No. 149

                                                Cambridge, October 22

Dear Leila,

Am I the maid who first
Devoured the fatal fruit
And felt the fall?

Am I the serpent cursed
To sink into the brute
And slide and crawl?

Is this the myth?
Is this to lie?
Is this the truth?
Is this too high?

                                                        Love,
                                                        Flora

No. 150

>Cambridge, October 24

Dear Leila,

Low, low, low,
Low on the land I lie

But hold, hold, hold
The hope of the scope of the sky.

>Love,
>Flora

No. 151

>Cambridge, October 25
>Anna Hazard Barker
>Nativitas

Dear Margaret,

Her birthday was October twenty-fifth,
And on her birthday she would give a gift
To you. She was like that. Then what could you
Give her? Give her your deepest love, then do
What love and life demanded: Let her go.
Yet sometimes we remember what we know,
And you did not forget what once you knew.
She leaned. Her eyes were such deep violet blue,
Were so like night, as they had never been
Before. You knew what you had never known
Before. She leaned on you. You saw. She saw.
You felt. She felt. It was a mystic awe.
It was the mystery, the mystic thrill.
She represented then the Beautiful.
You loved her more than any other woman.
You had to let her go. Her love was given
To, as it was sought by, the very one
Whom you loved more than any other man.

>Love,
>Julia

No. 152

>Cambridge, October 25
>Arthur Ames Merrill
>Natalis

Dear Leila,

Can I past thirty yet believe
That if I am so much in love
With him in him a love must live
For me? The gold leaf is alive.

>Love,
>Flora

No. 153

Cambridge, October 25
Influx of Knowledge

Dear Margaret,

Thank you for sharing sometimes even with me,
As you shared with James, with Caroline, with Waldo,
With William, with Elizabeth, with William,
Those letters, journals, poems, conversations.
How do I read them? How do I respond?

Love,
Julia

No. 154

Cambridge, October 26

Dear Leila,

What men and women do we greet
In Margaret's house on Ellery Street?
At this window thoughts are thought.
At this window books are wrought.
Here the mother is a maid.
Here the father is a god.
In this room the child we find
Emerges from the labor of the mind.

Love,
Flora

No. 155

Cambridge, October 27

Dear Leila,

Fiery euonymus,
Bronze and gold oaks,
Form a forge
Like the studio of Hephaestus
Under the azure flame from which he fell
And to which again he ascended.

Love,
Flora

No. 156

Cambridge, October 27

Dear Margaret,

Hercules was the hero of action
Yet it was passion that in the end
Lifted him through consuming fire
To unending apotheosis.

The conflagration of autumn
Though it does not burn consumes
But today the blue above it
Spreads endless.

Love,
Julia

No. 157

                                              Cambridge, October 28
                                              Saint Jude

Dear Margaret,

Jude should be my saint.
I faint
For a long hope.

Jupiter is my god.
I plod
Up the long slope.

Does his heavenly letter
With energy render me better
Vested to die?

Is there heavenly weather
When he and I are together
Templed in sky?

                                                        Love,
                                                        Julia

No. 158

> Cambridge, October 29
> Ludi Victoriae IV

Dear Leila,

Not all Jove's mortal sons are doomed to die.
The glutton and the drunkard gleam as gods,
Hardy and hard as acorns, soft as grapes,
Solid and strong as oak, as various
As wine in lift, liquidity, and flow.
The gold and purple happen every spring.
The gold and purple batten every fall.
The poem, greedy and intoxicated,
Rocks in the cradle, struggles up Olympus.

> Love,
> Flora

No. 159

                                        Cambridge, October 30

Dear Margaret,

You had not slept with Anna Barker
Since her marriage to Samuel Ward.
But Sam was away, and after the concert
You and she went to their elegant dwelling
At 3 Louisburg Square. You ached.
She was graceful and lovely. You loved her less.
The secret of your life was sealed
To her forever. Yet you took pleasure
In sleeping on Sam's pillow. You wished
For visions like his. You dreamed of drowning.

                                                          Love,
                                                          Julia

No. 160

Cambridge, October 31
The Birth of Keats

Dear Margaret,

That Beethoven should be deaf,
That Milton should be blind,
That young Keats should lie dead
Upon the shore of life
Is what we find
Certified as true
Before we lose your manuscript and you.

Love,
Julia

No. 161

                                        Cambridge, November 1
                                        All Saints

Dear Leila,

Contemplated and contemplative
In a wide space of wind
Beside the white picket fence
Rests a rose of rose,
A rose of sweetness and of softness
That rests upon the fence
And sustains no motion
But my emotion
And, if rest and motion are the same,
Contemplating
And being contemplated.

                                          Love,
                                          Flora

No. 162

                                              Cambridge, November 3

Dear Margaret,

Though far below thick cloud down here glints gold,
Too soon too dark glooms this November day,
This private solemn anniversary.
Why only after I pronounced my vows
Forever did I know I would be wrong
To keep not to abandon them? The truth
Comes when it comes. In its own time shines light.
Thus does the rose gleam gold from clasping bud,
Thus Dian gold from not unhunted hill,
Thus Venus gold from effervescent sea,
Thus sun gold from obnubilating night.

                                                        Love,
                                                        Julia

No. 163

                                       Cambridge, November 8
                                       Mundus patet

Dear Leila,

Is it entering into the self?
Is it escape from the self?

Is it a way of thinking?
Is it a substitute for thinking?

Is it doing, creating, control, Apollo?
Is it helpless servitude to the Muse?

Is it the most serious, most liberating, commitment?
Is it the addiction to a game?

Is it the mirage of the myth?
Is it the myth of the true?

Is it the profusion, the confusion, of the image?
Is it the austerity of abstraction?

Is it the blaze of the rose, the flame of the tree?
Is it the fire of the sky?

Is it the desire of the sky?
Is it the despair of the sky?

Is it the mere juggling of words?
Is it the sheer grandeur of words?

Is it the flighty gleaning of sounds?
Is it the mighty meaning of sounds?

Is it the binding of the real?
Is it the finding of the ideal?

Is it the choice of life?
Is it the voice of death?

Love,
Flora

No. 164

                                    Cambridge, November 9
                                    Terribilis est locus iste

Dear Margaret,

Your baby's body is buried
In soft Mount Auburn. Often you walked
There. There often I have walked.
People still ask if you were married.

You and your spouse lie deep
Tossed beneath the boisterous tide,
Lost to rough tough time and tide.
People still ask if we should weep.

Braving the breakers of Rome,
The terrible triumph and stark despair,
You tasted the triumph, you sipped despair.
People still ask if you sought home.

                                              Love,
                                              Julia

No. 165

> Cambridge, November 13
> Feriae Iovi

Dear Leila,

Oh, how I crave the beauty of the moon!

If on the Ides in perfect plenitude
The moon shines white in plenitude of beauty,
Is that bright beauty Jove's, is Jove that beauty,
Is Jupiter the father of the child?
Can I forget or shall, can, I remember
What happened once or many times in Rome?
Was I promiscuous? No, for the gods
Are aspects and relations, accidents,
Places and times, existences, ideas,
Emotions, feelings, sensibilities,
Differing thus and otherwise the same,
Otherwise one. Who more than Jupiter
Is different and the same, is one and all?

Vulcan can be the twenty-third of May,
Apollo be the thirteenth of July,
Jupiter be the thirteenth of September,
Jupiter be the fifteenth of October,
Jupiter be the thirteenth of November,
Jupiter be the Ides of every month,
Jupiter be the plenilunium
Of each lunation, Jupiter thus be.

Not only do I wonder at the thunder,
Admire in fright the lightning lightening,
Desire with sight, with sigh, the azure sky,
Banquet where banqueting is glorious,
Up on the everlasting Capitol,
Banquet magnificently, sacrifice,
Parade, play, paint, fear, feel, philosophize,
Know, make, remake myth, story, song, long dream,
But I observe the beauty of the light,
Worship the beauty of the bluest height,
Adore the beauty of the whitest moon,
Love mighty sire, and love the sire's child soon.

>   Love,
>   Flora

No. 166

>Cambridge, November 13
>Iovi Epulum

Dear Margaret,

Should I be eating more or eating less?
If I ate less would I cease to be full
Always as this day's moon is round and full?
If I ate more could I cease to be light
Enough to weigh what I weigh on that moon,
Cease to be light and frail enough to fear
Too strong a wind like one your ghost might fear,
Too dreadful for a sailing ship at sea?

>Love,
>Julia

No. 167

                          Cambridge, November 13
                          Iovi

Dear Leila,

He is the god of the weather.
How can he be the father
Of my own child of heaven,
Of an immortal that is born to me?

He is the god of the azure,
Bright sky. He is the treasure
Giving, as he is given,
The instant that is an eternity.

                          Love,
                          Flora

No. 168

> Cambridge, November 13
> Fortunae Primigeniae

Dear Leila,

In my understanding
Thus far I got:
The life of the child that is his
Might have an ending;
The subtle difference is
That it might not.

> Love,
> Flora

No. 169

                                                  Cambridge, November 16

Dear Margaret,

Had God spoken?
Had we been elected,

You to the Rome of the real, of the flesh, of the soul,
I to the Rome of the myth, of the lived tolled tale,
You to the Rome of the almost present future,
I to the Rome of the not yet absent past,
You to the Rome of the new revolution,
I to the Rome of the old devotion?

You were not drowned in the Tiber or in the Turano.
From your home you viewed the doomed damned palace of the pope.

I went into the chapel
And bowed my head.
I went to the refectory
And knelt for my bread.
God has spoken
To me, I said.

                                                                Love,
                                                                Julia

No. 170

Cambridge, November 17

Dear Margaret,

I though unworthy welcome worth.
Books spinning from the brain
Are footprints left upon the earth
And fructifying rain
And suns renewing mighty birth.

Love,
Julia

No. 171

                                        Cambridge, November 18
                                        The Death of Proust

Dear Margaret,

Fin, he wrote, then wrote a bit more.
If he had lived to be seventy-four
What sentence would he have brought to the full
And beyond?
Your drowned
Manuscript destiny brought to null.
Was your big book then ready for print?
His big book was ready. Faint
Is mine, though bigger, endless, dull.
Dull leaves are falling. Does bright fruit fall
In the end?

                                                     Love,
                                                     Julia

No. 172

Cambridge, November 19

Dear Leila,

You will not have forgotten Anthe.
Knowing my evil shall I speak of her,
Shall I speak of my good, shall I speak of good?
In this beginning of cold I am
Blasted already, my red going black,
My red life now a wound,
Another sample of a rose
Of a windy day. She is
The rose of the gold
That grows through the cold,
That is sweet in the heat,
That, however bad I am,
However badly damaged,
However blighted in the bloom,
In the very bud,
I will, like you, not have forgotten.

Love,
Flora

No. 173

> Cambridge, November 20

Dear Margaret,

Shall I name it Beacon or Fishkill Landing?
In the mountains, there do you feel free?
There, for you, was the pleasant life,
You said, of the free nun; there, for me,
The pledging life which I must call
That of the nun unfree. One fall
The purple mountains turned to gray,
For you to leave, for me to stay.

> Love,
> Julia

No. 174

Cambridge, November 23

Dear Margaret,

In six months will we annotate
The occasion of our birth?

By what prohibited port,
With what obsolescent ship,
In what inimical wind,
On what superundulous sea

Will we sail from the waters of the womb
Or slip down the edge of death?

Love,
Julia

No. 175

                          Cambridge, November 24

Dear Margaret,

When the pope abandons Rome
Does the father leave his home,
Forsake his wife and children, flee
His God-bestowed responsibility,
Or losing sight of Peter's dome
The pious devil leave God's people free?

                                  Love,
                                  Julia

No. 176

                        Cambridge, November 25
                        Saint Catherine of Alexandria

Dear Leila,

Is Margaret willing to live
Still for the sake of her precious child?
Is Julia willing to live
Still for the sake of her priceless child?

Is it a sin to see in a book
A baby? Does the question look
Simple to the Boston Sibyl
Who knows the tree of good and evil?

Is Margaret eager to die
If her dear, her little son, must perish?
Is Julia eager to die?
What on this earth does Julia cherish?

                        Love,
                        Flora

No. 177

                                    Cambridge, November 25
                                    Ad montem

Dear Leila,

I'm
Rhyme

Breath
Death

Why
Sky

Earth
Birth

You're
More

                                    Love,
                                    Flora

No. 178

Cambridge, November 26

Dear Margaret,

The Arlington beech may be leafless now. I cannot pay it a visit. I cannot dream of bicycle, taxi, bus, the car of a friend. Would an ambulance serve? I yearn for the guardian's grandeur, the gracious strength, the fageous sheen.

I watched the purple leaves turn verd. Did the green turn gold? Did the gold turn bronze? Did the bronze flit into the wind, flutter up to the sun? Could I go and see if the beech is bare?

I would bestow upon the boughs a dozen, a hundred, leaves of gold, medallions of the special ones, the helpers who helped me there, beside the tree, beyond the tree, within the home. Honor the kindly ones, I would say.

Gleam there, I would say, and wait the long wait for summer.

But nature would intimate, insist: A better beauty inheres in season. Let the tree speak of itself. Store the golden names in your heart.

Love,
Julia

No. 179

Cambridge, November 27

Dear Margaret,

Ideas float away.
Ideals slink off.
God is forgotten.
The gods are games.

Beech in Cambridge in November
Exists in various incarnations,
Persists in various rhythms,
Subsists in various degrees of leaf and unleaf.

The bare beech, stable and stately,
Exercises, exorcises, exhorts.
It is lordly. It is democratic.
It is teacherly and comradely alike.

Fagutal Jupiter may utter oracles
Of something remembered,
Of something desired,
Of something lovely and strong,
Of something that comes and goes,
Of something that remains.

The sunlight, even if feeble,
Gives a gift of cheer.
One can simply be,
Even for an hour or two.

The bare beech seems simple in the sun.
Complication comes with the cloudy afternoon.
Complexity accompanies the dusk.
Or was the clarity of noon complex?

The bare beech is rarely sheerly bare.
Something flutters darkly in the dark.
The dark will simplify the complex heavens.
Venus and Jupiter gleam but not as gods.

Love,
Julia

No. 180

                                        Cambridge, November 28

Dear Leila,

The oppression of the pen
Perhaps cannot be forgiven
Except by us
Who owe to it our existence.

We may feel sorry for ourselves
Perceiving chilled and withered petals.
We may feel sorry for our readers
Peering into ragged gardens.

We might feel sorry for our writers
Looking long with bleary vision,
Holding on with weary fingers,
But for them it is do or it is die.

Margaret wrote and Margaret perished.
Who dares to write that Margaret could not write?
Her garden gate stands open and within
Some trees drip blood, some offer us rich ruddy fruit.

                                                         Love,
                                                         Flora

No. 181

> Cambridge, November 29
> The Birth of Amos Bronson Alcott
> (1799–1888)
> The Birth of Louisa May Alcott
> (1832–1888)

Dear Margaret,

Islands of white shining cloud
In a celestial clarity of azure
Should not bear the burden of the name of cloud
As suggesting the negative, the nebulous,
When they suggest that even November,
That even the twenty-ninth of November,
Might not, even for a Jo March, be
A bad time to be born.
What is a good time to be born?

> Love,
> Julia

No. 182

>Cambridge, November 30
>Saint Andrew

Dear Margaret,

Yes, a man's a man.
We can rise in honor.
We can sit together.

Oh, a song's a song.
It can play the part.
It can say the heart.

Andrew, Thomas, Robert can
Be and make our texts and soon
Can for all that make our tune.

Here comes a woman listening.
A queen can rise, a sister sing.
Here's a thought, and here's a thing.

>Love,
>Julia

No. 183

Cambridge, December 1

Dear Margaret,

Why, moon, are you,

In a December evening,
In a beginning of December and of evening,

In the vicinity of Venus and of Jupiter,
In converse with Venus and with Jupiter,

Not science,
Not knowledge,

But a sliver of beauty,
But a sliver of the beautiful,

A quiet voice of beauty,
A silent voice shining of the beautiful,

I asked your beloved moon.

Love,
Julia

No. 184

> Cambridge, December 4–5
> Bona Dea

Dear Leila,

The thermometer shifts from fifty to twenty.
We may do something and call it plenty.

We may drink wine and call it milk.
The house with grape leaves may be fit.
The sacrifice may be a pig.

We may say something and call it much.
The sacred secrets we may clutch.

In this night we may do as Romans.
The men by now have all departed.
The women pray here, singing, dancing.

Are we women? Are we good?
Robin Hood in Barnsdale stood.

> Love,
> Flora

No. 185

> Cambridge, December 5
> Fauno

Dear Margaret,

Robin Hood in Barnsdale stood
And leaned against a greenwood tree.

If he invited me to dine
I would not have to pay, since he

Would look into my bank account
And offer instant charity.

But do not make a loan, I would then plead,
For I will never not be deep in need.

> Love,
> Julia

No. 186

Cambridge, December 6
Saint Nicholas

Dear Margaret,

Robin Hood in Barnsdale stood.
Shoot me dead I quickly said.

Love,
Julia

No. 187

> Cambridge, December 7
> Pearl Harbor

Dear Margaret,

Nothing is right,
Everything wrong.
There is no light.
Can there be song?

> Love,
> Julia

No. 188

>Cambridge, December 7
>Immaculatae Conceptionis Vigilia

Dear Leila,

If the conception is immaculate
Can we believe the birth will be embodied?
The minimalist who stuck two sticks together
Discoursed two hours on how more would have muddied
The pure idea. Flurries turned to flakes
That snowed upon us as we watched and studied,
Dodging the drops and gusts that numbed our fingers,
How gray and white were blooded or were bloodied
And, as we raised our faces to the skies,
How white and gray were laded or were ladied.

>Love,
>Flora

No. 189

                        Cambridge, December 8
                        Immaculatae Conceptionis Solemnitas

Dear Margaret,

The lady. The rocks. The grotto. The mud.
The lady! The lady was a vision.
Did I see her, did I see the shining vision,
Through the French girl's eyes,
Through the French saint's eyes,
Through the Jewish writer's eyes,
Through the film director's eyes,
Through the movie star's eyes,
Through the eyes of the American child,
The innocent little girl,
Innocent little socialist, little communist,
Little atheist innocent of religion?
Was this religion, the religious,
This emptiness breaking into beauty?
Was this the holy, the sacred,
This vacancy breaking into speech?
Was this the infinite, the eternal,
This nothingness bursting into song?
I am the Immaculate Conception.
The music was the sparkling of clear waters.

                        Love,
                        Julia

No. 190

                                    Cambridge, December 8
                                    Immaculatae Conceptionis Solemnitas

Dear Leila,

The clouds at dawn today in the east
Are very rosy and very wild.

From the conception to the assumption
Does there exist now the abstraction?

The clouds wrestle. The clouds embrace.
The cicadas sing now no longer.

If dawn today makes us immortal
Let someone remember to make us young.

                                                Love,
                                                Flora

No. 191

>Cambridge, December 8
>Tiberino in Insula

Dear Margaret,

On Tiber Island, longtime site of healing,
The wounded waited in the hospital,
Bloody from battle. Boys? No, Roman soldiers.
Came Tiberinus, Aesculapius
There came, the Brothers came, the Princess came.
Margaret, you came, you cared, you comforted.

>Love,
>Julia

No. 192

                                              Cambridge, December 8
                                              Tiberino, Gaiae
                                              Tiberino in Insula

Dear Leila Saint of Knowledge,

Will men be man, Gaius,
Women, woman, Gaia?

Do I ask what I am?
Do I do what I can?

In or near silence,
In or near Island,
In or near Tiber,

Did I pray for health,
Did I pray for death,
Did I hope for both?

Island was of earth,
Tiber was of birth.

The river was of ruth,
The tribune was of truth.

                                              Love,
                                              Julia Flora of the Tiber

No. 193

> Cambridge, December 9
> The Birth of Milton

Dear Leila,

Did the infant cry?
What can we justify?

Tiresias gone blind?
Eyes of the mighty mind?

Silence, speech, or song?
Tears brief or laughter long?

> Love,
> Flora

No. 194

                                        Cambridge, December 11
                                        AGONALIA

Dear Margaret,

Poetry lost, the shout and whisper last:
Up to the other, utter, utterance,
Down to despair, down down down down to dying.
How long will sound be being, how soon silence?

                                                      Love,
                                                      Julia

No. 195

> Cambridge, December 11
> AGONALIA INDIGETI

Dear Leila,

Where is Sol Indiges, to whom we call?
We sit within our windows watching water.
Today there is no sun. Indigenous
Is only rain. The universe is gray.
We sit and study. Do we understand?
We understand in myth, in art, in life
The grayness of the tragedy of woman,
The tragedy of women when their men
Are not quite worthy, not quite equal, not
Quite able to appreciate or answer
Their intellect, their artistry, their passion,
Their purity, their pure profound devotion.
Iphigenia and Antigone,
Cassandra and the daughter of Demeter,
Walk out and fall before our tearful eyes
On stage, on pages, in deep memory.
Rachel will act and Fanny Elssler dance
Before our rapt admiring gaze; their men
Offer distraction, doubt, and disappointment
Like Mariana's Sylvain in the tale.
But Julia was espoused to Jesus Christ.
Do we see Margaret with George Thomas Davis,
Samuel Gray Ward, William Hull Clarke, James Nathan,
Or Thomas Hicks, in Cambridge, Massachusetts,
Boston, Chicago, New York, finally Rome,
Or with Giovanni Angelo Ossoli,
With Love, with Death? Who is the bride of Death?
                                    Is it

Is it Antigone, Persephone,
Or Margaret as Marchesa Ossoli,
Or rather Margaret known as Mariana,
Or rather Julia known as Miriam?
Upon these will the sun now never shine?

       Love,
       Flora

No. 196

> Cambridge, December 15
> CONSUALIA

Dear Margaret,

Must I not squirm
Like the uncovered worm?

Have I a norm
For the resolved reform?

Am I so frail
I will not fail to fail?

Can I not smile?
This is the last mile.

> Love,
> Julia

No. 197

                                            Cambridge, December 19
                                            OPALIA
                                            The Birth of Anthe

Dear Leila,

Have you sensed the treasure
Of the wealth of December?

Have you known the fragrance
Of the rose of December?

Even with the feel of the weather
Of winter have you felt the spring?

                                            Love,
                                            Flora

No. 198

                                          Cambridge, December 19
                                          The Birth of Anthe

Dear Margaret,

Even in the dark days
I discern a delicate light.

Even in the dark days
I perceive how the aether beams.

Even in the dark days
My dark heart sparkles.

                                                  Love,
                                                Julia

No. 199

                                      Cambridge, December 19
                                      Anthe

Dear Leila,

There could be a sculpture. It would be of white marble. Would it be embellished with azure, rose, and gold? Would it remain in or return to its original immaculate white? Would it be the work of Phidias? Would it be the work of Hiram Powers? Would it be like a bust of Anna Hazard Barker? Would it be like a bust of Sarah Margaret Fuller? Would it be an Aphrodite? Would it be the Roman Venus? Would it be of that Mediterranean marble with subtle splendor able to reveal a fleshly sensuous real, a subsistent supersensual ideal, the aspects of the beautiful, the lineaments of the beautiful? Ah, would it be Anthe? Ah, would the flaming mind shine through?

                                                Love,
                                                Flora

No. 200

> Cambridge, December 19
> Io[vi?]

Dear Margaret,

Like you I sit at my window. Is it a god in bronze that I see within though I look without? Is it Apollo, Poseidon, Zeus? Was it fashioned by Hephaestus? Was that Vulcan? Are these Apollo, Neptune, Jove? Jove snows and snows and snows. He must be the bronze god. He must be the father of my child. He must be the sower of the snow. The snowplows intermittently scrape along Massachusetts Avenue. Otherwise the night is very quiet. The snowflakes are very quiet and very wild. As I watch at the window above the street, some of the flakes have reached my being. Flakes fall upon my spirit, into my spirit. Will I bear the child? The snow is white, the sky is white, the page is white. Will I bear the snow child, the sky child, the paper child? The father is the white night sky. The father is the strong bronze god. Will I bear the bronze child more lasting than bronze?

> Love,
> Julia

No. 201

                        Cambridge, December 21, 22, 23
                        Angerona and Volupia
                        Lares of the Sea
                        Mother of the Lares

Dear Leila,

Can it be Jack and Jill?
Is it too black and chill?
Is it too white and bright?
Is it nocturnal cold and blankness?
Is it diurnal freeze and blindness?
Is it, instead of the child, the two, the twins?
Is it the swan and the wolf,
The falling and the fallen snow,
The covering cloud and the uncovering azure,
Castor and Pollux,
Romulus and Remus,
The two Lares in their chapel,
The two values in their temple,
The true and the beautiful,
The truth and the beauty,
The knowledge and the sheen?
Do we know the snow from the ice?
Can we tell the dazzle from the dark?
Do the spirit and the matter make the hymn?
Do the words and the music make the song?
What will be great learning, what great art?
Which twin will be mortal, which immortal?
Will both twins be mortal, both immortal?
Are quintuplets, as there were that May
Of Julia's birth, all ready to be born?
The holy, good, true, beautiful, and whole?

                                               Born

Born dead, alive, aborted, fiercely breathing?
If the grand snowy swan has fathered them,
If the wild bronzy wolf has nurtured them,
They must have come to be, they must needs be.
Are giants climbing, angels floating down?
In the late sun gigantic icicles
Are shining swords.
In precipitate dusk angelic daggers
Are weeping ice.
Can daggers weep?
Do icicles die?
The little children live and laugh.
The children still go up the hill.

> Love,
> Flora

No. 202

                                          Cambridge, December 24

Dear Margaret,

But why all this of tree and rock?
But what all this on oak and stone?
I looked up high from bold New York.
I do recall where I was born.
There earth assumed a rocky guise
And trees could grow to scrape the skies.

                                                    Love,
                                                    Julia

No. 203

> Cambridge, December 25

Dear Margaret,

The blue sky
Was true sky
And the earth was dry
Enough that we could walk
About on it and talk.

With the singing
Of their winging
The choir of mourning doves
Swept and swooped into their sanctuary
Beneath the stiff green roof of rhododendron.
They did not form a mournful congregation.
This is indeed a very merry Christmas.
The thick green ceiling is the truthful witness
And vital succor for their lives, their loves.

We walked on warmed through still cold oaken groves.

> Love,
> Julia

No. 204

Cambridge, December 29–31

Dear Margaret,

This is what I have to say,
And this is the way I have to say it.

The straggling stems of the roses are the hints
Of something that is remembered that has been.

The ragged leaves of the roses are the hopes
Of something that is imagined that will be.

I say of something, of the presence and the absence,
What I say of someone, of the coming and the going,

Or what I say of the going of the roses
Is what I say of the absence of my Anthe.

Somewhere on this earth December is June in bloom.
Somewhere in this world Anthe wakes at home.

                Love,
                Julia

No. 205

> Cambridge, December 31

Dear Leila,

Margaret is what I know
And what (alarm) I do not know.

Julia is what I know
And what (uncouth) I do not know.

A word is what I know
And what (absurd) I do not know.

Heavens descend and blow.
Could there be sentences in snow?

To a brain must reach this show
And a Jove soon teach me how to know.

> Love,
> Flora

No. 206

                                        Cambridge, January 1

Dear Leila and Margaret,

Two consuls climb the Capitol
As Janus gazes from his hill.

Rome is luck, is joy.
Rome is we, is I.

But is Rome Rome
Or is it Ossoli?

And is Rome Rome
Or is it Mario?

And is it Rome
Or is it victory?

And is it Rome
Or is it Cicero?

And is it Rome
Or is it poetry?

And is it Rome
Or is it Angelo?

If it is not complex, profound,
At least it is not simple sound.

And if we should be fated
To face the trip back home

Over Dione's daughter's foam
It could be complicated.

                                        Love,
                                        Flora and Julia

No. 207

> Cambridge, January 1
> Aesculapio in Insula

Dear Margaret,

The fane of Aesculapius today
First graced the island where the Tiber parts
And where for weary soldiers as they lay
Wounded you tended flesh and warmed torn hearts.

> Love,
> Julia

No. 208

      Cambridge, January 1
      Emancipation Proclamation, 1863

Dear Margaret,

How can I tell you?
You died too soon.
President Lincoln.
Soldiers. Blood.
And still the slaves.
Emancipation.
President-Elect
Barack Obama.
About the election,
About my obsession,
Should I have sent
At least one letter?
Of big things
Should I have written?
Of great hopes
Could I have spoken?
What of those
Can a ghost know?

      Love,
      Julia

No. 209

Cambridge, January 1

Dear Margaret,

P. S. In the *New-York Daily Tribune* of January 1, 1848, I see what you write from Rome about America's "horrible cancer of Slavery." Can I know what the ghost has known? Further in your dispatch I can read about your hearing "the same arguments against the emancipation of Italy, that are used against the emancipation of our blacks." I read and I read. I write and I write and I write. What have we known? What can we know? What can we write of what we know? What can we know of what we write? You report, you analyze, you exhort. "I do not know what I have written," I read towards the end of your piece. I step into slush. I walk upon ice. Snow and shadow and sunshine rest upon the nearby Cambridge beech. What rests upon the mighty tree of knowledge? How can we open the weighty book of knowledge?

Love,
Julia

No. 210

Cambridge, January 3\
The Birth of Cicero

Dear Margaret,

Ego, etsi nihil habeo quod ad te scribam, scribo tamen quia tecum loqui videor. Thus, on May 22, 45 BCE, from his villa at Tusculum to his friend Atticus in Rome, Cicero begins a letter. There are letters and letters.

Love,\
Julia

No. 211

                                                   Cambridge, January 4

Dear Leila,

He could make anything boring
It has been said of scholar Scullard.
H. H. wrote of Rome.

She could make anything superficial
It can be said of poetaster Budenz.
Julia writes of what to whom?

She could make anything earthly heavenly lovely
It must be said of star of goddess Cytherea.
Venus speaks to dawn to evening gleam.

Venus today spoke crystal word
As though a whitish budding suddenly
Was in celestial meadow bloom.

Venus today spoke silver
As blue clear night approached on high
Low in the lazule dome.

                                                                Love,
                                                                 Flora

No. 212

                                            Cambridge, January 7

Dear Margaret,

It is preferable to sing
Even if no ears abide to hear us.

It is preferable to sculpt
Even if our statue crashing shatters.

It is better to write
Than not to write

Even if the leaves go flying out into the whirlwind,
Even if the sheets sink sodden down underneath the waves

Far off in an endless indifferent ocean
Or near and yet not reaching our possibly receptive native shore.

                                                     Love,
                                                     Julia

No. 213

                                                Cambridge, January 8

Dear Leila,

Is it better to write
If worthless words
If unworthy words
Deserve the sack
Deserve the sand

If Ms Minerva
Turns away
Storms away
Knocking the stack
Of books from the stand

If Ms Muse
Picks up the pen
Plucks up the pen
And puts it back
Into my hand?

                                                Love,
                                                Flora

No. 214

Cambridge, January 8

Dear Margaret,

Minerva,
Brilliant daughter
Of the shining mind of Jove,

Smile
Since if my mind
Is a tiny empty pool

Its desire
Is oceanic,
I cried to the gleaming god.

Love,
Julia

No. 215

> Cambridge, January 9
> Ianus piandus

Dear Leila,

He gnôsis.
Tò kalón.

To Janus
We atone.

Can Hellas
All alone

Be witness
To the tone

Of crisis
All my own?

> Love,
> Flora

No. 216

Cambridge, January 10–11

Dear Leila,

Fair Margaret at her window sat
 And watched the moon-bright sky.
Great Margaret at her window stood
 And saw the sun pass by.

To her the apple tree could speak,
 Her did the roses kiss,
To her the cold came through the cracks
 And froze the buds of bliss.

Far from the window she must roam,
 Far from the harbor sail.
Close to the shore she must go down
 Under the ruthless gale.

Down went her book, too. Now she is
 The written, not the writer.
What knowledge blows on her? She is
 The victim, not the fighter.

The night was black, the night was white,
 The air was snow and sleet.
In glided Margaret's grimly ghost
 And stood at Julia's feet.

I was killed once, I was killed twice,
 I am killed yet again.
My life and loveliness are lost
 Through your unlovely pen.

She ceased, but Julia was not moved
> By midnight's wintry weather.
They stayed there at the windowpane
> Like tree and tree together.

Love,
Flora

No. 217

Cambridge, January 16

Dear Leila,

Out there, chill and clear, light gleams.
In here, still so near, heat steams.

I can remember the men whom I have loved.
Arthur, Joseph, Mario: Shall I list them?

Silver and gold and oak and violet,
Garden and prairie, dew and avalanche.

Well I know my loved ones loved me less.
Was I loving thus less lovable?

Was I too odd, too free? Might I have been beguiled?
Only a god shall be the father of my child.

Love,
Flora

No. 218

>Cambridge, January 17
>Compleanno di Giovanni Angelo Ossoli
>(1821–1850)

Dear Margaret,

Tall, dark, and handsome is your love, your husband.
The letters which you write to him by hand,
The autographs in your own hand, salute him
As caro, mio caro, caro mio,
Amore, mio amore, mio bene.
Ossoli is a noble and a Roman.
What is he like to you? A violet.

>Love,
>Julia

No. 219

>Cambridge, January 20
>Inauguration, 2009

Dear Margaret,

At last in linear time a day
To be inscribed in cyclical time.

May the line last. May the sun stay.
May the great cycle rise sublime.

>Love,
>Julia

No. 220

>Cambridge, January 21
>Pulchritudinem sol et luna mirantur

Dear Leila,

To Beauty wonder of the sun,
To Beauty marvel of the moon,
To Beauty admiration of the sky,
I am yet wedded everlastingly.

Is it, with evening just begun
And night to fill the heavens soon,
Like this: glimpsed, watched, above earth's sod and bough,
Celestial depths of altitudes of blue?

>Love,
>Flora

No. 221

Cambridge, January 26

Dear Margaret,

Around, the cold.
Below, the snow.
Above, the blue.

All that as that.
All this as this.
That as this too.

What I am.
What I see.
What I do.

Love,
Julia

No. 222

Cambridge, January 27
Castor and Pollux

Dear Leila,

The darkening large expanse of azure
The brightening tiny point of silver
The vigil
Be vigilant
The twins

The heavy pounding of the horses
The heavy panting of the horses
The vision
See victory
The twins

The building gilding of the dawn
The bastioned dazzling of the day
The vistas
Free visitants
The twins

Love,
Flora

No. 223

                                                  Cambridge, February 4

Dear Margaret,

I try
Not to want
To die
But I can't.

I cross
Over ice.
What loss
Is the price?

You sit
In your gown
And wait
Till you drown.

I weep
At your going.
How deep
Goes my knowing?

                                                         Love,
                                                        Julia

No. 224

Cambridge, February 5
Concordiae in Capitolio

Dear Margaret,

Waldo lost them all too soon,
Father, brothers, wife, small son,
Too soon, you, the Margaret-friend,
Last, too soon, spark, gleam, of mind.
Concord, from the Capitol,
Cast benignity on all.

Love,
Julia

No. 225

> Cambridge, February 5
> Concordiae

Dear Leila,

Must they turn, forever tossed,
Forever dismembered,
In the violence of the sea,
In the silence of the grave?

Not for what they lost
Are they remembered
But for what they were able to be
And for what they gave.

> Love,
> Flora

No. 226

Cambridge, February 6

Dear Leila,

No more jingles.
No more platitudes.

Nonsense mingles
With these attitudes.

Promise tingles
At such latitudes.

Love,
Flora

No. 227

                                              Cambridge, February 9
                                              Plenilunium

Dear Margaret,

Is there a moon to moon over,
Is there a star to desire,
Is there a sun to be the center
Of the journey, of the journal,
Of the annals, of the anniversary?
Of the ellipse are there two foci?
Is there motus and is there quies?
Is there he gnôsis and is there tò kalón?
For all the yearnings are there all the words?
What if anything will my ultimate breath
Breathe in of reality,
Breathe into infinitude?

                                                            Love,
                                                            Julia

No. 228

Cambridge, March 9

Dear Mariana,

The crocus golden in the sun
   In sun is brief; too soon it dies.
It disappears in sleet and snow.
   I wish I were where Helen lies.

Does he thus speak who sang of love
   And death? Or is the song my own?
Or is it yours? And are you you
   Or are you Margaret all alone?

No Helen would have died for me,
   She said, or would have died for you.
For him she died for whom her heart
   Beat and stopped beating, ever true.

I wish my grave were growing green,
   He said, on fair Kirconnell Lee
And I were lying in her arms
   Who braved dread death to succor me.

Who is burd Helen? Is she love
   Or is she knowledge and the quest
For knowledge or the ultimate:
   Beauty, pure motion and deep rest?

When beauty dies do I die too,
   Unloved, unloving, knowing naught,
Under the ugly wave undone,
   Motionless, restless, placeless, caught?

Why when the snow has disappeared
   And days of golden sun return
Is there no body lying low,
   No crocus corpse to find and mourn?

                                              Love,
                                              Miriam

No. 229

> Cambridge, March 15

Dear Mariana,

Blue is the sky and bright the air
    And light or dark the crocus gleams
White, gold, white-purple, purple-white,
    Oh, purple, one in many streams.

Oh, all too late eternity
    Now calls me. I am moribund.
Oh, all too soon infinitude
    Summons. I am not wholly nunned.

High in the sky, low on the earth,
    The Ides are jovial. The god
Laughs and the blossoms laugh and I
    Wander and wonder if I could.

> Love,
> Miriam

No. 230

> Cambridge, March 22

Dear Margaret,

Kristi's crocuses,
Kristi's krokoi,
Kristi's balm,
In wind, in calm,
Under cloud, under sun,
On sod, on lawn,
Hold and show
The sheen of their own
Being and beauty.
Their globes and bowls
And openings
Hold, too, the feel
Of hands that held
Their origins,
Of mind that planned
Their burgeonings,
Of eyes that see
This white or gold
Or purple sheen
Existent, real.

> Love,
> Julia

No. 231

Cambridge, March 25

Dear Margaret,

The first philosophy
I seem to remember
As fragments of Greek
That reached my groping
And seemed to be
Of the one and the many.

The first daffodil
Seems to rise
Like a golden sun
Alone in its heaven
Of subtle greening.

The first little squills
Seem to star
A sky of lawn
Become all blue
With their multiples.

The fragments of my thought
Seem to accommodate
The many and the one,
Liberty and union,
The one and the many,
Equality and freedom,
The many and the one,
Myriads and me,
The one and the many,
The all and the I.

Is it lonely
Within the whole,
Azure, sunny,
Without the sole?

                                        Love,
                                        Julia

No. 232

Cambridge, March 26

Dear Margaret,

Union served
To mean the nation.
Liberty worked
To mean the states.

Union meant
Compromise.
Liberty meant
Enslavement as right.

The postequinoctial sun
Shines in cold heaven.
The novilunium
Hides in clear sky.

Words of history
Are words of time.
After disaster
Should come Easter.

Love,
Julia

No. 233

Cambridge, March 26

Dear Leila,

Why should the clarity have gone?
Clouds crowding close must be a sign.
Along with Margaret's flesh went down
The marble statue of Calhoun.
Her body, lost, did not remain
In any form but sank unseen.
His image was brought up again.
Why should I write? You must have known.

Love,
Flora

No. 234

Cambridge, March 27

Dear Margaret,

All men are born.
Can I cite your words,
Willing to write
Your pain and desire?

All men are born
Free and equal,
You wrote, quoting
Your memory, witness

To utterance deeply
American, darkly
American, worthy
Of hope and observance.

This verbal statement,
Not made in vain,
Stands there, you felt,
To shame and encourage,

Golden certainty,
Freedom, equality,
For the new nation
And every member.

This regards
Red men and black men,
You held. It was eighteen
Forty-three.

This regards
All men, you held.
This regards,
You held, women.

                                              Love,
                                              Julia

No. 235

> Cambridge, April 19
> CERIALIA

Dear Leila,

The white magnolia brightens
In the sun and in the breeze.
The cruelty of April
Is its addiction to the winds of March.
Under a sun of April
A breeze comes gusting
As a resuscitated wind of March.
In the spirit of the wind
I prophesied to Julia
As to Jochebed, to Miriam, to Moses.
Rap your cane on Massachusetts Avenue,
Stamp your foot on Massachusetts Avenue,
Pass smashing slashing through the sea of the breeze, of the wind,
Plant your staff here and here and here.

Here see the green blossoms of certain maples,
The green leaves of much green grass,
Here the yellow cornel,
The yellow forsythia,
The yellow daffodils,
The yellow tulips,
Here the orange tulips,
Here the red tulips,
The red blooms and fruits of many maples,
Here the purple azaleas,
The purple hyacinths,
The purple grape hyacinths,
The purple violets,
Here the blue squills.

Here see desire
In the blue of the blue squills.
Here see a sign
In a golden line
On a white tulip.
What land is this?
Is this Louisiana?
Is this Massachusetts?
Is this a noble path of the wind?
Here hear the promise.
Resonant, redolent,
Strongly, sweetly,
The goddess spoke
From the pink and white magnolia.

                          Love,
                          Flora

No. 236

                                                    Cambridge, April 26

Dear Margaret,

Near the earth are
The purple myrtles,
The violet violets.

Lifting a little
The blue forget-me-nots
Forget not blue sky.

From higher the white
Weeping cherry
Like Andromache

Through tears smiles.

                                                             Love,
                                                             Julia

No. 237

Cambridge, April 28
Floralia I

Dear Leila,

Do the mockingbirds mock
And the mourning doves mourn
If the weeping cherry

Weeps for joy?

Love,
Flora

No. 238

                                              Cambridge, May 1
                                              Floralia IV

Dear Margaret,

The boughs are all blossom.
The crabapple calls.
This bloom is beauty.
Hearken. Here
Sight and scent are sound.

Am I able to answer?
Fear finds my flesh.
Madness meets my mind.
Horror hunts my heart.
Horror haunts my heart.

                                              Love,
                                              Julia

No. 239

> Cambridge, May 11
> LEMURIA II
> Ma[niae]

Dear Leila,

Selves and slaves,
Struggles and surrenders,
Rights and wrongs,
Reasons and religions:

Of these I read.
My country, 'tis of thee
I cannot sing.
Woman in the Nineteenth

Century, Seneca
Falls, Elizabeth,
Margaret, far from me
Are, stand, speak.

Only light lilacs,
Bright dogwoods, true tulips
Touch, entrust.
Wistarias witness.

I wait, watch, listen.
Maybe then Margaret,
Even Elizabeth,
Come back and counsel,

Come near and comfort.

> Love,
> Flora

No. 240

                    Mount Auburn Cemetery, May 12
                    Fifteenth Anniversary of
                    The Death of Daniel Von Dwornick

Dear Margaret and Daniel,

Along the slim gray path
And over the thick gleaming green of the grass

We, Ruby and Julia, have come to honor you here,
You, Margaret, whose name is here but not your body,
You, Daniel, whose body is here but not your name,
You both, who died too young, who died too soon,
You, Margaret, at forty, in storm of wind and sea,
You, Daniel, at home, yet not yet thirty-three,
You, Margaret, knocked beneath the hostile wave,
You, Daniel, nursed within the tending love.

We name you both among the dogwoods,
Among the bodily excellences of the pink and the white dogwoods
Alive in their bright perfection of loveliness, living
Corporeality
That seems, in the sunlight, in the golden breeze,
Under the azure, the celeste, of the sky,

Spirit free, embodied, disembodied,
Spirit of delicacy, of splendor, of strength,
Honored and honorable and honoring.

                          Love,
                          Julia

No. 241

Cambridge, May 19

Dear Leila,

Iris and columbine entice, delight,
Intricate, intimate,
In this new verdant azure paradise.

God almighty first planted a garden,
Biblical, mythical.
Is there no garden if there is no god?

Slow is my motion to this greener Eden,
Physics with history,
Which is that rest that is ever to move.

                                            Love,
                                            Flora

No. 242

> Cambridge, May 23
> TUBILUSTRIUM
> Feriae Volcano

Dear Margaret,

Robinia and robin,
Fire and forge,
Trumpet and lustration,
War and peace,
Thought and feeling,
Truth and beauty,
You and I,
Not divided but one,
Not contrasted but each as two.
Oh, the throbbing of the white blossoms
Suspended high towards the blue of sky,
Oh, the shading of the golden melody
Ascended loud towards the white of cloud.
Some day something may be known
If in the interval of bloom and song
I can, like you, I ever can
(Oh, I never can)
Understand, can fashion,
Can be free and can be fit,
Can be forge and can be fire.
Oh, the purple luxuriance
Of the purple rhododendrons,
Oh, the aureate ruffles
Of the first roses of gold,
Oh, the mixed messages of swifts
                                    Twittering

Twittering and flitting far on high,
Oh, the subtle comments of the doves
Intimate, insistent, so near by.
Oh, have we not been born?
Oh, something might not die.

                                                Love,
                                                Julia

No. 243

Cambridge, May 30

Dear Margaret,

In the celestial blue the great
White clouds are old friends
Freshly welcoming.

Lush and elegant the great
White blossoms of the virgilias
Receive my visits.

I admit my wish.

My game I proclaim.
Can anyone blame

Mysticism,
Heroism,
Scholarship,
Poetry,
Philosophy?

I have rinsed my dish.

My self I confess.
Can anyone bless

Glutton (Munch!),
Poltroon,
Pedant,
Poetaster,
(Grumble!) Dunce?

Do I dance? I stumble.
For the fence I fumble.
Will I wince? I crumble.

Can I not manage to try
To be a little better — Why
Not — before I die?

>   Love,
>   Julia

No. 244

>Cambridge, June 13
>The Birth of Margaret Rodgers Budenz

Dear Margaret,

I wanna cry.
I wanna die.

I wanna weep.
I wanna sleep.

I wanna scream.
I wanna dream.

I wanna know.
I wanna go.

I wanna pray.
I wanna stay.

>Love,
>Julia

No. 245

        Cambridge, June 13
        Feriae Iovi

Dear Leila,

I want to see.
I want to be.

The roses smile
A little while.

        Love,
        Flora

No. 246

Cambridge, June 19

Dear Margaret,

Like the young Sibyl in my youth
   I joyed in immortality.
Like her in age I faced the truth.
   Like her I said, I want to die.

                           Love,
                            Julia

No. 247

                                            Cambridge, June 22

Dear Margaret,

An angel came in golden hair.
She rang the bell, she climbed the stair.

She bore my burdens, braved the rains
And winds to mitigate my pains.

Though Kristi was her earthly name
She was celestial in her frame.

Her smiles were sunny blossomings.
Her heart held fire. Her mind had wings.

                                                  Love,
                                                  Julia

No. 248

Cambridge, July 2

Dear Margaret,

I long for the lost god.
Why does the flower fade?
Why does the heavy cloud
Oppress the sky and the child?

Love,
Julia

No. 249

                                        Cambridge, July 5
                                        Entrance into
                                        Ursuline Novitiate 1956
                                        Widener Library 1965

Dear Margaret,

The climbing clematis in purple darks,
    Lace-cap hydrangeas spread in azure lights,
Proclaim that if my days and months are marks
    They call to depths still, summon still to heights.

                                                Love,
                                                Julia

No. 250

> Cambridge, July 8

Dear Margaret,

Since Kristi Olson the philosopher
    Pondering freedom and equality
Became my neighbor thoughts and words are her
    Deeds lifting littleness to liberty.
I am the small, the feeble, I aver,
    And she the tall, the regal, royalty.
Clematis can be cramped, crimped, stringy burr,
    Rise, expand, shine, purpureality.

> Love,
> Julia

No. 251

                                        Cambridge, July 19

Dear Margaret,

Who stares at the storm?
Who is awake in the wind?
Who is awash in the waters?
Who sleeps in the sea?

                                        Love,
                                        Julia

No. 252

Cambridge, July 19

To the Women of the Nineteenth Century
Dear Friends:

    Did you really exist? All these selves, your selves, come before me, come to me, singly, in pairs, in dozens. Perhaps because you and I cannot interact, your distinct selves are more vivid than those of my living friends, for yours are not diminished or dimmed, as theirs may be, by my own.

    Our president died on the ninth of July. The vice-president takes his place. Margaret dies on the nineteenth of July. You remain in your places. You remain. The second half of the nineteenth century remains. It is, it still is yours. Margaret does things for me, for you, then goes away. You do things for me, then go away. Thank you. I do nothing. But soon I, too, will go away.

Gratefully yours,
Julia Budenz

No. 253

Cambridge, July 19

Dear Margaret,

Acanthus and hibiscus now are blooming
In Cambridge, Massachusetts, under white
Blossoms of cloud on smooth blue lawns of sky.
Maria, Waldo, Henry, William, James,
Nathaniel, Anna, Samuel, Caroline, George,
Louisa, Ellis, Sarah, Frank, Sophia,
Lucretia, Elizabeth, Susan, Lucy live.
I cease. These blossom yet. I cease to name them.
I name you. Why do you not bloom among them?
Live on. You should be making history still.

Love,
Julia

No. 254

> Cambridge, July 30
> Fortunae Huiusce Diei

Dear Leila,

The gods are games
With which I play,
Numinous names
With which I say

The word that frames
The faltering way,
The word that claims
The luck of this day.

> Love,
> Flora

No. 255

Cambridge, October 10

Dear Leila,

Are they liars?
Must the Sirens lie?

The sugar maples fire me.
The morning glories ensky me.

The exquisite multicolored roses of October
Promise and fulfill, oh, oh.

Can I sing with the Sirens?
Must I lie with the Sirens?

Love,
Flora

No. 256

Cambridge, October 11

Dear Leila,

Will I ask Thomas Crawford?
Will I ask Margaret Fuller?
Will I ask Thomas Hicks?

Will I ask George Washington Greene?
Will I ask Samuel Eliot?
Will I ask George Stillman Hillard?

Will I ask Charles Sumner?
Will I ask Samuel Ward of New York?
Will I ask Samuel Ward of Boston?

Will I ask Julia Ward Howe?
Will I ask Jenny Crawford Campbell?
Will I ask Louisa Cutler Ward Crawford Terry?

Will I be Thomas Crawford's Orpheus of marble?
Will I be Margaret Fuller's Orpheus of rhyme?
Will I be Orpheus? Will I shade my eyes?

Will I shade my eyes against the brightness?
Will I shade my eyes against the darkness?
Will I be Cerberus? Will I close my eyes?

Love,
Flora

No. 257

                                                  Cambridge, October 12

Dear Leila,

I am Orpheus.
I look into the brightness.
I am blinded.

I am Orpheus.
I look into the darkness.
I look into myself.

I am Orpheus.
I no longer see.
I no longer sing.

                                                             Love,
                                                             Flora

No. 258

Cambridge, October 13

Dear Margaret,

As blind, as deaf,
As Laura Bridgman,

I press blunt fingers
Around the pen,

I press numb fingers
Onto the page.

Will I be rescued by Samuel Gridley Howe,
Florence Nightingale, Dorothea Dix,

Or mourn for wedded love with Julia Ward
Or hear and see the glory of the Lord?

Love,
Julia

No. 259

Cambridge, October 14

Dear Margaret,

Passing rose and clematis
I apologized like this:

Laura Bridgman, please forgive
My forgetting that you live.

You are not a metaphor.
What I feel is what you are.

Love,
Julia

No. 260

Cambridge, October 31

Dear Margaret,

Not because it is Halloween
Do I sit here tonight in horror.

The horror is ever dark inside me.
I am ever dark inside the horror.

The horror is always fat within me.
I am always thin within the horror.

I am myself ghost, specter, witch,
The masked, the muffled, monster, horror.

I hear rain slick outside on the street.
There is some trick. There is no treat.

                                  Love,
                                  Julia

No. 261

Cambridge, November 1

Dear Margaret,

Must the saints suffer? They rejoice
Others' sad hearts through act, thought, voice.

Will we be saints if we dispel
Tentacles of the earthly hell?

Might we be saints if we could find
The azure skies within the mind?

May we be saints if we can hold
A momentary flash of gold?

Love,
Julia

No. 262

Cambridge, December 25

Dear Leila,

I am the bride of Death,
I am the bride of Truth,
I am the bride of Beauty,

I am the mother of
Tritogenes, the son
Of three, the eloquent elf.

Here is enduring breath,
Here is maturing youth,
Here is alluring duty,

Here not some other love
But the creating one
In three, outselfing self.

Love,
Flora

No. 263

                                                Cambridge, December 26

Dear Leila,

Shall one year slip into another year?
Shall I begin to make my resolutions?
Shall I never again
Mention my azure sky,
Invoke my golden breeze?
Do my words weary, my candid phrases cloy,
My finest feelings and my fairest thoughts
Like dismal dawns of freezing rain repel
Even my disembodied audience
Even while I try to substitute
My most true heaven for my most valid hell?

                                                                Love,
                                                                Flora

No. 264

                    Cambridge, December 28
                    Holy Innocents

Dear Margaret,

In order to understand
The letters which I send to you
You have to understand
The voluminous tree of which they are some leaves
And wander through the ever-enlarging gardens
In which they grow as some of the various bloom
And contemplate the child
Of which they are the treasures and the toys,
Of which they are the gazings of the eyes,
Of which they are the beatings of the heart.
Is the child innocent, human, half divine?
Are our children safe or likely to be slaughtered?
Are our children of marble, bronze, gold, ivory?
The treasures are the textured texts,
In danger of the destiny
Of your Roman Revolution.
Are our children statues sinking in the sea?
Your baby brother Edward,
Born on your birthday,
Your small son Angelino,
Born of your body,
Rest in Mount Auburn.
Will my letters rest?
Will my letters be delivered?
Will my letters be lost beneath the tide?
Will we all meet in the land of the lost,
Converge in the universe of dissolution?
                                      Please

Please read these letters soon,
As they begin to exist.
Please play with my child,
While my child can play.

Love,
Julia

No. 265

Cambridge, January 1

Dear Leila,

What is your birthday? I am remembering

Sarah Margaret Fuller, born May 23, 1810.

What are our birthdays? I am remembering

James Freeman Clarke, born April 4, 1810;
William Henry Channing, born May 25, 1810;
Ralph Waldo Emerson, born May 25, 1803;
Julia Ward Howe, born May 27, 1819;
Julia Mairin Budenz, born May 23, 1934.

But how do we remember Margaret Fuller?

James Freeman Clarke (1852)
As published in
Memoirs of Margaret Fuller Ossoli (1852):

    The difficulty which we all feel in describing our past intercourse and friendship with Margaret Fuller, is, that the intercourse was so intimate, and the friendship so personal, that it is like making a confession to the public of our most interior selves. For this noble person, by her keen insight and her generous interest, entered into the depth of every soul with which she stood in any real relation. To print one of her letters, is like giving an extract from our own private journal.

William Henry Channing (1852)
As published in
Memoirs of Margaret Fuller Ossoli (1852):

    I have no hope of conveying to readers my sense of the beauty of our relation, as it lies in the past with brightness falling on it from Margaret's risen spirit. It would be like printing a chapter of autobiography, to describe what is so grateful in memory, its influence upon one's self.

Ralph Waldo Emerson (1852)
As published in
Memoirs of Margaret Fuller Ossoli (1852):

I remember that she made me laugh more than I liked; for I was, at that time, an eager scholar of ethics, and had tasted the sweets of solitude and stoicism, and I found something profane in the hours of amusing gossip into which she drew me, and, when I returned to my library, had much to think of the crackling of thorns under a pot. Margaret, who had stuffed me out as a philosopher, in her own fancy, was too intent on establishing a good footing between us, to omit any art of winning. She studied my tastes, piqued and amused me, challenged frankness by frankness, and did not conceal the good opinion of me she brought with her, nor her wish to please. She was curious to know my opinions and experiences. Of course, it was impossible long to hold out against such urgent assault. She had an incredible variety of anecdotes, and the readiest wit to give an absurd turn to whatever passed; and the eyes, which were so plain at first, soon swam with fun and drolleries, and the very tides of joy and superabundant life.

Julia Ward Howe (1910)
As described in
Julia Ward Howe (1916):

 A little later [after the centenary of James Freeman Clarke, for which Julia Ward Howe composed and read a poem] came a centenary which — alas! — she did not enjoy. It was that of Margaret Fuller, and was held in Cambridge. She was asked to attend it, and was assured that she "would not be expected to speak." This kindly wish to spare fatigue to a woman of ninety-one was the last thing she desired. She could hardly believe that she would be left out — she, who had known Margaret, had talked and corresponded with her.
 "They have not asked me to speak!" she said more than once as the time drew near.
 She was reassured; of course they would ask her when they saw her!
 "I have a poem on Margaret!"
 "Take it with you! Of course you will be asked to say something, and then you will be all ready with your poem in your pocket."
 Thus Maud, in all confidence. Indeed, if one of her own had gone with her,

with her, the matter would have been easily arranged; unfortunately, the companion was a friend who could make no motion in the matter. She returned tired and depressed. "They did not ask me to speak," she said, "and I was the only person present who had known Margaret and remembered her."

Julia Mairin Budenz (2010)
As recorded in
"The Margaret-Ghost" (January 1):

    I decided in 2007 to ignore and forget myself. I decided to write letters to Margaret Fuller about herself. I have never, I think, written so much about myself.
    Shall I think she and I can know as she and Goethe know? Shall I think she and I can love as she and Beethoven love? Shall I think she and I can laugh as she and the blue sky laugh?
    Am I not close to Margaret Fuller? I have a poem about her in my pocket. No one, I think, will ask to hear me read it on the twenty-third of May.

Leila, I am remembering our Margaret.

Love,
Flora

No. 266

Cambridge, January 1

Dear Margaret,

Some unannounced sun from the south
Touches my wall of books,
Gives my sober volumes a glow.
This is still the first morning.
My dirty windows face east.
This very year two centuries ago
You will be born, your mother's oldest child.
Today she must already know.
The sun has not been forecast for today.
All that has been said
Is cloud and snow.
All that must be said
Is resolution
Before the coming dissolution.
All that must be done
Is concentration
Before the ultimate disintegration.
This is the year for your, not for my, sun.
Your sun, this year, must be my new creation.

Love,
Julia

No. 267

Cambridge, January 5

Dear Leila,

How can the sun be lost? Must it be found?
Today there is no sun. Can there be day
Without the sun, without a sun? Today
No sun is shining. Will no sun today
Ever be shining? How thick are the clouds?
How wide must be the spreading of the clouds?
How cloudy is the clouding of the clouds?

Is this the weather, this the lost and found?
In all these clouds do we lose Margaret Fuller?
Can we find Margaret Fuller in the sun?
Can we find Margaret Fuller and ourselves?
Dig up the diaries, look up the long-lost years:

Sarah Margaret Fuller, 1810–1850;
Ralph Waldo Emerson, 1803–1882;
Samuel Gray Ward, 1817–1907;
Julia Ward Howe, 1819–1910;
Julia Mairin Budenz, 1934–20xx.

Margaret Fuller, journal (1844):

beautiful ones be happy. Keep on to heaven. And thou, S. did not the heart prompt to me sincere intelligent meaning! Go then. — Waldo said my device should be a ship at sea in a gale. Motto "Let all drive." —

Margaret Fuller, journal (1849):

ROMA, 1st Jan. 1849
    This year cannot fail to be rich in events most important for Italy, Europe, the world. Rome has at last become the focus of the Italian revolution and I am here.

Waldo Emerson, journal (1850):

On Friday, 19 July, Margaret dies on rocks of Fire Island Beach within sight of & within 60 rods of the shore. To the last her country proves inhospitable to her; brave, eloquent, subtle, accomplished, devoted, constant soul! If nature availed in America to give birth to many such as she, freedom & honour & letters & art too were safe in this new world.

Waldo Emerson, journal (1850):

She had a wonderful power of inspiring confidence & drawing out of people their last secret.

Waldo Emerson, journal (1850):

I have lost in her my audience. I hurry now to my work admonished that I have few days left.

Waldo Emerson, journal (1851):

S.G.W. says How can you describe a Force? How can you write the life of Margaret?

Waldo Emerson, journal (1851):

The unlooked for trait in all these journals to me is the Woman, poor woman: they are all hysterical. She is bewailing her virginity and languishing for a husband.

Waldo Emerson, journal (1851):

A tone of sadness was in her voice like the wail of the ocean. And from my earliest acquaintance I had a feeling as if some one cried *Stand from under!*

Waldo Emerson, journal (1851):

I had, I remember, some feeling in my early acquaintance with her of the unprofitableness of all this derision & joking & crackling of thorns under a pot. It was a superficial judgment. Her journals are throughout religious, tearful, tragic in their tenderness & compunction at shortcomings, and the tone of conversation was only the pastime & necessity of her talent.

Julia Howe, journal (1882):

April 27. Made to-day a good start in writing about Margaret Fuller. This night at 8.50 P.M. died Ralph Waldo Emerson, *i.e.*, all of him that could die. I think of him as a father gone — father of so much beauty, of so much modern thought.

Julia Budenz, journal (2010):

Could I meet Margaret on an ocean,
Meet Margaret in a revolution,
Meet Samuel Ward in bank, in art,
Meet Waldo Emerson in thought,
Meet Julia Howe in newly finding
Fuller so many years after the ending?
Now I must hurry to my work
With few days left and fragile bark.

Leila, the time kept passing. Was the loss
Continuously greater? Was it less?

The day seemed longer and before the cloud
Could darken further into night there cleared
The blue and in the clearing gleamed the sun
And brightness everywhere was felt and seen.

Love,
Flora

No. 268

                                                  Cambridge, January 27
                                                  Castor and Pollux

Dear Margaret,

Hot shines the sun.
Bright gleams the morn.
Will day be done?
Is there some bourn?

Can I be cold?
Can I be crying?
I must be old.
I must be dying.

This is my youth,
This my last duty:
Infinite truth,
Absolute beauty.

                                                                       Love,
                                                                       Julia

No. 269

                              Cambridge, February 17
                              Ash Wednesday

Dear Margaret,

Do I forget the good?
This is the call
To one and all
Which I would answer if I could,

The call that every man
And woman hears
With human ears
Which I will answer if I can.

Though truth and beauty must
Still summon me
Especially,
May I turn good before I turn to dust.

                              Love,
                              Julia

No. 270

                                  Cambridge, March 1
                                  The Birth of
                                  Seena Pappas Lopes, 1916

Dear Margaret,

Do you remember distant Arlington?
I never from that dismal Arlington
Wrote of my dear first roommate there,
The stranger who became the friend.

We knew what others did not know.

We knew the horror of the night,
The bodies there that would not work,
The workers there that would not come,
The helpers there that would not help.

We felt what others did not feel.

We felt the humor of the day.
We made the humor of the day.
We felt the pain, the wait, the pain.
Who made us cry? We made some laugh.

We understood what we could understand.

We understood the meaning of the hours.
We made the meaning of the hours.
And if our ravaged legs could scarcely walk
We understood our minds could dance.

                                              Love,
                                              Julia

No. 271

Cambridge, March 3

Dear Margaret,

Why are winds wild?
How are snowdrops cold?

We were anxious for August and a triumph fiery.
Will we make it to May and a promise flowery?

Moons come. Moons go.
Suns shine. Suns shy.

Love,
Julia

No. 272

                                        Cambridge, March 9

Dear Leila,

Between the cold and the cold
Could there slip a spell of sun,
Marvel of marble and gold
Of my own Pygmalion?

                                                  Love,
                                                  Flora

No. 273

> Cambridge, March 11
> The Birth of Torquato Tasso

Dear Margaret,

If you do not have
Enough to live on
Is it better to die?

What if you do not have
Enough to die on?

Was this winter a death
Under the frozen ground?

Was this winter a prison
Fixed closed on life?

The purple crocus opens
Filled with gold.

Little by little
The little flowers begin to flourish.

The crocus has enough.
How can we have enough
To live or die on?

> Love,
> Julia

No. 274

Cambridge, March 14
EQUIRRIA

Dear Margaret,

Generals of wind,
Troops of rain,
March on the glass.
May the power remain.

I am a pacifist.
There is a war
Upon my soul.
Must it be either-or?

Surely the sheer
Passion is single.
Beauty and truth
On one peak cannot mingle.

Will it be beauty?
Will it be truth?
Which will stand victor?
Could it be both?

The horses keep panting.
There is no breather.
The end is so near.
The answer is neither.

Love,
Julia

No. 275

Cambridge, March 16

Dear Margaret,

This is the house that Jack built.
My apartment building is disintegrating.
Cement came crashing.
My apartment is disintegrating.
Cracks crawl, scabs of plaster pall.
My clothing is disintegrating.
I walk in rags.
My body is disintegrating.
Sagging I totter, dragging a monster.
And is my mind disintegrating?
Stop, look, listen.
London Bridge is falling down.

Love,
Julia

No. 276

Cambridge, March 21

Dear Margaret,

I thought I was living with you in New York,
Not so much in the New York way down there
With the concerts and plays, the parties and salons,
The writers, editors, artists, poets, Poe
And Child and Cranch, reformers,
Associationists, the big excitements of city,

But up at Forty-ninth Street, along a dark lane,
With the East River on the east of you
Which to my wondering years from six to nine
Was the East River on the west of me
And with the window and the willow to the east of you
Which to my wistful years from six to nine
Was the window and the willow to the west of me.

I was living with you in New York,
But tonight here I am in Mount Auburn,
Not the Mount Auburn of the graves
But the Mount Auburn closer and closer to the grave.

Love,
Julia

No. 277

Cambridge, March 26

Dear Margaret,

If pain and penury are permanent,
If knowledge is no more,
If beauty beams no further,
Can behind the enormous red brick building
The immense blue sky shine blue?
The building is like a big red book.
To me it is closed.
The sky is like a big blue painting.
Once to me it stood open.
In the past I could almost walk through the great pages.
In the past I could almost step into the huge canvas.
At the book, the book, beloved red book, let me look.
By the sky, the sky, beloved blue sky, shall I die?

Love,
Julia

No. 278

Cambridge, March 27

Dear Leila,

I cannot try to do you justice, either cognitively or artistically. And why should I, since Margaret has done you more justice than anyone else is likely to do? Yet it must make me sad to give up at the very beginning the effort at poetic reproduction. Let me therefore sketch a few aspects of your impingement upon Julia's present existence.

Like Margaret and with Margaret, Julia looks on you and you are the clear blue sky, cold and distant as the Pole-star. If you are this, you must be of Julia's being. But maybe it is of Julia's past being, not of her present being. Or must Julia, like Margaret, with Margaret, recognize the unreality of your existence among us?

But I want to savor the phrases. What can it mean if you are the clear blue sky? What can it mean if this sky is cold and distant? What is the implication of the Pole-star?

What can it mean if suddenly this sky opens and flows forth a mysterious wind that bears with it one's last thought beyond the verge of all expectation, all association? Julia has known many winds. Some reveal and some kill. Is the last thought apocalypse or termination?

What can it mean if you are the mild sunset and put your friend to rest on a love-couch of rosy sadness, when on the horizon swells up a mighty sea and rushes over her till she plunges in its waves, affrighted, delighted, quite freed from earth? What are these waves of a mighty sea? What are these waves into which Margaret plunges? Will Julia plunge into these waves?

But that which matters is the night. What is the wildness of the dark sky of night? What is the link of the lake to the sky of night? Julia like Margaret looks into the lake, Leila, for you. Or does Julia run to the river, with the river?

I will not try to describe those nights of Leila, those nights which are yours. Margaret has described them. Julia like Margaret has lived them. Or are they a dying?

Love,
Flora

No. 279

                                        Cambridge, March 28
                                        Palm Sunday

Dear Margaret,

    Some things are repeated, and some things are not. Here I am in Mount Auburn Hospital, sitting on my donut cushion and swerving occasionally to drink in the blue course of the Charles River. That actually is the only drink which is permitted to me.

    But when the handsome Phil in his thick gray hair came to bring Holy Communion to the ninety-two year old Ethel in the bed on the other side of the room, I felt suddenly a repetition of the longing for holy food which I had experienced unexpectedly in Woburn two years before. Not wanting to repeat, I hesitated to detain the good man with my request as he was about to leave. It was lucky that I held my tongue. I am permitted neither wine nor bread. I am allowed no nutrients that can pass between my lips and down my throat. Domine, non sum dignus ut intres sub tectum meum. Can the Eucharist be administered intravenously?

                                                          Love,
                                                          Julia

No. 280

Cambridge, March 31

Dear Leila,

What does Margaret mean about the nights, your nights, since which she has been fearless and utterly free? And for Julia what could these nights mean? Leila, Saint of Knowledge, what do you know? Do you know all even while you are nothing?

Why to Margaret are there no requiems more? Why is death a name? Why do the darkest seeming hours sing Te Deum?

Is Margaret speaking about death, or is she speaking about a denial of death, or is she speaking about an escape from death? Is there no requiem because she lives, or is there no requiem because she may peacefully live or die? Do the darkest seeming hours sing Te Deum because there is something good in the universe, because there is something living in the universe? Margaret Fuller will be famous as one who accepted the universe. Thomas Carlyle, Henry James the elder, and William James the philosopher are among those cited.

Is the universe akin to night? What are Julia's nights in Mount Auburn? What are her nights in Mount Auburn Hospital, not too far from the graves? This hospital is an excellent one. That graveyard is a famous one. Is the hospital closer to the cosmos than the graveyard? Are the nights in the hospital much more in touch with worlds and worlds? Leila, you know more than perhaps you care to know from crybaby Julia and her faithful Flora. You know from us how it feels to carry around an abdomen that hurts and hurts, that never stops hurting. You know from us how it feels to be pulled from being stretched out on the high bed and escorted to the bathroom and back. You know from us what it is like to lie

on one's

on one's side in this bed skirting a reopened sacral decubitus and striving to write, to write. To write what? Why to write? Will this writing be in touch with the universe? Will it in any way be worthy of the universe? Will it in any way be worthy of Margaret Fuller? Will it in any way be worth surviving for? Or might Julia just as well give up and die? Might Julia just as well escape from all this pain? Might Julia just as well hope to float into the night? There is little hope of her surviving. There is little hope of her being granted time to write even as well as she can. Are these minimalizations self-pity? To what extent does she have a self? Does she have a self? She knows that she has nothing. She knows that like Leila she is nothing. She knows that all her pages may go floating with the Margaret-ghost, may go floating with her own ghost, into the night.

Oh, but she still has some blank pages. Eagerly her boney fingers reach out for the pen to fill the pages. What if these sheets of paper go up in smoke even as they are being filled? What if they blacken into night almost before they exist? What if during their nights of existence Julia is nearly fearless and almost free?

Love,
Flora

No. 281

Cambridge, April 7

Dear Margaret,

Do not resuscitate.

This is the white, or this is the black, answer.

This is the answer which the forms can understand.

This is the answer to the question which my gray mind has attempted to answer in its gray way whenever the inexorable demand for a non-gray response has been presented by the relentless black-and-white forms of responsible medical institutions that require my signatures shortly after I have entered their portals feeling almost in extremis and have begun to hear the shuffle of the pages as the papers are thrust before me.

Do not resuscitate. There it was. It was clear at last to my gray mind, and I signed.

I could hardly have done otherwise. It was merely that I could not comprehend the question.

Outside my window, beyond the big green patch of grass, the traffic moves both ways on Concord Avenue. The evening moves through gray to black.

In all medical institutions the nights are very black. It is better to try to keep the mind gray.

Do not resuscitate.

This is not the required white or black response to the sulky, sullen, sadistic attendants that attend upon the night.

Maybe once or twice there will be a non-discordant moment, there will be a smile. Maybe some night there will be a smile and a gentle adjustment of the entangling blankets.

Maybe the gray mind will manage to stay gray until a harmony, a concord, breathes and blossoms into resuscitation.

But lo, into this night, my night, our night, has already come, despite a suffering doubtless far deeper than mine, a slim woman with a little smile and a tone or semitone maybe human, maybe godlike, maybe marking, maybe making, a second of resurrection.

Love,
Julia

No. 282

>Cambridge, April 21
>PARILIA

Dear Margaret,

This is the midnight ride.
This is the midnight ride
Back, back.
I lie on my back.
This is the ride on my back,
Back to Mount Auburn,
To give my blood
To the life-thirsty ghosts,
To give my blood
To the life-testing needles.
What will I learn from
The ghosts? What will they say to me?
What will I learn from
The needles? What will they say of me?

>Love,
>Julia

No. 283

        Cambridge, April 27
        Floralia I, Pre-Julian
        The Death of Ralph Waldo Emerson, 1882
        The Death of Louis Francis Budenz, 1972

Dear Leila,

    From the big windows of the nursing home she can see not impossibly far away the pink and the white of cherry trees in bloom. Here there are no roses, but if there were she would not be able to see them. She cannot manage to rub her spotty eyeglasses clean, and like Margaret's her vision is poor. I speak, you must perceive, of Julia and of her vision. Shall I speak also of her visions?

    Could Margaret be out there on the road to Concord? Could the goddess Flora? Could the divine Leila? Could the divine Isis? Could Margaret's own ghost and Julia's father's ghost be hastening or loitering as they make their way to visit the ghost of Emerson in Concord? Why should the ghosts and the gods reappear on this day and in this place?

    In this place Julia's current roommate is one hundred three years old, but despite a sometimes joyful and sometimes pugnacious and sometimes peaceful and sometimes mischievous and sometimes tender and sometimes truculent and sometimes troubled translucence in her pallid face, she is far from ghostly. Even though she can no longer walk without support and can barely stand or hear or see, under her short white puffy curls some spirit fully alive, usually realistic, occasionally hallucinatory, still dwells in her old head. Yet, or therefore, it is not Edith who turns Julia's head towards the ghosts and gods processing or recessing today between Cambridge and Concord. Flora's brightly many-flowered robe, Leila's glisteringly black-and-white cloak, impinge upon her eye. Louis's ghost must have flown over from the grave in Newport, Rhode Island, and Margaret's must have floated along from her monument in Mount Auburn Cemetery. The breezes blow. But can Louis Budenz and Margaret Fuller blow in on the selfsame wind?

Julia has been scheming to relinquish her self and family and times and outlooks, substituting Margaret's life for her own. On the twenty-third of May in the year eighteen ten, what gusts or wisps of wind blew through Cherry Street in Cambridge? What breezes blow? They reach Julia if a window is opened, but Julia's self seems unchanged. Insofar as she has a self, insofar as she is a self — and how far that insofar extends she does not know — her self is hers and not Margaret's. On Julia and on Margaret the breezes may blow. Do they blow Margaret to Julia at the nursing home?

The breezes and the ghosts may be processing or recessing, but Julia is obviously regressing. Yet this is supposed to be a place of rehabilitation. And Julia during the restless nights senses herself, at least sometimes, placed between the self and the universe. Is this not a cosmic situation? She feels herself set between or participating in or conscious of the microcosm and the macrocosm. Deeper and deeper into the one she contracts; higher and higher into the other she expands.

Where are the gods and the ghosts? They are in the paracosm. They are of the poem. If they exist for Julia, they exist above all in the poem. Yet it is not necessary that they exist. What is necessary is that the poem exist. The poem ought to be processing or recessing between Cambridge and Concord. The poem is regressing. The poem can scarcely stand. The poem is ceasing to exist. For it the cherry trees blossom in vain. For it the roses may never bloom again. Are Flora's Roman roses now blooming anew in Rome? In the final quires of Flora's final book there might be no rose gardens, there might be no cherry trees, there might be no Flora except for me, a dandelion in the grass, a little clover blossom in the grass, a strip of grass trampled into a narrow path, a bulb too close to the surface stricken by hours of ice, not florabund or florebund or floribund but moribund, a heavy dead word, a lifeless light thin word that blows like a sterile fringe of pollen, like a dry edge of dry leaf picked up by the April wind from winter.

Love,
Flora

No. 284

                                    Cambridge, April 28 – May 3
                                    Floralia

Dear Margaret,

Over there, across the road, lilacs blossom
The perfect lilac purple of purple lilacs
Assuredly fragrant as radiant they rise.

The window bears no bars, but this is my prison.

If it were in the paracosm
That the lilacs bloomed
I would be able to smell them,

But since they are real I cannot.

                                      Love,
                                      Julia

No. 285

Cambridge, May 3
Floralia VI

Dear Margaret,

If only the meanness had a meaning. Of the meanness I will no longer speak. Of the meaning I will inquire only if there is something to inquire about.

Have I sacrificed everything for the sake of something before which my utter devotion crumbles now that the sacrifice is being accepted? As my body and my mind disintegrate, cannot their fragile remnants continue to be consumed until there is nothing that remains to be consumed? Cannot they be gloriously consumed? Can their work be act and passion in the self and in the universe? Am I still Miriam of the Lamb of God? What would you say to me about your beloved Iphigenia?

From the altar may there arise and spread and bless an incense as of lilacs. Whether it is worthy or whether it is unworthy, whether it disappears or whether it persists, it is a consummation. It is my offering to the cosmos. It is my joy in being and in having been. It is my fullest joy in knowing and in having known. It is my greatest joy in making and in having made.

If only the meaning has a meaning.

Love,
Julia

No. 286

Cambridge, May 12

Dear Leila,

Sacrifice
Laughter

Relaxation
Rapture

Passion
Pasture

Action
Azure

Song
Longing

The laughter
The longing

The sacrifice
The song

Love,
Flora

No. 287

> Cambridge, May 23
> The Birth of Sarah Margaret Fuller, 1810
> The Birth of Julia Mairin Budenz, 1934

Dear Margaret,

    I honor your epic.

    I honor your birth.
    I honor your life.
    I honor your writing.
    I honor you the writer.
    Be the writer!
    I honor the writing which I term your epic.
    I honor that November day, the last day of its writing, when it kept spinning out beneath your hand, when after your long walk on a noble exhilarating morning you sat down to write and did not put the last stroke till near nine in the evening.
    I honor that moment, near nine in the evening, when you felt a delightful glow as if you had put a good deal of your true life into what you had written.
    I honor your true life.
    I honor your epic, into which you put so much of it.

    I honor your epic of man and of woman, your epic of woman.

Of man and woman as you sing of them
I sing. Of woman as more singable,
As more unsung, I run behind you singing.
I run behind your epic holding on
To its unfoldings and its folds. I take
The measure of your footprint on the strand
Of this great world of time, of time before,
Of aftertime.

I run? I cannot run.
Neither my body nor my mind, which both
Used to go sprinting through the golden breeze
Seeming to skim the earth and feel the sky,
Can do more than with effort heavily
And slowly put one foot or put one thought
After one slowly, heavily, with effort,
Put. I can scarcely wish to move, walk, think.
I hold? My hands, my intellect, enfeebled,
Numb, and arthritic, can no longer hold
Things good and true and beautiful which once
They held or which I deemed or dreamed they held.
Can I hold on? How long can I hold on?
What measure can I take? How can I sing
With crackling, cracking, vapid voice, these lips
Listless and dry, this brevity of breath?
What measure can I take, what measure make,
Of you, of me, of prints of giant steps
Upon the endless shore, of baby steps
That wobble as they try to follow after?

Men step into the large footprints of man.
Throughout the long evolving centuries
Man has been the hero. Men have followed.
Men try and fail and tend to fall away.
Yet man has been a prince, a Hercules
Giving his mortal portion to the fire,
Then welcomed by the gods, an Orpheus
Unfettered sailing singing past the Sirens,
Untempted by enchantment that degrades,
Absorbed in art, fixed on philosophy,
Commissioned as a giver of the laws
Of nature moved to music and revealed
In hymns that told the secrets of the world,
Of nature seen deep in the mind of God.
But now Eurydice will find her voice
And call forth Orpheus, for woman is
                              The other

The other half of the same thought as man,
The other chamber of the heart of life,
Taking her turn now in the full pulsation,
A hero then. The earth waits for her queen.
We hope to see and reach the palace home.

Margaret, you dare to see and strive. I tremble.
Margaret, you dare to see and stride. I stumble.

Nevertheless I witness the procession
Of heroes stepping fleetly in your footsteps,
Or maybe you are following in theirs,
Studying and singing of their path,
Registering the catalogue of women.
Here, to begin my register of yours,
Are those with whom your catalogue is ended,
Women of intellect and of the pen,
Two prisoners of sickness, heroines
Of health: Miss Barrett and Miss Martineau.
Can such as these be heroines, be heroes?
These are old maids. "Miss" is ridiculous
As title for a warrior, a commander,
A virile man who lives and dies in glory.
Women of intellect and of the pen
Can beam the lamp of life from their prison window,
Illumining the nations. They grow old
As trees grow old, replete with grace and honor.
Age brings maturity and not decay
To such as these. For them to make their thoughts
Available they do not need health, youth,
Personal presence reaching with its charms.
Their hair turns white, their eye stays clear, their mind
Reaches our mind, their art brings strength and comfort
To sick and well, and from their lonely chamber
They see the glories of the universe.

I will, though sick in body and in mind,
Gaze toward the glories of the universe.
I will, I Ms. Budenz, I Miss Budenz,
Strive for the heroism of those Misses,
Barrett and Martineau, who emulate
Minerva, virile, feminine, artistic,
Wise, strong, quick, bold, bright, intellectual,
Warrior, weaver, virgin, victorious.
I plead with the fates to grant to my decay
Maturity of study, writing, art,
Courage to suffer, struggle, sweetly smile,
Not take myself too seriously yet make
My selfhood and that more essential self,
My poem, however poor these poor selves be,
My cosmic fact as long as they perdure,
Though sad or saccharine, my happiness,
My smile, my glad gift given to existence.
The application may be trivial.
When, after exile two months long, I found
Myself at home once more and, all alone,
Began to make the evening meal, I found
The kitchen sink clogged up, the drainpipe leaking.
I could have wept, but laughed, the analogy
With body and with mind proved so exact:
The plumbing of my body clogged or leaking,
Leaking or clogged the plumbing of my mind.
I plead with the fates to grant what you envisaged,
Margaret, instead: the springs of immortal refreshment
Unsealed within the soul. I will, I will,
Transformed, survive a little longer, drink
From springs of truth and beauty, rise from depths
To heights, from source to airy fountain,
From darkest twists of labyrinthine mine
To bright wide outspread radiance of sky.

I sound like the younger William Ellery Channing,
Emerson's friend, your sister Ellen's husband,
Poet to some, to others poetaster.
I sound like Philip James Bailey in his epic *Festus*.

I want to sound of you and of your epic.
I want to sound with you, to sing with you,
To think with you, to understand with you,
To hold your sky-blue banner with my hand,
Your blood-red carbuncle within my heart.
What Muse can help me in my echoing,
In my analysis, in my complete
Response? I bow my head and shade my eyes.
I peer up timidly and with despair
And shame to glimpse our comrades, our companions,
Our Homer, Virgil, Dante, Tasso, Milton,
Wordsworth. And shall I droop down to the dust,
Forever fix my vision on the ground?
Stars for me darken, flowers for me fade.

Margaret, what deities shall I invoke?

Goddess Flora, of the noontide bright,
Speak to me the language of the flowers,
Their hues, their shades, their shapes,
Their mixtures, textures, fragrances.

Goddess Leila, of the midnight black,
Speak to me the language of the stars,
Their sparklings, solitudes,
Shared patterns, figures, flagrances.

Margaret, these guardians as Muses spoke.

Fixed seems the stillness of the nocturnal heaven.
Within are stars ascending, stars descending.

Fixed seems the softness of the deep purple flower.
Irises are descending, are ascending.

Motion and rest, rest and motion,
Fire and air and earth and ocean,

Purple, red, orange, yellow, green,
And blue list things unseen, things seen.

I do not list the evils of my present
That shake my hopes for self and for the earth
And for the very universe, as then,
More than a century and a half ago,
While you were writing in eighteen forty-four
And publishing in eighteen forty-five
(Forgive the prosiness of my account,
For what pentameters accommodate
The prose of politics and government
Or of the plainest moral verity
Abstracted from the passion of the present?),
The threatened choice by president and people,
The Texan annexation, shook your hope
Of freedom and equality for all,
Woman and man and slave and citizen
In these United States, whose destiny
Was prophesied and promised, and for each
Human inhabitant throughout the world.
All are born free and equal: This is pledged
And this must be, you cried, and called on women,
Las exaltadas, as its moral makers,
As the preservers and as the advancers
Of the foundation set in space and time.

But here in space and time we stop, I stop,
For here it is, your bicentennial,
And I, though home at last, am weak, am ill.
I cannot stride with joy to Cherry Street
To celebrate the spot where you were born
Into this world of Cambridge and the cosmos
Or stroll delightedly up to Mount Auburn

                                                    To honor

To honor you among the boles and blossoms
Of that great garden. At your monument
I will not stand to read my poem for you
Before the crowd. I cannot read my poem
Of you to anyone except to you
As memory and present inspiration,
Or to your ghost as presence, aspiration,
Imagination. Shall I offer blood,
My blood, and hear you speak and speak with you?

Are you a vampire, some malevolent
Actor, or, passive, ineffectual,
A bloodless shade, a beggar without voice,
Greedy for gifts of recall and of converse,
A bloodless shade waiting beside the pit,
Or, unadmitted to the underworld,
Wandering graveless, waiting for burial,
Elpenor, Palinurus, Lycidas,
Shelley, unresting on the whelming wave,
Resting unresting on the unresting wave,
Desert of dust, and mountainside of ice,
Ever in motion, ever motionless,
Once living, therefore mortal, therefore dead,
Or literary, metaphorical,
The sound of words, a paragraph, a page,
A volume bound and slowly opening,
And yet a prophet, father, mother, friend,
Tiresius, Anchises, Anticleia,
Antigone, Cassandra, Agamemnon,
Deiphobus, Achilles, Hector, Glaucus,
Antiope, Alcmena, Leda, Tyro,
Musaeus, Tasso, Sappho, Saint-Martin,
Aspasia, Eloisa, Ratchewaine,
Panthea, Portia, Countess Colonel Plater,
Heroine in the Polish Revolution,
The Countess Zinzendorf, a fellow pilgrim
In the Count's mission, moral, practical,
Thinking, intelligent, with noble gifts
                                        Of mind,

Of mind, of manner, of deep character,
The nun, the Ursuline, the quietist,
Guyon, De Stael, creator of Corinne,
Writer, the splendor of whose intellect,
If flawed, if tainted, yet beams warmth and light
Into the most obscure New England schoolhouse,
Upon the little girls on their wooden bench,
Semiramis, Elizabeth of England,
Catherine of Russia, Isabelle of Spain,
Mary Stuart, Mary Wollstonecraft,
Mrs. Carter, Madame Dacier,
Madame Roland, Queen Emma, Saint-Simon,
Boehme, the Chippewa woman betrothed to the Sun,
Aztec Marina, seeress Frederica,
Grand Duchess Amelia, Lady Rachel Russell,
Lucy, the wife of Colonel Hutchinson,
Who looked out from the window of the Tower
And watched her husband carted to the scaffold,
Beatrice Cenci, Vittoria Colonna,
Joanna Southcott, Anne Lee, Channing, Kinmont,
Godiva, Boadicea, and the victim
Heroines, heroes' daughters, one the child
Of Agamemnon, Iphigenia, one
Macaria, the child of Hercules,
Sacrificed, sacrificing, girlhood, self,
Offering self in selfless sacrifice,
Like whom in what in them is excellent,
Womanly, manly, human, and divine,
Apollo, Jupiter, Minerva, Muse,
Vulcan, artistic, caring, dedicated,
Strong, feeling, intellectual, you might
Be visited as shades are visited
Or visit as a spirit deigns to visit,
Be visited by me or visit me,
Be spoken to by me and speak to me?

You are the poet and the heroine
And the consulted ghost of your own lay,
Myth, sermon, prophecy. Will you not drink
As ghost my sacrificial blood, that blood
Black in my pen, and drinking deeply draw
From possibility reality
In and beyond the world? Will I not drink
The stream still ever flowing from the heights
Of your thought?

      You thought and sought and you did find
The depths and elevations of your thinking,
Of your own mind. You sought and you did find.
You found great spirits that could speak to you,
Swedenborg and Fourier and Goethe,
Beethoven, Michelangelo, and Petrarch,
And more that thronged about you, men and women
Who wrote. They wrote with words, with shapes, with sounds.
These are the ghosts.

    Today I cannot go
To seek your ghost where others go to seek it,
Fluttering through the room where you were born
Or hovering around your cenotaph.

Yet somewhere, somehow, I must greet that ghost
In Cambridge on this anniversary,
And somehow, somewhere, I must celebrate
The birth of the hero.

     Shall Miranda serve
As version of this personage, you be
That of which she is representative?
Child early led to feel herself a child
Of the spirit, child who easily took her place
Not only in the world of organized being
But in the world of mind, a living mind,
The temple of immortal intellect,
             Never

Never a plaything, granted by her father
In so far as he himself possessed them,
Keys to the wonders of this universe:
Such is Miranda in your narrative,
Such are you in my story of your story.

Today, this twenty-third of May, I must
Enter your story, both your history
And the attendant myth. On Follen Street
And all about its entrances and exits
And portions of the nearby avenues
Shall I not both encounter your dear spirit
And honor your nativity? I look,
I listen. Sunlight gleams and breezes whisper.

The Follens and then, after you had perished,
Mary and, for a while, Elizabeth
Peabody and the widowed Mary's sons,
Her children by the late great Horace Mann,
Resided on the lovely Follen Street.
They all have vanished. Or do they, do you,
Subtly remain? Who peers from purple windows?
Who cons the purple shade of every iris?

Let us see or let us hear
Or let us hear and see

Robins throbbing trilling thrilling,
Doves uttering loves spelling telling,

Locust trees in lofty
Elegant conversation
As their tall slender bodies
Standing straight or gracefully inclining
And as their syllables in pendent blossoms
White and high and light and light and airy
Showering sweetness
Enhance their talk among themselves
Entrance us sharing from below,

The dark red kisses of the rosebuds
Widening into the pink and white of smiles,

The purple clematis with those eight-pointed stars,
These pure white parasols of mountain laurel.

Margaret, I praise your birth on this your day
With the solarity of earth and heaven,
Sidereality of heaven and earth,
Immersion and expansion in this May.

Margaret, I ponder what your ghost will say.
Let my life be beautiful, powerful, complete.
With one more moment to live I would wish the same.
Like you I will select the epic way.

You speak from both the present and the past,
This minute and the written words that last,
Printed and housed and reaching out to me,
Of *Woman in the Nineteenth Century*.

Love,
Julia

No. 288

Cambridge, May 23
Feriae Volcano

Dear Miranda,

Woman in the Nineteenth Century, as you must know by now, is denominated an epic by Julia Budenz in a letter written to Margaret Fuller earlier on this very day. In her epic Margaret prophesies a future in which human beings will attain community of life and consciousness of mind, will enter upon the liberty of law and the harmony of common growth. Then Apollo will sing to his lyre what Vulcan forges on the anvil, and the Muses weave anew the tapestries of Minerva.

In writing to you on this festival of Vulcan, I want to supplement what Julia was expressing to Margaret. I want to write about epic, about gods and heroes, heroines and goddesses, sacrifices and games, liberty and harmony, consciousness and community. I wonder how you will react. Please wait patiently. Even today I may manage to trumpet something or to timbrel something, to finger and hammer or to finger and shuttle or to finger and pluck. Wait for the multiflora rose. There is much too much, but wait for what there may be.

Love,
Florinda

No. 289

> Cambridge, May 23
> TUBILUSTRIUM

Dear Mariana,

There are lives, and there are letters.
There are births, and there are birthdays.
There are authors. There are actors.
There are heavens, hells, and earthways.

> Love,
> Miriam

No. 290

Cambridge, May 23
Ricorrenza

Dear Leila,

Over the roses,
Over the oaks,
Into the bluest sky,
Julia will go,
Or will it be I?

Love,
Flora

No. 291

                                              Cambridge, May 23
                                              Recurrence

Dear Leila,

Will it be into the roses?
Will it be into the oaks?
Will it be over the azure sky?
Will Julia truly, beautifully, go?
Will it be May or June or July?
Will Julia be
There then with me?

                                                         Love,
                                                        Flora

No. 292

>Cambridge, May 23
>Ricorrenza

Dear Leila,

Before my gaze
Gleam yellow, red, and blue,
The good and then the true
And then the beautiful.
Nevertheless, of these
Solely those sparkling two
For me are even almost possible:
Tremor of truth and burst of beauty, muse
And muse of all my days.
If only then I could
Hope that my heart might hold the good,
Might give the good.

>Love,
>Flora

No. 293

> Cambridge, May 23
> Recurrence

Dear Leila,

The more it is not poetry,
The more it is sheer prose,
The more it is mere verse,
The more I through the century
Do spur my candid horse
To pass and pass,
But like an ass,
But like an aureate ass,
It stops for the rose.

> Love,
> Flora

No. 294

                                      Cambridge, May 23
                                      Ricorrenza

Dear Leila,

To fit what is
I change the name
From poem to work,
From work to game.

There is no artistry.
Here is confession.
There is no honored genre.
Here is obsession.

There is no beautiful.
There is no true.
Here is no goodness.
Here is what I do.

                                      Love,
                                      Flora

No. 295

> Cambridge, May 23
> Recurrence

Dear Leila,

No, the sky opens. Hold.
There,
As is
Dawn red,
Noon blue,
It is,
As if
Sunset
Must be glimpsed in gold.

> Love,
> Flora

No. 296

                                      Cambridge, May 23
                                      Ricorrenza

Dear Leila,

Oh, the abstract, the ideal.
Ah, those amative abstractions.
Theory, my friend, is green.
Love, my love, I said to my love, glints purple.
Even if a mind be gray,
It will play.
It will hum.
It will eat
The amiable peach,
The amatory orange, the enamoring plum,
Juicy ideas of satisfactions.
Although the colors go unseen,
The mind will reach
The pure intellectual treat.
How can the great complexities be simple?
Oh, the more real than the real.

                                                    Love,
                                                   Flora

No. 297

Cambridge, May 23

Dear Mariana,

The beaten body
Of the donkey
With the human
Brain inside
That tries to say
I think I am
Can only bray

Love,
Miriam

No. 298

Cambridge, May 23

Dear Margaret,

What do they see
Who gaze at me?

The long-eared ass?
The greener grass?

What do I fear
Who plainly hear?

What do I feel
Who graze the real?

Love,
Julia

No. 299

Cambridge, May 23

Dear Leila,

If I feast my eyes
On the gorgeous glorious goddess
Isis, the good, the wise,

Must I stand there asinine,
Must I kneel initiated,
Must I function as the fine

Player of a complicated game
Or as the hero of an outrageous novel
Or as a heroine of epic fame?

Love,
Flora

No. 300

Cambridge, May 23

Dear Margaret,

Wie schön, o Mensch, mit deinem Palmenzweige
Stehst du. Is this the invocation standing
Behind the epigraph that is a prologue
To what I call your epic? Man, you gleam
Free through reason, strong through laws,
Through meekness great, and rich through treasures
Which long your bosom held concealed from you.

Wie schön, o Mensch. This is the opening.
Even if you do not agree with all,
Margaret, your lines are verses seven to nine
Of the first stanza of the many stanzas
That constitute the poem which you cite,
Though my speech must be strictly unpoetic.
The whole initial stanza sounds like this:

As lines are heard and beats are heard and rhymes

1	5	a
2	4	a
3	4	b
4	5	c
5	5	c
6	3	b
7	4	d
8	4	d
9	5	e
10	5	f
11	5	f
12	6	e

Schönheit or Wahrheit sings forth with such chimes.

Hearing all this we can call out with you,
Though my speech must be skew and still prosaic.
Just as you willed to pluck another's song,
We sacrifice our verses to another's
That we may comprehend your invocation
To human being, human person, human,
To man, to hero, doer, thinker, artist.

Yet fully to invoke and understand,
Poetry, German, Schiller, Schiller's *Artists*,
Vocabulary, tense, case, punctuation
Must stand behind our reading and before
Our minds. Rich treasures must not lie concealed.
Without the language can we grasp the matter?
Can we be grand without the grammar?

Love,
Julia

No. 301

Cambridge, May 23

Dear Margaret,

"Mrs Farrar has given me Schiller's works,"
You wrote from Boston to James Freeman Clarke in Kentucky.
You had just been spending ten very happy days
At Mrs Farrar's harmonious home in Cambridge
And there had received Clarke's two good letters.
It was October eighth of eighteen thirty-three,
During an escape from the isolation of Groton.

"I was delighted," you wrote to Clarke of the gift.
"After all I think I can get
More intimate with my dead than with my living friends."
Have I been, can I be, intimate with you,
Writer whose writing I have read, I can read,
Spirit who famously haunted Henry James,
Ghost to whom in Cambridge I come close?

Love,
Julia

No. 302

Cambridge, May 23

Dear Margaret,

"Schiller does not thrill but he exalts us."
Did you write this in your private journal?
"Moral force is commensurate with
His intellectual gifts, & nothing more."
If I can only grow well and strong enough
To go to Houghton will I be able to know you?
Broken in branch and bole will I ever know?
Thrilled by rose and sky will I ever thrill?

Love,
Julia

No. 303

Cambridge, May 23

Dear Margaret,

Your letters are never addressed to me,
But I read them as if they are.

"She left nothing behind her," wrote Henry James,
"Her written utterance being naught."

"What comes up is the wonderment of *why*
She may," James asked himself, "be felt as haunting."

She would, he pondered, "doubtless have been surprised
To know that talk may be still" (it was nineteen three),

"After more than half a century, made about her."
Is your writing heard today? It is twenty ten.

I think now of your letters, not addressing
The five books published during your too-short life.

I do not now begin to count or mention
Your articles in periodicals.

I seek now not deep thoughts, profound emotions.
These I will speak of further in my future

If this, that future, lasts for me, for you,
As yours, for me, endured two centuries.

Schiller is on my mind now. Schiller was
On yours, in yours, and in your words and works

Often. Your letters speak to me of this
Often. I read, I hear, but copyright

Infringes on my liberty to copy.
This copyright is not yours, is not mine.

I sit in silence reading as your letters
Keep speaking loudly, silently, to me.

Your letters speak to me of Schiller's *Artists*,
Which as my letters show is on my mind,

Which as your letters show I must acknowledge
As more to you than just an epigraph.

Efforts, despairs, accomplishments all mingle
As sometimes summer, winter, spring in May.

May thirteenth, eighteen thirty-seven, Groton.
Back from teaching in Boston.
Autograph letter, signed M. F.
Massachusetts Historical Society.
FL 6.292–296.
To James Freeman Clarke (1810–1888).

"I have now been at home ten days and am still quite unwell, yet, I think, better and growing better."

"I will try to tell you what I have done with my classes in the way of study."

"With my more advanced pupils I read . . . Schiller's Don Carlos, Schiller's artists and Song of the Bell besides one lesson in wh I gave a sort of lecture on Schiller . . . ."

May thirty-first, eighteen thirty-seven, Groton.
About to leave for teaching in Providence.
Autograph letter, signed S. M. Fuller.
Boston Public Library.
FL 1.280–281.
To John Sullivan Dwight (1813–1893).

"Miss Tuckerman writes me that you are desirous to know what I have done in the way of translation. I am truly ashamed when I think of my large promises and small performance."

"My book of translations is but a sorry sight . . . ."

"I have translated great part of Das Ideal und das Leben, and about half of die Künstler, but I am altogether dispirited by the result and cannot, at present, summon courage to go on."

September twenty-seventh, eighteen forty-four, Cambridge.
About to leave for journalism in New York.
Autograph letter, signed S. Margaret Fuller.
Cambridge Public Library.
FL 3.231–232.
To Sarah Hodges (1825–1910).

"I am highly gratified with this mark of regard from your Aunt and yourself."

"The desk is the very thing of all in the world I should be most pleased to receive."

"In Goethe the Iphigenia and Tasso would now reward your patient attention and the thoughtful poems by Schiller, such as 'The Artist,' stimulate the thinking powers."

And you go on to grow, to know and know,
To write and write, to publish and to publish.

What can I write before I write no further?
What can I read before I read no longer?

What can I learn before I learn no better?
What can I know before I know no more?

Soon may I tell what you have been, have done.
Soon may I say what you have said, have written.

Love,
Julia

No. 304

> Cambridge, November 2
> All Souls

Dear Margaret,

Is knowing growing in my soul?
Clouds are expanding in the heavens.
Cancer is growing in my flesh.

Is noon suffused with blue and gold?
My mind is rising to the sky.
Beauty is growing in my heart.

> Love,
> Julia

No. 305

                Cambridge, November 3
                Departure from Ursuline Convent 1965

Dear Mariana,

Arboreal is this gold, this blue celestial.
The sky is azure clarity and blaze,
Blazing, serene, deep, tremulous in depth,
Unmoved, unmoving, on its broad bright surface.
The maples are of many golds, delightful,
Fiery, plenitudinous yet decking
The earth with ineluctable descent
Of scents, of flames of fragrance, of a real
Substantial and ethereal, departing.
Does the sky, too, descend, touch us, depart,
Leaving a fragmentation in the heart?

Did Julia leave her Blithedale on this day,
Beneath a nebulous, a nubilous,
Novembrian New England heaven, upon
A dimming, darkening, New England earth,
Leaving behind, not in a riverbed
But in the dry constriction of a cell,
The long black veil, the long black robe with long
Wide sleeves that reached far past the reach of hands
And long serge skirt that brushed black-polished shoes,
Leaving the crucifix, thick leather belt,
Big dangling rosary, gold wedding ring?
She had been wedded to her lord and king.

Should fact with fiction intermingle? Fiction
Inhabits its own world. Fact interferes
Harshly, obtrusively. And yet the master
Permits his personage, Miles Coverdale,

                                          Within

Within his fiction, novel, or romance,
To be handed a letter from Miss Margaret Fuller,
Living and active in the fictional
Time of the novel, dead, drowned, by the time
Of the novel's writing and its publication.
A friend of mine, Miles says of Margaret Fuller,
One of the most gifted women of the age,
In whom there were a certain curve of the shoulders
And a partial closing of the eyes that showed
Just for a moment on the fictional
Priscilla as she held the real letter —
Or the unreal letter of the real person.
In a real letter written from Brook Farm
On the thirteenth of April in eighteen forty-one
To Sophia Peabody, his fiancée,
It was not a letter received from Margaret Fuller
That Hawthorne stressed but her irascible,
Not fictional but very factual,
Her very actual and transcendental
Cow: the historical and kicking heifer.
From Margaret Julia may expect a letter.

                              Love,
                              Miriam

No. 306

>Cambridge, November 4
>The Death of Anne Miller Whitman 1984

Dear Mariana,

How could I make myself resemble,
Priscilla asked, Miss Margaret Fuller,
Merely by holding her letter in my hand?

The cow is very fractious, Hawthorne
Believed. Sophia knew best whether
She resembled her mistress in this character.

Why should Julia ever resemble
Margaret Fuller or ever clasp
In trembling hand a letter from a ghost?

>Love,
>Miriam

No. 307

> Cambridge, November 8
> Mundus patet

Dear Margaret,

Comfort care. Do not resuscitate.
The message bold in black is now affixed
Firmly upon my white refrigerator door.

The heavens open only and descend
Now only in the gray of rain. Across
The earth a spirit stirs and breathes a gray of wind.

> Love,
> Julia

No. 308

Cambridge, November 11

Dear Leila,

Knowledge was what I pursued.
Knowledge is what I desire.

How it was I should have told.
How it is I should be telling.

What I said was how it felt.
What I reveal is how I feel.

Love,
Flora

No. 309

> Cambridge, November 13
> Iovi Epulum

Dear Leila,

Here is that blue.

Here is that blue laughing large across
The sky above.
What is above the sky above?

Here is that blue.

Here is that blue listening little in
The self within.
What is within the self within?

Here I am,

Without belief,
Without illusion,
Without (can it be?) even the ego of being,

With the minuteness,
With the immenseness,
Of the divine imagination,

With the pervasiveness,
With the persuasiveness,
Of that blue.

There is that azure.

> Love,
> Flora

No. 310

> Cambridge, December 1
> Pietati ad Circum Flaminium

Dear Margaret,

The hospital bed has arrived.
I can hear it hum.
I can pull myself up.
How high can I try to arise?

> Love,
> Julia

* * *

Section Two
Woman in the Nineteenth Century

* * *

Section Three

The Wings of the Dove

* * *

Part Four

Of Knowledge by the Tree

* * *

Standing I clasp the trunk. . . .
I reach for what I see. . . .
Do I totter?
What is there?
Does something fall?

Question?
Suspension. . . .
Infinitude.
Finis!

Part Five

Tree

Is it the strand, the shore? It is the tree.
At the edge of the spreading garden grows the beech,
Massive, now purple, green now, now all gold,
Now branching pewter, pearly now, now gemmed
And geminating needles, points that fashion
Coppery lace and proto-purple rose,
Beside the ocean or beside the sea,
Beside the river or beside the lake,
Beside the pool. And is the pool the hole
Outside the whole, a hole within the whole,
Diminutive, diminishing, still more
The less, the negative, negating, null,
The lacking, ever large in mirroring?

How shall I say this?
How shall I not say this?
Shall I not say it if I cannot say it right?
The flower is the tree is the sky,
Somehow, if only faintly, known,
Somehow, and utterly, loved,
Somehow themselves and not themselves,
Not themselves but the very selves
So known, thus loved,
Even if colorless yet of purple passion,
Even if passing yet with aureate aura,
Even if nothing all.

* * *

Part Six

Knowledge of the Tree

* * *

When I had known infinity,
When I had known eternity,
I was known by mortality.

Wandering through paradise
I tasted sweets so sweet they had
To alternate with absences,

With presences so full of pain
They proved that evil was the real
Afar and near, apart and in.

Sweets gleamed resplendent on the tree.
Deception disappointed fall.
The question was which happened to be last.

Part Seven

Of the Tree

No. 1

Is it a tentative?
Is it an end?
Is it an ecstasy?
Stretch, elm, extend . . .

No. 2

Did I not know the roses and the lilies?
Did I not con the maples and the elms?
Did I not probe the blue of blue heaven?

Did I not see
Between the minutest azure
Of a Cambridge garden's flowering forget-me-nots
And the immensest azure
Of unforgettable spreading Massachusetts sky
The mediation of a gray or golden tree?

No. 3

Is tree truth, tree trust?
Is there a kind of heaven,
Is there a tree of heaven,
Bloom, branch, and bole,
Growing from the soul,
No, growing far beyond the universe,
A motion and a rest,
A knowable, known tree,
What I yearned to know,
What I seemed to feel,
What I tried to tell?

No. 4

Fin. Maintenant je peux mourir.
And then a few lines more.
The golden breeze.

Flos, caelum, arbor, aura aurea.
The golden rose. The sky.
The golden breeze. The tree.

The terrible tremendous love.
The tree. The sheen.
The tree of the knowledge of the sheen.

No. 5

The golden breeze plays playful in the foliage.
Graceful, gracious, the maples and the elms
Play the game that is the dance that is the oratorio.
Squills, hyacinths, hydrangeas, morning glories
Engage in antiphons with the sky.

This is a picture.
Paintings do not have conclusions.
I have watched five gardens wanting to bloom.
The tree is an epic without an end.
The beauty is breaking my heart.

No. 6

Where candles flicker you can get burned.
Where constellations glimmer you might aspire.
It was the lamp that told the truth.
It was the sky that blessed the love.
Psyche knows Amor at last.

No. 7

The golden breeze. The golden bough.
The gate of ivory. The gate of horn.
When I go in will I come out again?
Now come the dreams.

No. 8

O all ye that pass by the way,
I, Flora, have been authorized to say
That Julia, my author, is ready to be ended.
She pleads, yet, that I may
Last centuries, outlast her little day,
Be amaranth. Take, read. Be not offended.

Index of Titles

A FERRAGOSTO LA ROBINIA DEL
 GIAPPONE A CAMBRIDGE NEL
 MASSACHUSETTS 3:441
A PARLAR DE' SUOI SEMPRE VERDI RAMI
 3:439
Aceraceae (*section title*) 4:100
Adam 2:39
Adaptation 1:63
Advent 1:96
Advent: December 4, 2004 4:409
Aeneas in Carthage: December
 1, 2004 / Pietati ad Circum
 Flaminium 4:406
Aeneid: July 2005 / Attollens umero
 famamque et fata nepotum. 4:520
Aeneid: July 2005 / Per superos atque
 hoc caeli spirabile lumen . . . 4:521
Aeneid: July 2005 / Prouehimur portu
 terraeque urbesque recedunt.
 4:517
Aestivation 2:35
Affect and Effect 1:73
After Compline, January 6 2:95
Afterward 1:68
Again Bright, Gray 3:418
Agan, Again: January 18–19, 2004
 4:301
Agonalia: January 9, 2004 4:294
Aition 2:26
AL SUON DE' DETTI 3:449
Alexandrians: November 17, 2004
 4:402
All that I loved is lost or will be lost.
 5:73

ALLA SALUTE 3:455
Allegory 1:16
Alles Epithymies 2:120
Amor 3:5
An azure 5:148
Anamnestic 1:116
Anapneusis 1:69
And January 3:722
Anima 1:59
Animation 2:37
Anne, Bronze, Gold 3:419
Anniversary —
 February 15, 2007 / In Memory of
  Billy Carr 4:559
 March 21, 2002 4:190
 April 13, 2000 / In Memory of
  Nadya Aisenberg 4:125
 May 12, 2000 / In Memory of
  Daniel Von Dwornick 4:126
 August 22, 2004 / Polly / Mary
  French Freeman / Mrs. Robert
  Tibbetts Blazo / . . . / Mary
  Freeman 4:386
 October 6, 2000 / Thetis and Peleus
  4:133
 November 4, 2000 / In Memory of
  Anne Miller Whitman 4:143
Another Chance 4:101
Anthe —
 February 15, 2004, m. 4:324
 February 27, 2005 4:462
 May 7, 2002 4:195
 May 8, 2002 4:196
 June 7, 2001 4:155

Anthe (continued)
  June 16, 2004 / Cras veniet vestris ille secundus aquis. 4:354
  July 1, 2005 4:504
  November 2, 2003 4:277
  November 29, 2006 / Vigil of St. Andrew 4:547
  November 30, 2006 / Feast of St. Andrew 4:548
  December 3, 2006 / First Sunday of Advent 4:549
  December 19, 2000 4:144
  December 19, 2004 4:417
Anthe's Dance 2:125
Anthe's Hand 2:124
Anthem: August 30, 2004 4:395
Aphrodite: November 16, 2004 4:401
Apollo: February 19, 2004 4:330
Apollo: July 13, 2005 4:522
Apollo: November 13, 2004 4:398
Apollo: December 23, 2003 / Il. 15.355–366 4:284
APPENDICE: LEONARDO OLSCHKI E L'USIGNUOLO DI COLOMBO 3:448
April 3:687
April 1 4:96
ARBOR 3:418
ARBOR VICTORIOSA 3:438
Archaeology 4:36
ARDOR 3:415
As it becomes more difficult to live 5:116
As the water came down through the ceiling 5:125
Ashore 4:51
Asseveration 1:64
Assumption 2:41
Astronomia Nova 1:104
At 2:44
At times the measures measure out the times 5:96
Augustine 2:42

Banquet, The 1:48
Barrier 4:55
Beech 2:80
Before Liftoff 2:115
Before Vespers, August 6 2:137
Behind the Door 4:65
Behind the Mist 4:60
Bells 2:17
Benediction 3:424
BIBLIOTECA COLOMBIANA 3:453
Biding bloom is small, The 5:88
Biennial 2:140
BIOGRAFIA 3:444
Birthday Card (or A Birthday Card) —
  February 24, 2007 / Sheila Connolly 4:562
  February 26, 2002 / Justine Louise Budenz 4:181
  February 26, 2005 / Justine Louise Budenz 4:461
  March 11 – April 25, 2002 / Torquato Tasso 4:193
  March 11, 2002 / Josephine Theresa Budenz Palermo 4:184
  March 11, 2007 / Josephine Theresa Budenz Palermo 4:563
  March 19, 2002 / Minerva 4:188
  March 27, 2003 / Mary Anne Miller 4:253
  March 31, 2003 / Rose Shawfeng Wang / Mother Fidelis, O.S.U. 4:256
  April 6, 2003 / Lucas John Palermo 4:262
  April 8, 2003 / Joan Ellenbogen Geller 4:264
  April 30, 2007 / Regina Barbara Catherine Fucito Merzlak 4:568
  May 5 / Ombretta Frau 5:24
  May 23 / Julia Mairin Toledo Budenz 5:28
  June 8, 2002 / Julia Tseng Chen / Mother Angela, O.S.U. 4:203

Birthday Card (*continued*)
  June 13, 2000 / Margaret Rodgers Budenz 4:129
  July 13 / Gaius Julius Caesar 5:36
  July 17, 2000 / Louis Francis Urban Budenz 4:130
  July 17, 2005 / Louis Francis Urban Budenz 4:526
  July 20, 2004 / Francesco Petrarca 4:363
  September 19, 2001 / Nicholas Horsfall 4:173
  October 15, 2001 / Publius Vergilius Maro 4:174
  October 25 / David Perkins 5:25
  November 19, 1999 / Catherine Biggs Carpenter 4:120
  November 19, 1999 / Frederick Turner 4:122
  November 19, 1999 / Helen Degen Cohen 4:121
  November 24, 2001 / Joanna Maria Budenz Gallegos 4:175
  November 24, 2006 / Joanna Maria Budenz Gallegos 4:545
  November 24 / Joanna Maria Budenz Gallegos 5:63
  December 11 / Elaine Gillis Storella 5:19
  December 16, 1999 / Jane Austen (1775–1817) / Ludwig van Beethoven (1770–1827) / Claudia Samuels (1945–1999) 4:123
  December 16, 2001 / Cookie / Virginia Walsh / Mother John Bernard, O.S.U. / Mrs. Albert Joseph Furtwangler / Ann Copeland / Ginny 4:176
  December 23 / Alice Jane Karo 5:23
  Rome, March 13, 2001 / Mariateresa Scotti 4:148

Bis: March 11, 2004 4:336
Black Hole, A 1:111
Blessing 3:426
Blue Monday 2:61
Blue the skies. 5:141
Bounds that Let Breeze in 3:508
Breakfast: December 23, 2004 4:419
Breath 2:100
Bridge 3:490
Brief Grammar, A 3:418
BUON VIAGGIO 3:487
But what is how 5:157
By the Tree (*book part*) 5:3
By the Tree of Life 1:25
Calendar 2:18
Can I face this day? 5:118
Candle, The 1:36
Candor 2:21
Cardinal 2:22
Castle 2:76
Cell 2:52
CHIARA MATRAINI 3:475
CHIAROSCURO 3:477
Child and Parent: July 2005 4:515
Choir 2:56
Cinquefoil 4:61
Circumference 4:106
Clearing 1:19
Climates 2:73
Cloistering Game: May 25, 2004 4:338
Colloquium on Epic: March 11, 2005, a.m. 4:465
Comedy 3:430
Commemoration 1:112
Commencement: June 13, 2004, Ovis Idulis 4:350
Comparing 1:89
Complaint 4:62
Compleanno: May 23, 2004 4:337
CONGEDO 3:446
Consequence 1:78
Consequence: December 25, 2004 4:421

Considerations 1:60
Context 2:67
Conversations with the Italian 3:430
Cor: January 6, 2004 4:293
CORINNA O PINDARO 3:471
CORINNA, O L'ITALIA 3:471
Correction in Red 4:94
Criticism 1:61
Crockery 1:11
Crown, The 1:45
Cry of Flora Baum: June 13, 2004 /
  Quinquatrus Minusculae 4:347
Dactylography 2:153
Daedalus: July 2005 4:512
DAGLI ALBERI ALLE CASE 3:460
DAL 13 AL 14 SETTEMBRE 3:484
DALLA COROLLA AL CALICE 3:459
Darling Buds of May 2:19
Dating: Cynthia and Endymion 4:134
Day is heavy, The 5:128
Days and Deeds: July 30, 2004 4:372
De Fortuna: May 2005 4:501
De Senectute: May 2005 4:500
De Tempestate: May 2005 4:502
Death of the Author: December 9,
  2004 4:413
December 3:721
December 21 2:94
DEH PEREGRINI CHE PENSOSI ANDATE
  3:482
Delphi 2:221
Demeter 2:138
Description 4:59
Design of Flora Baum —
  April 1, 2007 / Fortunae Virili
    4:565
  April 4–10, 2007 / Ludi Matri
    Magnae 4:566
  April 21, 2007 / Parilia 4:567
  April 28 – May 3, 2007 / Ludi
    Florae 4:572
  May 1, 2007 4:569
  May 2, 2007 4:570

Design of Flora Baum (*continued*)
  May 3, 2007 4:571
Desire 4:75
Deus disintegrated. Saints dissolved.
  5:75
Deus meus, quare me dereliquisti?
  5:76
Diagram, The (*book part*) 2:151
Diary of Flora Baum —
  02/02/02 4:177
  02/22/02, Cara Cognatio 4:178
  02/23/02, Terminalia 4:179
  02/24/02, Regifugium 4:180
  03/03/03, Variae Lectiones
    4:225
  03/03/03, Videlicet 4:226
  03/03/03, Videre Licet 4:224
  January 9, 2005 / Agonalia 4:423
  January 10, 2005 / Sant' Aldo,
    Eremita 4:424
  January 11, 2005 / Carmentalia
    4:426
  January 12, 2005 / *Od.* 1.417–420
    4:427
  January 13, 2005 / *Od.* 1.443–444
    4:428
  January 14, 2005 / Saturn's Titan
    4:429
  January 15, 2005 / Carmentalia
    4:430
  January 16, 2004 4:298
  January 16, 2005 / Almost
    Midnight 4:435
  January 16, 2005 / Sunday
    Afternoon 4:432
  January 16, 2005 / Sunday Evening
    4:433
  January 16, 2005 / Sunday Night
    4:434
  January 16, 2005 / The Eighth Day
    4:431
  January 17, 2005 / *Od.* 11.487–491
    4:437

Diary of Flora Baum (*continued*)
  January 17, 2005 / St. Anthony
    4:436
  January 17, 2005 / Webster 4:438
  January 18, 2005 / Factors 4:442
  January 18, 2005 / On Ice 4:440
  January 18, 2005 / On Thin Ice
    4:441
  January 18, 2005 / Theocritus, *Id.*
    16 4:443
  January 18, 2005 / Winter 4:439
  January 19, 2004 4:302
  January 19, 2005 / King Orpheus
    4:444
  January 20, 2004 4:303
  January 20, 2005 / The Eve of St.
    Agnes 4:445
  January 21, 2005 / St. Agnes 4:447
  January 21, 2007 / Feast of St.
    Agnes 4:551
  January 21, 2007 / Midnight 4:553
  January 21, 2007 / Nearing
    Midnight 4:552
  January 22, 2005 / St. Vincent
    4:448
  January 23, 2001 4:145
  January 23, 2005 / Ianualia 4:449
  January 24, 2005 / *Aen.* 6.440–476
    4:450
  January 25, 2001 4:146
  January 25, 2005 / Agonenses
    4:452
  January 26, 2005 / Resonance
    4:453
  January 27, 2005 / Castori et Polluci
    ad Forum 4:454
  January 27, 2005 / St. Angela
    Merici 4:455
  January 27, 2005 / Synthesis 4:456
  February 4, 2007 4:555
  February 5, 2007 / Feast of St.
    Agatha 4:556
  February 7, 2003 4:210

Diary of Flora Baum (*continued*)
  February 7, 2007 4:557
  February 8, 2007 4:558
  February 13, 2001 / Parentalia 4:147
  February 21, 2003 / Feralia 4:211
  February 22, 2003 / Cara Cognatio
    4:212
  February 23, 2003 / Terminalia
    4:213
  February 24, 2003 / Cum
    Tarquinius Superbus fertur ab
    urbe expulsus 4:215
  February 24, 2003 / Regifugium
    4:214
  February 25, 2003 / Argyrótox'
    4:218
  February 25, 2003 / Publish or
    Perish 4:217
  February 26, 2003 4:219
  February 27, 2003 / Equirria 4:220
  March 1, 2002 / Feriae Marti /
    Iunoni Lucinae 4:182
  March 1, 2003 / Feriae Marti 4:221
  March 1, 2003 / Feriae Marti /
    Iunoni Lucinae Exquiliis quod
    eo die aedis ei dedicata est per
    matronas 4:223
  March 1, 2003 / Iunoni / Natalis
    Martis 4:222
  March 5, 2002 4:183
  March 6, 2003 4:227
  March 7, 2003 / Sanctae Perpetua
    et Felicitas / Carthage, 203
    4:231
  March 7, 2003 / Vediovis inter
    Duos Lucos 4:228
  March 9, 2003 / Santa Francesca
    Romana / First Sunday of Lent /
    Arma Ancilia Moventur 4:232
  March 11, 2003 / 459th Birthday of
    Torquato Tasso 4:233
  March 11, 2003 / Two 4:234
  March 11, 2003 / Worlds 4:235

Diary of Flora Baum (*continued*)
  March 12, 2003 / Three 4:238
  March 12, 2003 / True Confession 4:237
  March 12, 2003 / Wednesday in the First Week of Lent 4:236
  March 13, 2003 4:239
  March 15, 2003 / Annae Perennae 4:240
  March 18, 2002 / Afterward 4:187
  March 18, 2003 / Plenilunium 4:243
  March 19, 2003 / Quinquatrus / Feriae Marti / Minervae 4:244
  March 20, 2002 / Spring 4:189
  March 20, 2003 / Equinox 4:245
  March 21, 2003 / Equinox 4:246
  March 22, 2003 / Saturday 4:247
  March 23, 2003 / Lutatius quidem clavam eam ait esse in ruina Palati incensi a Gallis repertam qua Romulus Urbem inauguraverit 4:251
  March 23, 2003 / Quinquatribus Ultimis 4:252
  March 23, 2003 / Sunday 4:249
  March 23, 2003 / Tubilustrium 4:248
  March 23, 2003 / Twilight 4:250
  March 25 4:95
  March 31, 2003 / Lunae in Aventino 4:254
  March 31, 2003 / Monday 4:257
  March 31, 2003 / Pridie Kalendas Aprilis 4:258
  April 3, 2003, Thursday 4:259
  April 4, 2003 / Ludi Matri Magnae 4:260
  April 6, 2003 4:261
  April 7, 2003 4:263
  April 9 4:97
  April 12, 2003 / Ludi Cereri 4:265
  April 13 4:98

Diary of Flora Baum (*continued*)
  April 13, 2003 / Atrium Libertatis 4:271
  April 13, 2003 / Iovi 4:270
  April 13, 2003 / Iovi Victori, Iovi Libertati / Palm Sunday 4:266
  April 13, 2003 / Ovis Idulis / Iovis Fiducia 4:269
  April 13, 2003 / Passion Sunday 4:267
  April 13, 2003 / The Ides of April 4:268
  April 14, 2003 / Ludi Cereri / Monday in Holy Week 4:273
  April 14, 2003 / Ventus ab occasu grandine mixtus erit 4:272
  April 15, 2003 / Fordicidia 4:274
  April 24, 2005 4:467
  April 25, 2005 4:468
  April 26, 2005 4:469
  April 27, 2005 4:470
  April 28, 2005 4:471
  April 29, 2005 4:472
  April 30, 2005 4:473
  May 1, 2005 4:474
  May 2, 2005 4:475
  May 3, 2005 4:476
  May 4, 2005 4:477
  May 5, 2005 4:478
  May 6, 2005 4:479
  May 7, 2005 4:480
  May 8, 2005 4:481
  May 9, 2005 4:482
  May 10, 2005 4:483
  May 11, 2005 4:484
  May 12, 2005 4:485
  May 13, 2005 4:486
  May 14, 2005 4:487
  May 15 5:66
  May 15, 2005 4:488
  May 16, 2005 4:489
  May 17, 2005 4:490
  May 18, 2005 4:491

Diary of Flora Baum (*continued*)
  May 19, 2005 4:492
  May 20, 2005 4:493
  May 21, 2005 4:494
  May 22, 2005 4:495
  May 23 5:67
  May 23, 2005 4:496
  May 24 5:29
  May 25 5:30
  May 25 5:68
  May 31, 2004 4:343
  June 1, 2002 / Iunoni Monetae 4:198
  June 11, 2002 / Fortunae Reduci in Foro Boario 4:205
  June 11, 2004 / Matri Matutae, Fortunae Reduci 4:345
  June 13 5:31
  June 13 5:69
  June 13, 2004 / Iovi Invicto 4:349
  June 15 5:70
  June 16, 2004 / Bloomsday 4:352
  June 20, 2002 / Summano ad Circum Maximum 4:206
  June 20, 2004 / A Solstice 4:359
  June 20, 2004 / A Sunday 4:358
  June 20, 2004 / Reddita quisquis is est Summano templa feruntur ... 4:356
  June 20, 2004 / Romani veteres nescioquem Summanum ... coluerunt ... 4:357
  June 20, 2004 / Summano ad Circum Maximum 4:355
  July 5 5:32
  July 6 5:33
  July 7 5:34
  July 14, 2005 4:523
  July 15, 2005 4:524
  July 16, 2005 4:525
  July 27, 2005 / Margaret Deaumer Rodgers Budenz 4:531
  July 28, 2005 4:532

Diary of Flora Baum (*continued*)
  July 29, 2005 4:533
  July 30, 2004 / Fortunae Huiusce Diei in Campo 4:370
  July 30, 2005 4:534
  July 31, 2005 4:535
  July 31, 2005 4:537
  July 31, 2006 4:538
  August 1, 2006 4:539
  September 11 5:54
  September 21, 2006 / Publius Vergilius Maro 4:542
  October 11 5:55
  October 15, 2006 / Publius Vergilius Maro 4:543
  October 20 5:39
  October 21 5:40
  October 21, 2006 / Former Feast of St. Ursula 4:544
  October 23 5:49
  October 25 5:56
  October 26 5:5
  October 26 5:57
  October 29 5:58
  November 1, All Saints 5:60
  November 4, 2003 4:279
  November 5 5:6
  November 6 5:8
  November 8, Mundus patet 5:61
  November 11 5:62
  December 1 5:12
  December 8 5:13
  December 8, 2003 / 4:25 p.m. EST 4:280
  December 8, 2003 / 5:45 p.m. EST 4:281
  December 15, 2003 / Consualia 4:283
  December 20 5:16
  December 24, 2003 / Reflection 4:285
Delphi, Bysios 7 2:143

Diary of Flora Baum (*continued*)
    First Sunday of Advent 5:11
    Friday, June 7, 2002 / Vesta aperitur 4:202
    Friday, June 22, 2001 4:160
    Friday, June 29, 2001 4:164
    Friday, July 13, 2001 / Apollini 4:167
    Friday, July 27, 2001 4:170
    Friday, November 10 5:53
    Good Friday, April 13, 2001 4:150
    Halloween 5:59
    Kalends of Sextile / Sixth Year of President George W. Bush 4:540
    Monday, April 1, 2002 4:192
    Monday, June 3, 2002 / Venus passes 1.6° north of Jupiter 4:200
    Monday, March 17, 2003 / Liberalia, Agonalia 4:242
    Monday, March 18, 2002 4:186
    Saturday, April 21, 2001 4:151
    Saturday, June 16, 2001 / Big Sister 4:158
    Saturday, June 23, 2001 4:161
    Saturday, May 11, 2002 4:197
    Spy Wednesday, April 11, 2001 4:149
    Spy Wednesday, March 27, 2002 4:191
    Still July 7 5:35
    Sunday, March 17, 2002 4:185
    Sunday, June 2, 2002 4:199
    Sunday, June 10, 2001 4:156
    Sunday, June 17, 2001 / Monumentum 4:159
    Sunday, June 23, 2002 4:207
    Sunday, June 24, 2001 / Forti Fortunae trans Tiberim / Nativité de saint Jean-Baptiste 4:162

Diary of Flora Baum (*continued*)
    Sunday, August 5, 2001 / Saluti / Saluting / Laura Benedetti / Catherine Biggs Carpenter / Mona Harrington / David Bradford Marshall / Elaine Gillis Storella 4:172
    Sunday, 7 p.m., December 5:14
    Thanksgiving 5:9
    Thursday, July 12, 2001 / Ludi Apollinares VII 4:166
    Thursday, July 26, 2001 4:168
    Thursday, November 9 5:52
    Tuesday, April 2, 2002 4:194
    Tuesday, July 10, 2001 4:165
    Tuesday, June 26, 2001 4:163
    Tuesday, November 7 5:50
    Wednesday, April 25, 2001 4:152
    Wednesday, August 1, 2001 / Spei in Foro Holitorio 4:171
    Wednesday, December 5:15
    Wednesday, June 13, 2001 4:157
    Wednesday, June 5, 2002 / Semoni Sanco Dio Fidio in Colle 4:201
    Wednesday, June 6, 2001 4:154
    Wednesday, November 8 5:51
Did I recognize 5:159
Difference (*book part*) 1:113
Direction 1:14
Discrimination: March 2, 2005 4:464
Disintegration is also, The 5:94
DISSI 'L VER 3:439
Dominica 2:64
Doxology: August 22, 2004, Sunday 4:388
Duet: August 9, 2004 / Letitia and Flora / For Elizabeth Reeke and Julia Budenz 4:376
ECO 3:446
Effect and Cause 1:77
Elements 4:58
Eleusis 2:228
Embrace: December 8, 2004 4:412

INDEX OF TITLES

Encore: March 10, 2004 4:335
Encounter 1:20
End, The 1:26
Entry 3:87
Epiphany (*book part*) 1:31
Epiphany: January 6, 2007 4:550
Epistemology 2:132
Epistles 3:73
Epitaph 4:208
Epodes 3:63
EPPUR SI MUOVE 3:432
Equinoctial Gravitation 4:93
Equipoise 2:11
Eschato-Parousia 4:73
ET ALLARGÒ LA MANO 3:436
Eve 2:31
Even in Homer levees do not hold. 5:134
Exegesis 1:65
Exile 3:29
Fable: July 2005 4:511
FACENDOMI D'UOM VIVO UN LAURO VERDE 3:440
Facing the absolute 5:111
Fagaceae (*section title*) 4:209
Fairy Tale 1:101
FASCETTA 3:445
Father and Daughter: / Monday, January 5, 2004 4:290
February 3:673
February 29 4:89
Festschrift: December 19, 2007 / Dr. Lyle 4:579
Fifth Movement 4:536
Filament, A 2:19
Finale: March 9, 2004 4:334
Finding 1:85
Finis: March 7, 2004 4:332
Finitude: March 8, 2004 4:333
FIORI TOSCANI 3:485
Fioritura: May 30, 2004 4:341
Fire Escape, The 2:173
First Movement 4:276

Fishing 4:29
Five 5:65
Flora 2:119
Flora and Cora 2:104
Flora and the Maecenates 2:99
Flora Baum, Archaeologist 3:113
Flora Baum, Astronomer 3:110
Flora Baum, Botanist 3:9
Flora Baum, Employee 2:111
Flora Baum, Factotum 2:110
Flora Baum, Faineant 2:113
Flora Baum, Filer 2:106
Flora Baum, Geographer 3:114
Flora Baum, Historian 3:6
Flora Baum, Mathematician 3:11
Flora Baum, Secretary 2:108
Flora Baum, Shelver 2:107
Flora Baum, Student 3:115
Flora Baum, Thinker 3:6
Flora Baum, Typed 2:109
Flora Baum, Typist 2:105
Flora Baum's Curse 2:88
Flora Baum's Meditation 2:90
Flora Baum's Portrait . . . 2:121
Flora Baum's Prayer 2:89
Flora Baum's Prophecy 2:93
Flora Baum's Renunciation 2:91
Flora Baum's Thesis Proposal 3:70
Flora Baum's Vision 2:92
Flora Urania Baum 4:66
Flora: February 8, 2004 4:316
Flora: February 9, 2004 4:318
Florale 2:25
Floralia (*book part*) 3:135
Floralia: April 28 – May 3, 2001 / In Honor of Barbara Wismer McManus 4:153
Four 5:38
Fourfold Purple 1:13
Fourth Movement 4:457
FRA LOR CHE 'L TERZO CERCHIO SERRA 3:450
Fraction 1:55

Freeze and Flood 4:140
From 2:45
From the Well 1:17
Fulfilment, A 2:68
Furrinalia: July 25, 2004 / Nunc vix nomen notum paucis. 4:367
Furrinalia: July 25, 2005 4:528
Further 2:116
Futures: August 22, 2004 / Beata Virgo Maria Regina 4:387
Gambles: August 18, 2004 / Non moriar sed vivam . . . 4:385
Games: August 18, 2004 / Il. 23.373–400 4:384
Garden of Hephaestus, The 2:145
Gate 3:424
Genesis: December 4, 2004 4:408
Geography 4:28
Go to him, he is shining with beauty, she said. 5:85
Golden Bowl, The: July 21, 2004 / "Oh, splendid!" 4:364
Golden Bowl, The: July 26, 2004 / "Why, it has a crack." 4:368
Golden Rain 4:42
Golden Rose, The: July 27, 2004 / . . . the helpless regret is the barren commentary . . . 4:369
Grace 3:490
Grammar, A 4:76
Grammar of Flora Baum: June 13, 2004 / Minervae 4:348
Halley's Poem 3:427
He brought her back. 5:156
Heartwood 3:432
Heaven 1:22
Hector: February 8, 2004 4:315
Hector: February 9, 2004 4:317
Helicon 2:234
Here is some sun and some blue after days of grays and rain. 5:105
Heuristic 1:6

Hic Templum: November 19, 2004 4:405
Hierophanies 2:71
Hieros Gamos: Epiphany, 2004 4:292
His Vision 3:424
History, The (*book part*) 2:85
Homer and Ion: July 2005 4:514
Homer, too, is it 5:124
Homer, Virgil, 5:158
Homer: December 21, 2004 4:418
Homère Lyricisé 2:83
Hours of mere survival, The 5:79
How shall I say this? 5:570
Hypothesis 2:114
I Can Rarely Remember 1:7
I did not die while I stared heavenward, 5:78
I Dreamed 4:32
I Won't Say Yet 1:81
I Won't Talk of Love 4:31
Ianus: January 9, 2004 4:295
If little lovely multitudes of blossoms 5:91
If multitudes of blossoms 5:92
If the autumn anemones were nameless 5:143
IL 12 SETTEMBRE: IL SANTISSIMO NOME DI MARIA 3:484
IL BIGLIETTO 3:458
IL COLPO E LA COLPA 3:463
IL DISCORSO 3:480
IL LUSSO 3:458
IL MIO BEL VELO 3:449
IL PARADISO 3:473
IL PARTITO 3:472
IL PATRIMONIO 3:473
IL POETA 3:461
IL PURGATORIO 3:457
IL ROMANZO DI CORINNA 3:470
IL TIGLIO 3:454
Iliad (*book part*) 2:81
Illumination 2:59
Imagines: February 11, 2004 4:320

Immaculata: February 11, 2004 4:319
In my soul there is a lack. 5:138
IN PARTE OV' ERA 3:451
IN QUELLE PAROLE CHE LODANO 3:482
In September 5:147
IN SETTEMBRE LE ROBINIE DEL GIAPPONE A CAMBRIDGE NEL MASSACHUSETTS 3:481
In the Grass 4:68
In the Room 4:34
INDICE 3:444
Indulgence 2:36
Ingredients 1:80
Intentions 2:69
Intercalary 3:674
INTERMINATI SPAZI DI LÀ DA QUELLA 3:431
Interpretation 2:131
Invocation 5:27
Iris: December 14, 2003 / Il. 15.168–173 4:282
Is Anemou: December 25, 2003 4:286
Is beauty hoar, 5:137
Is it not unfeeling, 5:115
Is it the strand, the shore? It is the tree. 5:569
Is sky the end? Now here on earth 5:99
Is the smile of the roses 5:108
Is this all? Is this gracious gleam the end 5:150
Is this enough? Can that have been enough? 5:163
Is this the lore: 5:135
Isabel Again 4:38
Isabel and Kemp Owen 4:37
It is hard to imagine. 5:95
It might be March. 5:72
It Was 4:105
It Was Nice 1:88
Ithaca 2:213
January 3:519
January 5 1:28
January 6, 1 a.m. (Watch on a Shoestring) 1:33
January 6, 1 p.m. 1:51
January 6, 5 a.m. 1:34
January 6, 5 p.m. (Watch in a Pocket) 1:52
January 14 1:56
Joseph Orcome: July 2005 4:506
Journal 1:91
June 3:703
June 21 2:136
Kemp Owen Again 4:45
King Orpheus (*section title*) 4:275
Knowledge (*book part*) 5:165
Knowledge of the Tree (*book part*) 5:573
L'8 SETTEMBRE: LA NATIVITÀ DI MARIA 3:483
L'ALBERO GENEALOGICO 3:459
L'INVITO 3:454
L'OCCASIONE 3:479
L'UCCELLO MOTTEGGIATORE 3:453
LA CENA 3:455
LA COLOMBA 3:456
LA DISIATA VOSTRA FORMA VERA 3:442
LA LETTERATURA 3:467
LA MEMORIA 3:472
LA POESIA 3:463
LA POETESSA 3:462
LA RICERCA 3:479
LA VEDUTA 3:457
LA VITA 3:462
Labor Day 2:46
Lace-cap hydrangeas, The 5:127
Lady's Confession, The 4:44
Lady's Fear, The 4:47
Lady's Next Song, The 4:46
Last Night I Crossed 4:53
Last Night You Came 4:54
Late the Sweet Birds 2:59
Later 1:70
LAUREA 3:450
LAUREOLA 3:442

LAURO 3:436
LAURORA SCRIPSIT 3:441
Lay of the Last Monk (*book part*) 4:3
Legend: July 2005 4:510
Lemma 1:87
Letter: June 9, 2002 / Rose Shawfeng Wang / Mother Fidelis, O.S.U. 4:204
LETTERA AL PROFESSOR FONTANELLA 3:486
LEVOMMI IL MIO PENSER 3:437
Libraries, The 3:717
Life of the Author: May 2005 4:497
Life: In Honor of Celia Dubovoy 4:119
Lilies are not trees, The 5:131
Lilium, Platycodon: July 24, 2004 4:366
Limen Lumen 2:103
Limitation 1:62
Lineation 2:69
Lines 1:15
List of the Lister: May 2005 4:499
Living in March 4:90
LO SVILUPPO 3:478
Location 2:74
LOCUS LOCANDUS 3:427
Love of the Lover: May 2005 4:498
LUCUS A NON LUCENDO 3:491
Lullaby: August 27, 2004 / Memoria Tiberina 4:394
Lupercalia: February 15, 2005 4:460
Lyre, Harp, Violin (*book part*) 4:23
Macaronic 3:486
MACCHIATO 3:487
Magnificat 2:33
March 3:684
Margaret-Ghost, The (*section title*) Nos. 1–310 5:167
Mario Pacelli: July 24, 2005 4:527
Martial 8.69 3:517
May 3:703
Measure 4:108

Mēden Agan: January 18, 2004 4:300
Meeting in Light 4:52
Meeting in Texas: March 11, 2005, p.m. 4:466
Meetings 4:63
Memorial: January 24, 2007 / Salsa 4:554
Message 4:30
Metaphor becomes the simile, The 5:100
Migrants 2:65
Minstrelsy 2:38
Minute mysteries of winter buds, The 5:164
Mirroring 2:12
Mneme 2:146
Molpodora's Gift 2:129
MONNA INNOMINATA 3:464
MONNA NOMINATA 3:475
More 4:80
More: February 6, 2004 4:313
Most: February 7, 2004 4:314
Mother's Day Card: May 14, 2000 / Margaret Rodgers Budenz 4:128
Much Too Much: January 17, 2004 / *Il.* 16.156–166 4:299
Muddy Reflection 1:105
Muse 2:139
Must the grammar of beauty 5:89
My Flower 1:102
Mysterium Microcosmographicum 4:70
Myth of Scipio, The 3:717
Mythistorema 2:134
Mythologies: July 2005 4:509
Narcissus 1:79
Native Daughter 2:101
Near the Charles 2:102
Next Door 4:56
No One 4:72
Nocturne 2:117
Noisy sea, The 5:117

INDEX OF TITLES

Nomenclature: August 10, 2004 / Mimi / Connie / Mary Constance Freeman Hanson Wentworth Wickham / Mary Freeman 4:377
Not Very Deep 4:33
Not yet the night. 5:113
NOTE AI SONETTI 1-16 3:443, 3:460, 3:477
November 2:15, 3:721, 4:78
November Fourth 3:492
Nursery Rhyme: August 6, 2004 / Mimi / Connie / Mary Constance Freeman Hanson Wentworth Wickham / Mary Freeman 4:373
Nursery Rhyme: August 7, 2004 / Julia Toledo and Julia Flora 4:374
Nursery Rhyme: August 8, 2004 / Scamandrius Astyanax Hectorides 4:375
Nursery Rhyme: August 27, 2004 / Volturnalia / Iulia Flora Tiberina 4:393
O L'INFERNO 3:456
O VOI CHE PER LA VIA D'AMOR PASSATE 3:480
Oaks are standing free, The 5:126
Oboe's Song, The 4:35
October 3:721
October Twelfth 3:428
October Thirteenth 3:492
October Fifteenth 3:428
Odysseus: July 2005 4:516
Odyssey (*book part*) 2:147
Odyssey and *Iliad*: July 2005 4:513
Of Knowledge by the Tree (*book part*) 5:561
Of the Tree (*book part*) Nos. 1–8 5:579
Of This Day: July 30, 2004 4:371
Oh . . . 5:162
Olden-time, old-fashioned, 5:106
Oleaceae (*section title*) 4:74
One 5:4
One, The 4:113
One Tree 1:23

One Tree, The 1:24
Oracles 2:144
Orpheus: January 1, 2004 4:288
Orpheus: February 28, 2005 4:463
Orpheus: June 16, 2004 / Zephyro date carbasa, nautae. 4:353
Orpheus: November 3, 2003 4:278
Orphics: January 1, 2004 4:289
Overlap 2:28
PARCA-VILLAGGIO 3:487
Passage 1:92
Path Approaching, The (*book part*) 1:9
PER POCO IL COR NON SI SPAURA 3:430
Persephone 2:96
Phegonaia 2:130
Photograph, A 1:12
Photophilia 4:142
Photophobia 4:141
Physics of Flora Baum: July 23, 2004, Neptunalia 4:365
PIANGETE, AMANTI, POI CHE PIANGE AMORE 3:481
Picture fills, The 5:121
Place, The 4:69
Placing, Timing: January 21, 2004 4:306
Playground 1:103
Please come down from the chariot and pull 5:139
Pleiades, Vergiliae: January 21, 2004 4:304
POCO MANCÒ CH'IO NON RIMASI IN CIELO 3:435
Poem Is as the Season, The 2:78
Poem Is as the Year, The 2:79
POETA FUI 3:483
Poetry: November 14, 2004 4:399
Point One 3:418
Point Two 3:419
PONS 3:492
Poor Flora's Almanack: February 6, 2004 / 3:47 a.m. EST 4:312

Poor Flora's Criticism: January 25, 2004 4:307
Poor Flora's Decision: February 16, 2004 4:326
Poor Flora's Election: January 28, 2004 4:308
Poor Flora's Forecast: February 15, 2004, a.m. 4:323
Poor Flora's Heroism: February 18, 2004, Evening 4:329
Poor Flora's Lection: January 29, 2004 4:310
Poor Flora's New Criticism: February 14, 2004 4:322
Poor Flora's Optimism: January 31, 2004 4:311
Poor Flora's Prevision: February 15, 2004, p.m. 4:325
Poor Flora's Repentance: February 13, 2004 4:321
Poor Flora's Revision: February 18, 2004 4:328
Poring over the poem of obituaries 5:140
PORTA 3:429
Portico 2:53
Portrait of Cretogenes Zographos . . . 2:123
Post-Maian 2:29
Prayer of Flora Baum: June 11, 2004 / Matri Matutae et Fortunae Reduci 4:346
Prayer: July 2005 4:518
Precision 1:75
PRESSO A L'EXTREMO 3:443
Problems 2:5
Program, The (*book part*) 2:3
Prolegomena 2:135
Prorrhesis 2:87
Proto-Pasch 2:149
Psalm: July 2005 4:519
Pygmalion 1:117
Question 2:133

Question and Address (*section title*) 3:424
Question and Answer 3:493
Question and Answer (*section title*) 3:493
Question and Question 3:518
Question? 5:565
QUESTIONI FAMILIARI 3:465
QUESTIONI MONDIALI 3:466
QUESTIONI NOMINALI 3:464
QUESTIONI RELIGIOSE 3:465
QUESTIONI VITALI 3:466
Quintile 3:717
Recall 1:72
Receiver 4:115
RECENSIONE 3:447
Reception 4:114
Recipe 4:116
Red Friday 2:66
Relations 2:8
Rendition 2:72
Res: January 9, 2004 4:296
Resume 1:82
Revolution 2:51
Rhymer on the Verge of Anthe's Land 4:81
Rhymes and/or Reason 3:496
Ride 2:16
Rigamarole 2:75
Ring, The 1:42
Rite of the Call, The 1:35
Robins. Lilacs. Trees 5:86
Roma 3:115
ROMA 3:468
Roman Sonnets 3:704
ROMEA 3:452
ROMEO 3:474
ROMOLO PROFUMATISSIMO 3:434
Romulus Religiosulus 1:86
Root is what I know, The 5:142
Rosaceae (*section title*) 4:118
Roses of Shadow 2:40
Rotation 2:57

INDEX OF TITLES

Round 2:14
Rounds If Not Treason 3:499
Ruins 2:62
S'ANNEGA IL PENSIER MIO E IL NAUFRAGAR M'È DOLCE 3:431
SAGGIO DI FLORA BAUM 3:448
Saint Agnes of Rome: January 21, 2004 4:305
Saint Philip Neri: May 26, 2004 4:339
Sainte Aude: November 18, 2004 4:404
Schooling: February 13, 2005 4:458
SCIENZA NUOVA 3:447
Scion 2:20
SE 'L DESIR NON ERRA 3:437
Season 2:176, 2:186, 2:191, 2:202
Seasonal Wishes: 2007 / For Mona Harrington 4:575
Second Movement 4:396
Seferis 2:118
SEMPRE 3:461
September 3:718
Sequel 1:74
Sequence 1:76
Sequence: November 12, 2004 4:397
Seventh Day, The 4:117
Seventh Movement 4:577
Sextile 3:717
Shadow 4:87
Shaking 1:93
Shall I recount the miles and hours of distance 5:130
She entered twenty-two and blonde, 5:129
Sheen 2:24
Sheen, The 2:207
Sibyl (*book part*) 4:19
Sicut et Nos (*section title*) 4:110
Sidereus Nuncius 1:106
Silver Fountains 2:49
Similitude 2:9
Simulation 2:77
Sixth Movement 4:574

Sky 2:173, 2:187, 2:204
Sloughing 1:84
SOFFIETTO EDITORIALE 3:445
Solstice 2:32
Some Day 4:57
Someone 4:27
Someone Homeric might say to some other, 5:80
Something still glows. Is it a Troy in flames? 5:98
Sometime Too Hot 2:34
Sometimes It's Hard 1:115
SONETTI PETRARCHESCHI 3:435
SONETTI PREROMANI 3:469
Song of Tam Lin 4:48
Song of the Loathly Lady 4:41
Sonnets to the Italian 3:435
Sounds out of Season 3:494
Spiration: August 23, 2004 / Volcanalia 4:389
Spring, A 1:18
Spring Fever 3:12
Sprinklings: December 10, 2004 4:416
St. Anne: July 26, 2005 4:529
Standard Time 4:102
Standing I clasp the trunk.... 5:564
Statement 1:27
Stelling 4:83
Stories of Sylvia Pezographos 2:126
STUDI LEOPARDIANI 3:430
Studio 2:55
SUGGERIRE, ISPIRARE 3:474
Sum (*book part*) 1:3
Summer's Lease 2:31
Sunday Morning 1:71
Synchrony: November 15, 2004 4:400
Tam Lin (*section title*) 4:26
Television 3:490
Temper 4:135
Tempest 4:136
Tempi 2:10
Temple 2:54, 2:176, 2:194

Tempo 4:137
Term: June 11 – August 17, 2004 / Nomina mutarunt: hic deus, illa dea est. 4:383
Testing 4:138
Text 2:60
Text Depicting Throna: December 5, 2004 4:410
Thank you, I said. To whom? 5:82
Thanksgiving 3:491
That Time of Year 2:58
Theater 2:141
Then must the future be forgotten and forgone 5:107
Theogamy 2:142
Theorems 2:78
These torrents merely flow from the bathroom ceiling. 5:122
Thesis 3:491
They were both standing, and the sword had shattered. 5:84
Third Movement 4:422
Third Spring 2:97
This Night 1:100
This posthumous existence 5:155
Three 5:26
Three oaks standing. Shall I advance 5:87
Three, The 4:111
Thule: June 11, 2005 4:503
Time and Tide 4:49
Times with the Tease in 3:503
To 2:43
To Bruce Bennett, Richard Rorty, Quintus Horatius Flaccus, et al. 3:494
To Hear the Harps of Heaven 2:6
To Love That Well 2:50
To visit the virgilias one goes 5:103
Touches 1:66
Touching the Lyre 2:7
Trace: August 17, 2004, Tiberinalia 4:381

Tradition: August 17, 2004 / Iano ad Theatrum Marcelli 4:379
Trail: August 17, 2004, Portunalia 4:380
Trans World 3:489
Transfiguration 2:40
Transition: August 15–17, 2004 / Megalýnei hē psyché mou ... 4:382
Transubstantiation 2:13
TRASLATO 3:478
Tree 2:5, 2:175, 2:186, 2:190, 2:204
Tree (book part) 5:567
Tree fell like a wounded warrior, The 5:132
Tree of knowledge grows in Paradise, The 5:93
Tree of Knowledge, The (book part) 5:71
Trimming 2:70
Triptych ... 2:122
Tritogenes: July 2005 4:507
Trouble was, The 5:112
TROVARE, SCOPRIRE 3:467
Troy 2:207
Truth and Tree: August 15, 2004 / Mimi / Connie / Mary Constance Freeman Hanson Wentworth Wickham / Mary Freeman 4:378
Tune for Spring 4:99
Turdus Migratorius: May 28, 2004 4:340
TUTTI LI FEDELI D'AMORE 3:476
Two 5:18
Two, The 4:112
UDRALLO IL BEL PAESE 3:470
ULMUS-OLMO 3:440
Umbrageous Vision (book part) 3:263
Umbra 3:265
UMBRA-OMBRA 3:489
UN SECONDAMENTO 3:476
UNA COSA VERA, BUONA, BELLA 3:434

Unfriendly Elevator, The 4:64
Unnamed 3:424
Unshaken 1:94
Up and Down 4:107
Urbiculture (*book part*) 3:3
Utrasque 4:104
Utrique 4:103
Vade Mecum: February 20, 2004 4:331
Valentine 4:84
Valentine: February 14, 2005 4:459
Vaunt 1:58
VEDEVA A LA SUA OMBRA 3:438
Veil, The 1:39
Vergil / Virgil 3:490
Versed Sine 3:493
Version 1:29
VIA 3:417
VIAGGIO-VILLAGGIO 3:487
Viaticum: January 11, 2004 4:297
VIRGILIA 3:485
VIRGILIO 3:469
Vis Anemoio: December 26, 2003 4:287
Vis Insita 4:88
VISIO 3:423
Vision (*section title*) 3:519
VITA NUOVA O MONDO NUOVO 3:452
Vita: August 24, 2004 / Mundus patet. 4:390
Vocation 5:37
Warm Springs 4:50
Was it dualistic? 5:81
Was This 4:79
Watching 1:21
Waves Receding, The (*book part*) 1:53
We 1:90
We know well that there are 5:123
Weekday in Ordinary Time 2:48
Well, dear old self, 5:109
What are these marks that mark the fading page, 5:90

What else is there? Traverse five gardens. 5:114
What Happened 1:67
What Henry Said 4:43
What is a failure? Such a simple thing. 5:104
What Then Is Love but Mourning . . . 2:128
What to Tell, What to Ask: June 13, 2004 / Sunday of the Body and Blood 4:351
What Would Happen 4:39
When He Went Away 1:57
When I had known infinity, 5:576
Whether the roses were the weather or 5:102
Whether Weather 4:139
Which tree was this? There were so many trees. 5:133
White dogwood bright by darkest purple beech 5:83
Who were the fighters? They were lusty youths 5:101
Why does she remember with horror 5:119
Why have I failed? 5:97
Widener: July 5, 2005 4:505
Wings of the Dove, The (*section title*) 5:559
Wings of the Dove, The: August 2006 4:541
Winter Bud 3:109
Witness 1:5
Woman in the Nineteenth Century (*section title*) 5:557
Yellow Leaves 2:50
Yet remember. 5:110
Yet There Seem 4:40
Your Country 4:85
Your Right Hand 1:95
Zeus. Wicked. Agamemnon names. 5:74

The Gardens of Flora Baum

Set in 11-point Scala OT, the Open Type
version of the typeface created in
1990 by Dutch type designer
Martin Majoor and first
used for printing
programs at
Vredenburg Music
Centre, Utrecht. The name
honors Milan's La Scala opera house.

Printing: Lulu.com

Book design: Roger Sinnott